Employment and Work Relations in Context Series

Series Editors

Tony Elger
Centre for Comparative Labour Studies
Department of Sociology
University of Warwick

Peter Fairbrother
Centre for Research on Economic and Social
 Transformation
Cardiff School of Social Sciences
Cardiff University

The aim of the *Employment and Work Relations in Context Series* is to address questions relating to the evolving patterns and politics of work, employment, management and industrial relations. There is a concern to trace out the ways in which wider policy-making, especially by national governments and transnational corporations, impinges upon specific workplaces, occupations, labour markets, localities and regions. This invites attention to developments at an international level, marking out patterns of globalization, state policy and practice in the context of globalization and the impact of these processes on labour. A particular feature of the series is the consideration of forms of worker and citizen organization and mobilization. Thus the studies address major analytical and policy issues through case study and comparative research.

CHANGING PROSPECTS FOR TRADE UNIONISM

Comparisons between Six Countries

Edited by

Peter Fairbrother and Gerard Griffin

continuum
LONDON • NEW YORK

Continuum
The Tower Building, 11 York Road, London SE1 7NX
370 Lexington Avenue, New York, NY 10017-6503

First published 2002

British Library Cataloguing-in-Publication Data
A catalogue record for this book is available from the British Library.

ISBN   0-8264-5612-X (hardback)
       0-8264-5811-4 (paperback)

Typeset by YHT Ltd, London
Printed and bound in Great Britain by Biddles Ltd. www.biddles.co.uk

CONTENTS

List of Contributors   vi

List of Abbreviations   vii

1 Introduction: Trade Unions Facing the Future   1
Peter Fairbrother and Gerard Griffin

2 Unions in Australia: Struggling to Survive   21
Gerard Griffin and Stuart Svensen

3 Unions in Britain: Towards a New Unionism?   56
Peter Fairbrother

4 Unions in Canada: Strategic Renewal, Strategic Conundrums   93
Gregor Murray

5 Irish Unions: Testing the Limits of Social Partnership   137
William K. Roche and Jacqueline Ashmore

6 Unions in New Zealand: What the Law Giveth ...   177
Raymond Harbridge, Aaron Crawford and Kevin Hince

7 American Unions at the Start of the Twenty-first Century:
Going Back to the Future?   200
Paul Jarley

8 Conclusion: The State of the Unions   238
Gerard Griffin and Peter Fairbrother

Index   257

Contributors

Jacqueline Ashmore is on the staff of the National Centre for Partnership in Dublin.

Aaron Crawford was a Research Fellow in the Industrial Relations Centre, Victoria University of Wellington.

Peter Fairbrother is a Professor in the Centre for Research on Economic and Social Transformation, Cardiff School of Social Sciences, Cardiff University, and an Honorary Professor in the National Key Centre in Industrial Relations, Monash University.

Gerard Griffin is Professor and Director, National Key Centre in Industrial Relations, Monash University.

Raymond Harbridge is Professor of Management at La Trobe University, Melbourne.

Kevin Hince was formerly Professor in the Industrial Relations Centre, Victoria University of Wellington.

Paul Jarley is the Gatton Endowed Professor and Director, Center for Labor Education and Research at the University of Kentucky.

Gregor Murray is a Professor in the Industrial Relations Department at Université Laval in Québec City.

William K. Roche is a Professor in the Graduate School of Business, University College Dublin.

Stuart Svensen was a Research Fellow in the National Key Centre in Industrial Relations, Monash University.

Abbreviations

ABS	Australian Bureau of Statistics
ACTU	Australian Council of Trade Unions
AFL	American Federation of Labor
AFL–CIO	American Federation of Labor–Congress of Industrial Organizations
AIRC	Australian Industrial Relations Commission
ALP	Australian Labor Party
AWIRS	Australian Workplace Industrial Relations Survey
CCU	Confederation of Canadian Unions
CEQ	Centrale de l'enseignement du Québec
CEW	Committee on the Evolution of Work
CIO	Congress of Industrial Organizations
CIU	Congress of Irish Unions
CLC	Canadian Labour Congress
CSD	Centrale des syndicats democratiques
CSN	Confederation des syndicats nationaux
EMU	European Monetary Union
EU	European Union
EWC	European Works Council
HRDC	Human Resources Development Canada
ICFTU	International Confederation of Free Trade Unions
ICTU	Irish Congress of Trade Unions
ILO	International Labour Organization
LMRA	Labor Management Relations Act
LRC	Labour Relations Commission
NAFTA	North American Free Trade Agreement
NEA	National Education Association
NLRB	National Labor Relations Board
NZCTU	New Zealand Council of Trade Unions
NDP	New Democratic Party
OECD	Organization for Economic Co-operation and Development
PDs	Progressive Democrats
PESP	Programme for Economic and Social Progress

PNR	Programme for National Recovery
PQ	Parti Québécois
TDC	Trade Development Council
TUC	Trades Union Congress
TUF	Trade Union Federation

1 INTRODUCTION: TRADE UNIONS FACING THE FUTURE

Peter Fairbrother and Gerard Griffin

Trade union movements in many countries face uncertain futures. After three decades of extensive economic restructuring at both national and international levels, often accompanied by major legislative reforms, the way forward for unions is unclear. Throughout the 1980s and into the 1990s, in most developed economies, union membership has declined massively and union leaders and their members have lost their former prominence and place in the polity. Taken together, this amounts to a massive reversal of union fortunes and raises questions about the role, and indeed the future, of unions. For example, will trade unions be able to re-establish their past salience in both the bargaining arena and in the polity? Or, given the uncertainties of internationalized economies and states, will the first decade of this new century see further declines in union strength and power? This book examines these and related questions by exploring the background, current roles and prospects of trade unions in six predominantly English-speaking countries. We commence with some introductory remarks on the role and context of trade unionism, identify the extent of membership decline and justify our choice of both the comparative method and the range of countries studied.

Role and Context

We contend that trade unionism must be understood both in its specific national context as well as within the broader parameters of international links and relations. The union form of organization is one that is rooted in the complex of labour–capital relations. These relations embrace the direct control of labour within specific labour processes, the managerial regulation of labour through large-scale private and public corporate structures, labour as a commodity within wide labour markets, and the political regulation of labour through the state. Unions must address, at least to some extent, all of these features, responding to and addressing the processes of restructuring and recomposition that are taking place. In the abstract, this restructuring is part of the process of the recomposition of the labour–capital relation at the point of production and service; it is part of the complex and mediated processes of supervision and direction of the sale of workers' labour power in the modern economy (for a version of the following argument, see Fairbrother, 2000a).

Thus unions are institutions where workplace relations are the pivot for the day-to-day experience of much trade unionism. It is on the basis of this form of collective organization in various national contexts that representatives negotiate on behalf of the membership, the leaders of who represent this membership in a variety of forums, including political ones. This is a view of unions as 'intermediary organisations' positioned as collective organizations representing workers to employers and the state (Müller-Jentsch, 1988). It is predicated on an assumption that trade unions are organizational entities that, theoretically at least, are distinct and separate from the state and employers. Of course, union leaderships may enter into alliances with the state or employers or be drawn into cooperative relationships at both employer and state level. It is in this respect that arguments are developed about the autonomy and independence of unions as well as the degree to which unions should cooperate with employers or the state in the pursuit of union policy.

While the focus of the study is on national trade union movements, exploring the way that trade unions have organized, mobilized and operated in conditions of economic decline and insecurity of employment, it is also necessary to consider the context in which unions as a whole organize and operate. There are, of course, notable differences from one national context to another. The British model of unionism has been one where there has been a traditionally strong emphasis on workplace organization, particularly in the manufacturing sector, albeit within established and relatively stable forms of union organization beyond the workplace. In contrast, and with some exceptions, Australian unions historically have focused their strategies and energies on institutions away from the workplace. These differences exist also in non-English-speaking countries: unions in Scandinavian countries have had powerful, entrenched workplace forms of organization, as well as strong organization beyond, while the French union movement has been organizationally weak at the workplace but has displayed a remarkable capacity to mobilize workers from time to time.

For many union members – some would argue, most members, most of the time – trade unionism begins and ends at the workplace level. It is here in the course of work, on a day-to-day basis, on individual issues as well as collective ones, that members begin and learn their trade unionism. It is also at this level that trade unionism comes to life, in organizing and questioning the detail of the wage relationship. As well as operating locally, however, unions as a whole must also operate at a regional, national and increasingly international level. They deal with managements, with governments and with governmental and non-governmental agencies. In the European context, unions have looked to the supra-state level – the European Union – and, as well as dealing with the International Confederation of Free Trade Unions (ICFTU), they have developed links and relationships with other national union movements. The way unions as a whole organize and operate has a bearing on the fate and fortunes of workers as union members at a local level. To understand and appreciate these different methods of operation, it is useful to locate unions in their historical and comparative context.

Trade unions historically were rooted in the occupational communities of skilled workers or, as Hyman (1994) puts it, 'the relatively undifferentiated work situation of labour in the expanding sectors of mass production' (p. 117). For much of the post-war period, there was an expansion of mass production and mass consumption, giving rise to arguments about the relationship between macro-economic policies and forms of mass production, associated with Fordism. Critical to these arrangements was the state as the 'regulator of economic relations and provider of social benefit and protection' (*ibid.*). It has been argued that trade unionism for much of this period was a product of and contributor to these patterns of relationships. The patterns of unionism inevitably varied in these circumstances, distinguished by Hyman as a contrast between unions based on 'narrow membership constituencies' which generally pursue job-related concerns, while more broadly based unions often 'address a wider range of issues' (p. 121).

Union movements in many liberal democratic countries entered a phase of relative stability and subsequent membership expansion in the 1950s and 1960s. In these countries there was a dramatic increase in unionization, reflected in the expansion of union membership as well as the signs of an emergent union consciousness and practice in hitherto quiescent areas, such as the public sector. These developments were part of the changing labour markets in many countries during this period, the consolidation of trends in the 1920s and 1930s towards the establishment of the basis of mass-based manufacturing industries, exemplified most clearly by the automobile industry. A second feature of this period, less often remarked upon, is that there was an increasing convergence in industrial relations practices and procedures across different occupational groups and sectors. The public sector unions developed strategies and practices in their approaches to bargaining and negotiation that mirrored practices long evident in other sectors, such as manufacturing.

Not all countries, of course, followed this pattern. In the USA, for example, union density peaked in the early 1950s and commenced a long-term period of decline. A second country covered in this volume, Australia, also saw declining density during the 1960s when the union movement initially failed to organize the newly emerging white-collar workers. Overall, however, the 1950s, 1960s and much of the 1970s were boom decades for trade unions.

This growth in union power inevitably spilled over into the broader economic and political systems. In a number of countries, particularly Western European nations, successive governments attempted to use incomes policies as key instruments in the management of the economy. The goal of such policies was increased productivity. In Britain, these initiatives provided part of the impetus for the stimulation of workplace activism, particularly in the manual occupations, in the public sector (and beyond) as workers attempted to address the outcomes of these policies. Concomitantly and relatedly, there was an increased involvement of unions in the polity. Building on assumptions of liberal democracy, as a political form where a plurality of interests had a positive part to play in elaborating notions of citizenship and rule, the case was developed for formal recognition of unions as important political actors in the state (Dahl, 1961, 1985; Flanders, 1970). Even critics of liberal democracy developed analyses that placed the trade union movement as a key institution in the political compromises and accommodations that characterized much of the post-war development of liberal democratic states (Miliband, 1969, 1982; Hyman, 1989). Trade unions were then, even from within competing perspectives, seen as an integral part of liberal democratic rule.

A central aspect of union involvement in the polity was the links and relationships between unions, particularly the confederations, and political parties. One important aspect of these relationships was that unions were encouraged to look beyond their immediate sectional concerns and to locate their activity within broader social frameworks, such as establishing the infrastructure of a welfare state. In a number of countries, such as the UK and Australia, this took the form of a partnership with their respective labour parties. It gave rise to arguments that trade unions had a responsibility for industrial issues, while the political parties were, by definition, concerned with political questions. At conferences and through discussion, unions and their political partners developed approaches that addressed economic and political issues. These patterns of linkages and involvement were evident in various ways. At the most transparent level, union federations in a number of countries, including the Australian Council of Trade Unions (ACTU), the Irish Congress of Trade Unions (ICTU) and the Trades Union Congress (TUC) in the United Kingdom, came to formal agreements with political regimes whereby the 'economic' interests of trade unions were recognized, either through legislation, consultation or formal cooperation. In some countries, these agreements led to formal centralized bargaining.

It is against this background that arguments about the decline of trade unions in the 1980s and 1990s have been developed. At a general level, it is argued that, in comparison with the 1960s and 1970s, trade unions no longer have a marked presence with respect to either the economy or the polity. Even the traditional linkage between unions and labour parties are, at best, uneasy. In the economic arena, unions face more confident managements, implementing policies of restructuring often without explicit reference to unions. No longer are trade union leaderships party to the formulation of policy and programmes which take into account the specific concerns and interests of their memberships. In other words, the power and influence of trade unionism over the last two decades has suffered a decisive setback.

Unions have begun to explore strategies for rebuilding themselves and addressing the dramatic seepage of membership during the 1980s and 1990s. More generally, a range of national union leaderships has begun to examine the bases of union organization, focusing specifically on the circumstances for membership recruitment and retention. In these debates about the ways unions might develop, some commentators have deployed two models of unionism to focus the diagnosis of problems and their solution. First, a service model of unionism has been elaborated, where the argument was that unions should reorganize so as to serve their memberships more effectively and efficiently (for example, Bassett and Cave, 1993). From the point of view of union organization and operation, leaders are there to support and service a relatively passive and atomized membership. Second, an alternative model has been a view of unionism where the emphasis is on organizing and providing the basis, as Hyman suggests, for a 'living collectivity' (Hyman, 1989, p. 179). In this account, the membership is an active participant, contributing to the development of the collective focus and organization of the union (Bronfenbrenner and Juravich, 1998). More generally, debates about these distinctions and their complex interrelationship have become the grist of recent debate about trade unions and trade unionism (Fiorito *et al.*, 1995; Hyman, 1994). It is increasingly argued that the presentation of these models as stark contrasts is misleading and that a more nuanced account is necessary which acknowledges the interrelationship between servicing and organizing in practice (Boxall and Haynes, 1997, pp. 572–3).

In the light of recent history, unions face major challenges as they come to terms with the changes that are taking place in the economy and the polity. The recent history of trade unionism in advanced capitalist countries has stimulated debate about the nature of the problems faced by unions and their responses (Hyman, 1994; Johnston, 1994; McIlroy, 1997; Boxall and Haynes, 1997; Kelly, 1997; Bronfenbrenner *et al.*, 1998; Peetz, 1998). It is of course important to acknowledge the contradictory features of union organization and activity and the way outcomes may involve sclerosis or renewal, both within the workplace or beyond (Pocock, 1998; Fairbrother, 2000b). How unions respond to these challenges is critical for an understanding of how unions might develop and prosper.

Problems – Membership as the Exemplar

The problems faced by trade unions, can be summarized quite simply: in most of the industrialized societies, particularly in OECD countries, trade unions are declining rapidly in membership, power and influence. For unions, the halcyon days of the decades following the end of the Second World War are long forgotten. The questioning of the centrality of trade unionism as a social partner that commenced in the late 1970s and flowered in the 1980s resulted in a greatly weakened union movement in the 1990s. Frenkel (1993, p. 3) offered the bleak assessment that 'the future of unionism in the core advanced societies is more problematic today than it has been in any period since the Great Depression'.

Membership density demonstrates most clearly and most simply this decline of unionism. A recent report of the International Labour Organization (ILO, 1997) concluded that the trade union movement had 'fallen on hard times' and was 'experiencing serious difficulties almost everywhere'. More specifically, of the 70 countries for which comparable data could be gathered, 'about half had seen a considerable drop in their membership in absolute figures over the last ten years' (p. 6). Given the increased labour force, density rates dropped dramatically: in 35 of the countries, density had decreased by more than 20 per cent over this time period. Overall, of the 92 countries for which the ILO was able to gather data in 1995, 48 of these countries, more than half, had a density rate of less than 20 per cent.

The Report does make the obvious and correct point that union power and influence are not determined solely by density rates. Indeed, a large, 'tame' union movement is not necessarily more powerful than a small, 'militant' one. Nevertheless, numbers do count; the level of membership is still, in the words of Visser (1992, p. 24) a 'critical resource'. Such dramatic changes in membership must, inevitably, spill over into and reduce union authority. A strong argument can be advanced that governments and other organs of the state interact in a qualitatively different manner with lower-density union movements. High levels of voluntary membership confer on unions an undoubted legitimacy to speak on behalf of the workers they cover. Contrasting the number of industrialized states that had 'social contracts' with their union movements in the 1960s and 1970s with the equivalent number in the 1990s would seem to lend considerable support for this contention.

Inevitably, given the dimensions of the decline, the causes of this change have been much investigated. The most common factors referred to in these studies include:

- structural shifts in the economy

- employer attitudes and ideology

- public policy/changing relationships between unions and governments

- the changing nature and needs of employees.

Structural shifts in the economy and the changing nature of work, and consequently of workers, is an automatic starting point. The combination of globalization and technology has produced, as noted above, very different labour markets to those of the 1970s. At the sectoral level, trends such as declining employment in manufacturing and the increasing dominance of the service sector – the former a traditional stronghold and the latter a weak enclave of trade unionism – threaten the basis of union density. Further, the growth of what has become known as the peripheral workforce – the part-time worker, the casual worker and the under-employed worker – directly attacks this density.

During the 1980s and the 1990s, employers and employer groupings increasingly adopted – or, in the case of countries such as the USA, continued with – anti-union policies. In many cases, these policies were couched in terms of better human resources management. The primary employment relationship, this argument went, should be that between the employer and the individual employee. In this scenario, as employers sought to increase employee involvement and commitment to their organizations, unions were increasingly regarded as outside third parties and thus potential threats to the primary relationship. Union membership was, accordingly, to be discouraged wherever possible. Other employers accepted that their employees would be represented by unions but choose to follow less conciliatory practices than in the past. Many such employers adopted proactive policies geared at achieving significant employee labour market flexibility. In such circumstances, many unions were unable to respond adequately to these strategies.

The changing ideology of employers paralleled that of many governments. From 1945 onwards, most industrialized countries had legitimized, and, in many cases, enshrined in law, the concept of a collective employment relationship. In short, public policy supported trade unionism. Indeed, as noted above, in a number of unions were, arguably, incorporated into the power structure. The post-oil-price economic shock of the 1970s queried this relationship between state and unions. During the 1980s, a much more antagonistic relationship between governments and unions emerged with the election of conservative governments in, for example, Britain and the USA. The election of conservative state and federal governments in Australia and in New Zealand during the 1990s resulted in aggressively anti-union legislation that had a major impact on all facets of trade unionism (for example, see Hince, 1996). Even in countries with centre to left-of-centre governments, a less cordial relationship tended to emerge; at a minimum, and particularly at the 1990s developed, the hitherto favoured position of unionism was significantly eroded.

A final possible influence that is found in much of the literature is the concept of individual choice among employees. This argument postulates that the nature of employee needs have changed and that, specifically, a range of personal characteristics, attitudes and employment experiences influence an employee's demand for unionism. The challenge for unions is to persuade these new consumers that they should indeed choose to purchase membership. As the role of the employee as an industrial and political citizen changes – exemplified by shifting social relations in the production, service and consumption arenas – so too does the conception and bases of collective organization and action. Under these circumstances, the verities of the past may no longer suffice.

Possibilities and Prospects

While many trade union movements suffered significant setbacks during the last two decades of the twentieth century, the environment in which they operate is unlikely to become less hostile during the first decade of the twenty-first century. They will continue to face unprecedented challenges as a result of the globalization and liberalization of investment and trade. This environment has led generally to a weakening of union bargaining power and to a hardening of employer opposition to unions, manifested in a range of strategies ranging from the 'psychologisation' of the employment relationship (McKinley and Taylor, 1996; Roche and Turner, 1994) to an increasing use of more traditional and direct anti-union measures such as the victimization of union activists (Bronfenbrenner and Juravich, 1998). In turn, many governments have adopted neo-liberal policies aimed at withdrawing the state from the labour market. Such governments have undermined minimum employment standards and severed or degraded state recognition of, and support for, unions. This has, in general, resulted in the decentralization of bargaining structures from the national and industry levels to the workplace or enterprise levels (Katz, 1993).

These developments will continue to be associated with rapid changes in production technologies and employment. Capital mobility has facilitated the shutting down of production in many traditional industrial areas, and the construction of new plant in other areas (Belanger and Murray, 1994; Towers, 1997). In the face of increasing competition, work has undergone rapid transformation in order to maximize surplus value and transfer risk through such means as lean production, downsizing, casualization and contracting-out (Parker and Slaughter, 1997). Neo-liberal governments have downsized, privatized, and otherwise reinvented themselves in the image of the new, competitive private sector (Osborne and Gaebler, 1992). Facing increasing pressures to cut costs and balance budgets, social democratic and labour governments have often followed suit. Not surprisingly, unions find it difficult to organize in this environment because of employer opposition, the impact of state policies and the difficulty of achieving significant gains for members (Dagg, 1997). In addition, decentralization of bargaining has placed greater demands on the resources of unions, leaving a smaller share for recruitment and organizing.

In addition to these economic and political changes, it has been argued that there has been a growth of individualistic attitudes and a corresponding reduction in belief in the value and efficacy of collectivism. Changing patterns of demography, education, income and consumption, it has been asserted, has led to a blurring of class boundaries, with adverse implications for unionization given its traditional masculine, blue-collar, 'tough guy' image (Kelly, 1998; Pocock, 1998; Zoll, 1996). While most recent studies of attitudes towards unions have so far failed to find evidence of increased public antipathy towards unions, it cannot be assumed that this will automatically continue to be the case (Bild *et al.*, 1998; Gallie, 1996; Lind, 1996; Peetz, 1998; Waddington and Whitston, 1997). More pertinently, it may be the case that there will be a growing scepticism among workers about the form of trade unionism that prevailed for most of the twentieth century.

The ability of unions to respond effectively to these changes has been hindered in many instances by long periods of accommodation with governments and employers during which unions frequently evolved into managers of discontent, bureaucratic machines necessary to engage in routine collective bargaining, member servicing and corporatist politics (Boxall and Haynes, 1997; Fairbrother and Waddington, 1990). This led, in many cases, not only to institutional inertia, but also to the atrophy of workplace structures and rank-and-file activism, making such unions particularly vulnerable to membership loss in the event of a withdrawal of state support or employer recognition.

While unions and union movements are clearly affected by their environments, they also have the capacity to make strategic responses to those forces, and those changes will in turn have an influence on those environments. These responses may include:

- taking a more cooperative or militant orientation towards employers and governments

- making organizational or structural changes, such as mergers

- transferring resources between servicing and organizing activities

- changing geographical orientation; for example, transferring resources between local, regional, national and international initiatives

- broadening or restricting the range of services offered

- making a change in philosophical direction; for example, negotiating individual contracts for members

- attempting to shift the locus of bargaining

- building or severing alliances with political parties or community groups

- launching or terminating specific campaigns.

Unions have tried a range of these and other strategies, without any obvious panacea emerging. Mergers may have both positive and negative consequences for unionization and the overall effect appears to be, at best, neutral (Chaison, 1996; Millward, 1994; Peetz, 1998). Unions in many countries have attempted less militant and more cooperative strategies, with mixed and often negative results (Lawler, 1990; Masters, 1997; Undy *et al.*, 1996). Attempts have been made to increase the participation in unions of women and minority groups (Chen and Wong, 1998; Needleman, 1998). In some countries unions have been developing new political alliances, or redefining existing ones (House of Commons Employment Committee, 1994; Mazzocchi, 1998). Some unions have forged alliances and participated in joint campaigns with community groups (Fine, 1998). In an endeavour to counter the power of global corporations, there has been a renewed interest in the formation of international unions, federations and campaigns (Breitenfellner, 1997; Lipow, 1996; Ramsey, 1997).

There has been much discussion within many union movements about the need for increasing the focus on organizing. Despite the development of flagship programmes such as the Organizing Institute in the USA and Organising Works in Australia, the commitment of unions generally to increasing resources on organizing has been questioned (Masters, 1997) and doubts remain as to whether organizing campaigns are cost effective (Voos, 1984). Peak union bodies have initiated campaigns to demonstrate union effectiveness, such as the AFL–CIO's 'America needs a raise' campaign and the ACTU's eight-hour-day campaign. There has been an increase in corporate campaigns in which unions attempt to shape the behaviour of management by targeting specific companies considered to be acting unfairly (Jarley and Maranto, 1990; Prewitt, 1997).

What do all of these developments portend for the future of unions? There are a variety of views about this, bounded by those who take a linear view of history, and those who see cyclical patterns. At one extreme there are those who argue that unions cannot survive the de-collectivist onslaught and that new forms of workplace regulation, such as legislated minimum employment standards and works councils, must emerge if the rights of workers are to be protected (Freeman and Rogers, 1993). At the other extreme are those who argue that the decline of unionism is part of a cycle that will inevitably swing back to favour unionization (Kelly, 1998; Masters, 1997). They have seen it all before. In their view neo-liberalism is a replay of mid-nineteenth-century policies that have produced mid-nineteenth-century outcomes (a rump 'labour aristocracy' protected by unions, and an unorganized mass of unskilled, exploited workers). From the late nineteenth century, the latter group organized collectively against their exploitation and, after some bitter struggles, succeeded in gaining recognition. As industry consolidates, and as resentment among today's exploited workers intensifies, it is argued that a similar process will occur. These new industries are now consolidating into ever-bigger corporations in which managements have greater incentives to engage in collective and multi-employer bargaining. New factory-like workplaces such as call centres are emerging that will concentrate workers together, reducing the costs of organizing.

Between the two extremes there are a variety of other possibilities. Unions will survive if they adopt a panacea such as becoming more or less political, democratic, responsive, militant, cooperative, international, regional and so on. Others see unions as in danger of becoming extinct in some countries such as the United States, but surviving elsewhere, for example in Britain (Towers, 1997). Alternatively, unions may survive in regions with strong union traditions, but will die out in other regions (Martin, Sunley and Wills, 1996). Still others believe that while unions will continue to decline numerically, they will increase in wealth and power by becoming more efficient and effective (Bennett and Delaney, 1993).

It would be extremely difficult to provide even partial answers to the variety of questions raised by these varying interpretations. Nevertheless, we hope to make a contribution to these debates and assess which explanations and scenarios are the most plausible and best fit the evidence. These contra-dictory trajectories taken by the union movements of the countries studied here provide a number of lessons, which will be discussed in the concluding chapter.

Focus of the Book

The central focus of this book is to outline and analyse how trade unions have responded to the problems confronting them. We accept that in most countries unions have been, and largely remain, in numerical decline. Specifically, we are concerned to discover how they have responded to this decline; to determine the current state of unions as an indicator of how successful their responses have been; and to assess their immediate future prospects. We have chosen to pursue these questions in a comparative manner focusing on unions in six predominantly English-speaking countries: Australia, Britain, Canada, Ireland, New Zealand and the USA.

Use of the comparative method has a long and venerable history in industrial relations research, particularly post-World War Two (see, for example, Clegg, 1976; Kerr *et al.*, 1962; Poole, 1986; Walker, 1967). While the method does have pitfalls as well as potential, to use Schregle's (1981) terms, its use requires little justification. There has been an upsurge in comparative studies of unionization in recent years, inspired at least in part by the downward trajectory taken by the union movements of many OECD countries.

Most comparative studies of unionization can be placed into one of two groups. One tendency has been for individual researchers to compare a spectrum of OECD countries (Bean and Holden, 1992; Clegg, 1976; Griffin *et al.*, 1991; Visser, 1987, 1992; Western, 1997). The number of countries studied varied from six to eighteen, with all but one study covering more than ten countries. Clegg's six-country study was impressionistic, but as the number of countries analysed in each study has increased, so has reliance on the quantitative analysis of available country-level data. These studies have generally found positive relationships between unionization and the degree of bargaining centralization, the presence of the 'Ghent' system of unemployment insurance, the incumbency of labour and social democratic governments and public sector size; and a negative relationship between unionization and unemployment. While the existence of such relationships is generally accepted, there are sufficient departures from the trends to limit their utility. Unionization rates in France and Australia, for example, declined sharply in the 1980s despite the existence of relatively sympathetic governments and bargaining environments (Griffin and Svensen, 1996; Jefferys, 1996). In addition, these studies typically do not take account of potentially important influences on unionization such as the behaviour of employers, employees and their organizations (Corneo, 1995).

The second main group of comparative studies examines differences between two countries. These are often concerned with accounting for different unionization outcomes between countries with similar industrial relations institutions (see Rose and Chaison, 1985, 1996; Swenson, 1989). The choice of such 'close pairs' allows, where appropriate, institutional, economic, cultural and historical factors to be held constant. Less commonly, the comparison involves countries with similar unionization outcomes but different institutions (see Jefferys, 1996) and, occasionally, countries with different unionization outcomes and different institutions (see Maurice *et al.*, 1986). These paired studies enable researchers to go beyond the limitations of macro data and permit explanations enriched by cultural, historical, institutional, behavioural and other insights. However, the conclusions yielded by this method have limited generalizability beyond the countries examined.

There is a third comparative approach that has been employed extensively in comparative industrial relations: case studies of more than two countries written by a team of individuals with expertise in the countries concerned. Some of these comparative studies are relatively unstructured and readers are left largely to draw their own conclusions from the materials presented (for example, Ferner and Hyman, 1992). Others adopt a more structured approach, with each case study addressing a common set of questions aimed at developing or testing analytical models or theoretical arguments (see Locke *et al.*, 1995a).

The team case-study methodology has not been widely utilized for the comparative study of unionization, although Frenkel (1993) employed it in a study of unions in the Asia-Pacific region. The present study of six English-speaking countries uses a semi-structured case-study approach. Heeding the warning of Strauss (1992) about the dangers of premature theorizing in comparative research, we did not begin with the idea of testing a particular analytic model. Instead, the conclusions have been built up inductively from the evidence uncovered. In order to facilitate comparison, we commenced with a common set of issues, deliberately made general enough to permit the description of unique local characteristics, and to avoid skewing the conclusions toward a priori hypotheses.

The existence of different national models of industrial relations, or of some supranational model, is not assumed. While it is possible to point to some differences in emphases between unions in, say, European countries and those of predominantly English-speaking countries, such stereotypes are of less significance than the considerable divergence historically between industrial relations systems within these groups of countries. Despite recent changes arising from the common economic and social pressures of globalization and liberalization, these systems are a long way from convergence. Indeed, one of the paradoxical effects of globalization appears to have been the proliferation of alternative models of industrial relations not only between but within nations (Locke *et al.*, 1995b). Three of the six countries in our study are federations in which responsibility for industrial relations is shared between two layers of government.

The choice of six predominantly English-speaking countries does warrant justification. Our rationale is both relatively straightforward and, we think, appropriate. The steps in our choice were as follows. First, as noted above, we wished to utilize the comparative method to test our research questions. Second, we did not consider our own two countries, Australia and Britain, to be a large enough group to allow sufficient comparisons. Either, or indeed both, could be outliers in terms of union experience. Third, keeping in mind the contention that the diversity of experiences found in comparative studies is, potentially, both a strength and a weakness, we decided to focus on a relatively small group of union movements. Subsequently, we reasoned, the study could be extended if appropriate. Fourth, we wished to focus on a relatively homogeneous group of countries, insofar as that is possible. A number of similarities exist between all or many of the six countries. These include:

- a common language for a majority of each population, allowing and facilitating relatively quick exchange of ideas and beliefs through both print and electronic forms of communication

- based on this dominant common language, a not hugely dissimilar societal culture

- relatively common political systems, including Labour Parties in most of the countries and similarities in the role of the state

- a significant commonality in legal systems

- traditional, historic links between these countries.

Accordingly, we decided to focus our study on the fortunes of trade unions in Australia, Britain, Canada, Ireland, New Zealand and the USA.

In some respects, it is convenient to divide the six countries into pairs. Ireland, for example, shares a voluntarist industrial relations model with the UK archetype. Similarly, a distinct Australasian model of industrial relations evolved, characterized until the 1980s by state-operated compulsory arbitration tribunals and, more recently, by labour-market deregulation. Canada and the USA share a system in which a union, after demonstrating workplace support through a certification election, becomes the exclusive bargaining agent entitled to negotiate a legally binding contract with the employer. Even within these pairs, however, there exists much variation. In Ireland, unions have been incorporated into a centralized system of tripartite bargaining, while in the UK they were effectively marginalized during two decades of Conservative rule. In New Zealand, the change from centralization to deregulation was abrupt, while in Australia it has been more leisurely. Canada's unionization rate has remained almost constant for the past quarter of a century, while that of the USA has declined to the extent that many commentators believe the union movement to be beyond resuscitation, at least in the private sector (Freeman and Rogers, 1993; Green, 1996). It is the task of this book to examine such similarities and differences, and to deduce what principles may underlie these patterns.

Conclusion

It is argued in this book that trade unions as institutions remain embedded within the social relations of production. How they organize and operate depends on the complex of relations at the workplace level and beyond. Trade unions carry with them their own histories and traditions and must respond to particular sets of relations in different sectors and regions according to the occupational composition of their memberships. Many unions faced declining memberships, as economic and political restructuring proceeded. In some instances, it became difficult for unions to maintain an organized presence at workplace level. As the balance of power in many workplaces shifted towards managements, it became even more difficult for union negotiators to represent their memberships in an ongoing and regular way. The apparent strength of many unions in the 1970s was revealed as rather hollow and insubstantial at a local level, at the workplace. With restructuring and the shifting relations between labour and capital, there can be no one fixed pattern of organization and activity. It is possible that some trade unions will simply disappear – as happened to the third largest trade union in New Zealand in the mid-1990s – or wither in the face of the uncertainties of work and employment. Others will reconstitute themselves and begin to organize in the light of these changing circumstances and conditions, perhaps beginning to develop forms of unionism that parallel those elsewhere. This book aims to provide a stocktake of unions in six countries and to assess what role is being played by trade unions, as collective organizations, in the ongoing process of restructuring the relations between labour and capital.

References

Bassett, P. and Cave, A. (1993) *All for One: The Future of the Unions*, Fabian Pamphlet No. 559, London: The Fabian Society.

Bean, R. and Holden, K. (1992) 'Cross-national differences in trade union membership in OECD countries', *Industrial Relations Journal*, **23** (1), 52–9.

Belanger, J. and Murray, G. (1994) 'Unions and economic restructuring: introduction', *Relations Industrielles*, **49** (4), 639–56.

Bennett, J. and Delaney, J. (1993) 'Research on unions: some subjects in need of scholars', *Journal of Labor Research*, **14** (2), 95–110.

Bild, T., Jorgensen, H., Lassen, M. and Madsen, M. (1998) 'Do trade unions have a future? The case of Denmark', *Acta Sociologica*, **41** (3), 195–207.

Boxall, P. and Haynes, P. (1997) 'Strategy and trade union effectiveness in a neo-liberal environment', *British Journal of Industrial Relations*, **35** (4), 567–91.

Breitenfellner, A. (1997) 'Global unionism: a potential player', *International Labour Review*, **136** (4), 431–555.

Bronfenbrenner, K. and Juravich, T. (1998) 'It takes more than house calls', in K. Bronfenbrenner, S. Friedman, R. Hurd, R. Oswald and R. Seeber (eds) *Organizing to Win: New Research on Union Strategies*, Ithaca and London: ILR Press, pp. 19–36.

Bronfenbrenner, K., Friedman, S., Hurd, R., Oswald, R., Seeber, R. (eds) (1998) *Organizing to Win: New Research on Union Strategies*, Ithaca and London: ILR Press.

Chaison, G. N. (1996) *Union Mergers in Hard Times: The View from Five Countries*, Ithaca: ILR Press.

Chen, M. and Wong, K. (1998) 'The challenge of diversity and inclusion in the AFL–CIO', in G. Mantsios (ed.) *A New Labor Movement for the New Century*, New York: Garland Publishing, pp. 213–31.

Clegg, H. (1976) *Trade Unionism Under Collective Bargaining: A Theory Based on Comparisons of Six Countries*, Oxford: Basil Blackwell.

Corneo, G. (1995) 'Social custom, management opposition, and trade union membership', *European Economic Review*, **39** (2), 275–92.

Dagg, A. (1997) 'Worker representation and protection in the "New Economy"', in *Report of the Advisory Committee on the Changing Workplace*, Government of Canada; http://www.reflexion.gc.ca/menu_e.cfm.

Dahl, R. (1961) *Who Governs? Democracy and Power in an American City*, New Haven: Yale University Press.

Dahl, R. (1985) *A Preface to an Economic Theory of Democracy*, London: Polity Press.

Fairbrother, P. (2000a) 'British trade unions facing the future', *Capital and Class*, **41**, 15–56

Fairbrother, P. (2000b) *Trade Unions at the Crossroads*, London: Mansell.

Fairbrother, P. and Waddington, J. (1990) 'The politics of trade unionism: evidence, policy and theory', *Capital and Class*, **41**, 15–56.

Ferner, A. and Hyman, R. (eds) (1992) *Industrial Relations in the New Europe*, Oxford: Blackwell.

Fine, J. (1998) 'Moving innovation from the margins to the centre', in G. Mantsios (ed.) *A New Labor Movement for the New Century*, New York: Garland Publishing, pp. 139–69.

Fiorito, J., Jarley, P. and Delaney, J. (1995) 'National union effectiveness in organising: measures and influences', *Industrial and Labor Relations Review*, **48** (4), 613–35.

Flanders, A. (1970) *Management and Unions: The Theory and Reform of Industrial Relations*, (2nd edn), London: Faber and Faber.

Freeman, R. B. and Rogers, J. (1993) 'Who speaks for us? Employee representation in a non-union labor market', in B. Kaufman and M. Kleiner (eds) *Employee Representation: Alternatives and Future Directions*, Madison: IRRA, pp. 13–79.

Frenkel, S. J. (ed.) (1993) *Organized Labor in the Asia-Pacific Region: A Comparative Study of Trade Unionism in Nine Countries*, Cornell: ILR Press.

Gallie, D. (1996) 'Trade union allegiance and decline in British urban labour markets', in D. Gallie, R. Penn and M. Rose (1996) *Trade Unionism in Recession*, Oxford: Oxford University Press, pp. 140–74.

Green, M. (1996) *Epitaph for American Labor: How Union Leaders Lost Touch With America*, Washington, DC: AEI Press.

Griffin, G. and Svensen, S. (1996) 'The decline of Australian union density: a survey of the literature', *Journal of Industrial Relations*, **38**, 505–47.

Griffin, L., Botsko, C., Wahl, A. and Isaac, L. (1991) 'Theoretical generality, case particularity: qualitative comparative analysis of trade union growth and decline', *International Journal of Comparative Sociology*, **32**, 110–36.

Hince, K. (1996) 'The impact of the Employment Contracts Act on union membership, structure and organisation', in G. Griffin (ed.) *Industrial Relations in New Zealand: Five Years of Deregulation*, Melbourne: National Key Centre in Industrial Relations.

House of Commons Employment Committee (1994) *Third Report: The Future of Trade Unions*, Vol. 1: Report and Proceedings of the Committee, London: HMSO.

Hyman, R. (1989) *The Political Economy of Industrial Relations: Theory and Practice in a Cold Climate*, Basingstoke: Macmillan.

Hyman, R. (1994) 'Changing trade union identities and strategy', in R. Hyman and A. Ferner (eds) *New Frontiers in European Industrial Relations*, Oxford: Blackwell, pp. 108–39.

International Labour Office (1997) *World Labour Report 1997–98: Industrial Relations, Democracy and Social Stability*, Geneva: ILO.

Jarley, P. and Maranto, C. (1990) 'Union corporate campaigns: an assessment', *Industrial and Labor Relations Review*, **43**, 505–24.

Jefferys, S. (1996) 'Strategic choice for unions in France and Britain: divergent institutions with converging options', in P. Leisink, J. Van Leemput and J. Vilrokx (eds) *The Challenges to Trade Unions in Europe: Innovation or Adaptation*, Cheltenham, UK: Edward Elgar, pp. 171–85.

Johnston, P. (1994) *Success While Others Fail: Social Movement Unionism and the Public Workplace*, Ithaca, NY: ILR Press.

Katz, H. C. (1993) 'The decentralisation of collective bargaining: a literature review and comparative analysis', *Industrial and Labor Relations Review*, **47** (1), 3–22.

Kelly, J. (1997) 'The future of trade unionism: injustice, identity and attributes', *Employee Relations*, **19**, 400–14.

Kelly, J. (1998) *Rethinking Industrial Relations: Mobilisation, Collectivism and Long Waves*, New York: Routledge.

Kerr, C., Dunlop, J., Harbison, F. and Myers, C. (1962) *Industrialism and Industrial Man*, London: Heinemann.

Lawler, J. J. (1990) *Unionization and Deunionization: Strategy, Tactics, and Outcomes*, Columbia, SC: University of South Carolina Press.

Lind, J. (1996) 'Trade unions: social movement or welfare apparatus?', in P. Leisink, J. Van Leemput and J. Vilrokx, *The Challenges to Trade Unions in Europe: Innovation or Adaptation*, Cheltenham, UK: Edward Elgar, pp. 105–20.

Lipow, S. (ed.) (1996) *Power and Counterpower: The Union Response to Global Capital*, London: Pluto Press.

Locke, R., Kochan, T. and Piore, M. (eds) (1995a) *Employment Relations in a Changing World Economy*, Cambridge, Mass: MIT Press.

Locke, R., Kochan, T. and Piore, M. (1995b) 'Reconceptualizing comparative industrial relations: lessons from international research', *International Labour Review*, **134** (2), 139–61.

Martin, R., Sunley, P. and Wills, J. (1996) *Union Retreat and the Regions: The Shrinking Landscape of Organised Labour*, London: Jessica Kingsley Publishers.

Masters, M. (1997) *Unions at the Crossroads: Strategic Membership, Financial and Political Perspectives*, Westport, CT: Quorum Books.

Maurice, M., Sellier, F. and Silvestre, J. (1986) *The Social Foundations of Industrial Power: A Comparison of France and Germany*, Cambridge, Mass: MIT Press.

Mazzocchi, T. (1998) 'Building a party of our own', in G. Mantsios (ed.) *A New Labor Movement for the New Century*, New York: Garland Publishing, pp. 281–93.

McIlroy, J. (1997) 'Still under siege: British trade unions at the turn of the century', *Historical Studies in Industrial Relations*, **3**, 93–122.

McKinley, A. and Taylor, P. (1996) 'Power, surveillance and resistance', in P. Ackers, C. Smith, and P. Smith (eds) *The New Workplace and Trade Unionism*, London: Routledge, pp. 279–300.

Miliband, R. (1969) *The State in Capitalist Society*, London: Weidenfeld & Nicolson.

Miliband, R. (1982) *Capitalist Democracy in Britain*, Oxford: Oxford University Press.

Millward, N. (1994) *The New Industrial Relations*, London: Policy Studies Institute.

Müller-Jentsch, W. (1988) 'Industrial relations theory and trade union strategy', *The International Journal of Comparative Labour Law and Industrial Relations*, **4** (3), 177–90.

Needleman, R. (1998) 'Women workers: strategies for inclusion and rebuilding unionism', in G. Mantsios (ed.) *A New Labor Movement for the New Century*, New York: Garland Publishing, pp. 175–96.

Osborne, D. E. and Gaebler, T. (1992) *Reinventing Government: How the Entrepreneurial Spirit is Tranforming the Public Sector*, New York: Plume.

Parker, M. and Slaughter, K. (1997) 'Advancing unionism on the new terrain', in B. Nissen (ed.) *Unions and Workplace Reorganization*, Detroit: Wayne State University Press, pp. 208–25.

Peetz, D. (1998) *Unions in a Contrary World: The Future of the Australian Trade Union Movement*, Melbourne: Cambridge University Press.

Pocock, B. (1998) 'Institutional sclerosis: prospects for trade union transformation', *Labour and Industry*, **9** (1), 17–36.

Poole, M. (1986) *Industrial Relations: Origins and Patterns of National Diversity*, London: Routledge and Kegan Paul.

Prewitt, M. (1997) 'Unions embrace new tactics vs. operators', *Nation's Restaurant News*, 12 May.

Ramsey, H. (1997) 'Solidarity at last? International trade unionism approaching the Millennium', *Economic and Industrial Democracy*, **18**, 503–37.

Roche, W. K. and Turner, T. (1994) 'Testing alternative models of human resource policy effects on trade union recognition in the Republic of Ireland', *International Journal of Human Resource Management*, **5**, 721–53.

Rose, J. B. and Chaison, G. N. (1985) 'The state of the unions: United States and Canada', *Journal of Labor Research*, **6**, (1) 97–111.

Rose, J. B. and Chaison, G. N. (1996) 'Linking union density and union effectiveness', *Industrial Relations*, **35** (1), 78–105.

Schregle, J. (1981) 'Comparative industrial relations: pitfalls and potential', *International Labour Review*, **120** (1), 15–30.

Strauss, G. (1992) 'Creeping toward a field of comparative industrial relations', in H. Katz (ed.) *The Future of Industrial Relations*, Ithaca, NY: Cornell University Press.

Swenson, P. (1989) *Fair Shares: Unions, Pay, and Politics in Sweden and West Germany*, Ithaca, NY: Cornell University Press.

Towers, B. (1997) *The Representation Gap: Change and Reform in the British and American Workplace*, New York: Oxford University Press.

Undy, R., Fosh, P., Martin, R., Morris, H. and Smith, P. (1996) 'British trade unions' strategies in a hostile environment', in P. Leisink, J. Van Leemput and J. Vilrokx (eds) *The Challenges to Trade Unions in Europe: Innovation or Adaptation*, Cheltenham, UK: Edward Elgar, pp. 223–38.

Visser, J. (1987) In Search of Inclusive Unionism: A Comparative Analysis, PhD thesis, University of Amsterdam.

Visser, J. (1992) 'The strength of union movements in advanced capital democracies', in M. Regini (ed.) *The Future of Labour Movements*, London: Sage, pp. 17–52.

Voos, P. B. (1984) 'Does it pay to organize? Estimating the cost to unions', *Monthly Labor Review*, **107** (6), 43–4.

Waddington, J. and Whitston, C. (1997) 'Why do people join unions in a period of membership decline?', *British Journal of Industrial Relations*, **35** (4), 515–46.

Walker, K. (1967) 'The Comparative Study of Industrial Relations', *Bulletin of the International Institute for Labour Studies*, No. 3.

Western, B. (1997) *Between Class and Market: Postwar Unionization in the Capitalist Democracies*, Princeton: Princeton University Press.

Zoll, R. (1996) 'Modernization, trade unions and solidarity', in P. Leisink, J. Van Leemput and J. Vilrokx (eds) *The Challenges to Trade Unions in Europe: Innovation or Adaptation*, Cheltenham, UK: Edward Elgar, pp. 77–87.

2 UNIONS IN AUSTRALIA: STRUGGLING TO SURVIVE

Gerard Griffin and Stuart Svensen

Introduction and Context

Throughout the nineteenth century both the development of trade unionism and the emerging system of industrial relations paralleled the experiences found in other English-speaking countries. Although *ad hoc* combinations of workers, formed with a view to raising wages, were recorded as early as 1795, the first workers' organizations resembling trade unions were trade societies established in the 1830s. Some of these operated mainly as benefit societies through which workers could insure themselves against unemployment, sickness and other adversities. Other organizations acted to protect the interests of their members through industrial action and attempts to regulate the supply of labour. Due to a repressive political climate and generally unfavourable economic circumstances, most working-class organizations prior to the 1850s were small and short-lived (Turner, 1978, pp. 9–19). The 1850s was a watershed decade both for the labour movement and Australia generally. Free immigration accelerated as a result of the discovery of gold, and the population trebled in this decade. Convict transportation was halted in all colonies except in Western Australia, where it continued into the 1860s. The gold rushes created labour shortages, leading to high wages and favourable conditions for collective organization. An influx of new immigrants, overwhelmingly British, used to the idea of unionism and possessing organizing skills also helped. The first Australian branch of the British-based Amalgamated Society of Engineers was formed in 1852 by 26 emigrant engineers on board their ship to Australia. Over succeeding decades and until the 1890s, Australian unionism developed along predictable lines. The initial unions were mainly craft unions, small and locally based. Unions covering semi-skilled and unskilled workers commenced operations during the 1870s as did the first inter-union organizations. The 1880s saw the emergence of larger unions, typically through amalgamation of local unions. By 1890, some 350 unions were in existence (Quinlan and Gardner, 1995).

A series of major strikes in 1890–1, together with a subsequent severe and protracted economic recession, had several important consequences for unions; cumulatively, they changed dramatically the nature and character of Australian trade unionism. First, there was a collapse in unionization and the industrial strength of unions. The extent of the collapse is difficult to measure, but the number of unions appears to have approximately halved by 1894 (Quinlan and Gardner, 1995). Inter-union councils were also hard hit; the New South Wales Labor Council had eight affiliates with 41,267 members in May 1891, and this was reduced to eight affiliates with 401 members by 1899 (Markey, 1988, p. 319). A second major consequence of the strikes was the expansion of political activity. Plans to increase unions' representation in parliament predate the strikes of the early 1890s. These strikes, however, undoubtedly acted as a catalyst for the development of workers' political organizations and labour leagues, which ultimately grew into the Australian Labor Party (ALP). As discussed later, many trade unions have been longstanding affiliates of the ALP. A third outcome was the creation of an arbitration-based system of industrial relations. Most historians see the 1890s strikes as being pivotal to the creation of the Australasian system of compulsory conciliation and arbitration (Markey, 1989). While there were some experiments in conciliation and arbitration prior to 1890, these schemes were invariably voluntary, and a key defining feature of the Australasian system post-1890 was its compulsory element (Mitchell, 1989).

The arbitration system, particularly new federal legislation in 1904, had a profound influence on the development and character of unionism. The 1904 Act encouraged the formation and registration of representative organizations, leading to an immediate surge in both the number of unions and union density. The increasingly favourable economic conditions of the early twentieth century also aided union recovery. Union density was estimated to be only 6 per cent in 1900. By 1920, this unionization rate had increased to over 50 per cent, a rate largely maintained over the next six decades. Registration, and the arbitral system generally, had a number of additional consequences for trade unions, such as significant state regulation and control of their internal affairs and, as will be discussed later, their industrial strategies.

Overall, for much of the twentieth century, and based on the arbitral model, trade unions were an accepted and integral part of the centralized Australian industrial relations system. From the early 1980s onwards, however, unions started to lose this privileged position. Membership decreased alarmingly and power and influence in the economy, in the polity and in society generally declined. In a dramatic reversal of fortunes, unions are now struggling to survive as a viable force in the twenty-first century. This chapter outlines and analyses these developments, focusing on union membership, structure, governance and the relationship with the state and political parties. It then examines how unions have responded to the various crises they faced and provides an assessment of the current state of the union movement. It ends with a somewhat pessimistic analysis of the future roles of trade unionism in Australia.

Unions, the State and Political Parties

This section explores the relationship between the union movement, the main judicial arm of the state interacting with unions – the Australian Industrial Relations Commission (AIRC) – and the Australian Labor Party. It commences with a very brief discussion of union relations with other political parties.

The Communist Party maintained a strong association with sections of the union movement from the 1920s to the 1980s. The party never achieved significant electoral success; no Communists were elected to federal parliament, and only one member was elected to a state parliament. Nevertheless, at various times and places the party attracted a significant minority vote. For example, in coal-mining districts in the 1930s and 1940s, the party regularly polled over 20 per cent and sometimes came close to winning seats. The party also enjoyed successes at the local government level. Many union officials in mining, the waterfront and other industries were party members and the party was able to secure considerable influence industrially, leading to the reaction from the right-wing, mainly Catholic 'Industrial Groups' that had success in wresting control of some unions from Communists in the early 1950s.

The effects of the Labor Party battles of the 1950s gradually ebbed. The breakaway right-wing Democratic Labor Party never attracted a sizeable industrial or political following, and its main achievement was to keep the ALP out of office federally until 1972. The Communist Party survived the attack from the right but was weakened by factional splits in the 1960s and 1970s. The once proud Communist Party of Australia liquidated itself following the fall of the Soviet Union.

The conservative political parties, particularly the Liberal/National coalition parties and their predecessors, have had few linkages to the union movement. While such parties invariably take a general, pro-business position, conservative governments have not traditionally been overtly hostile towards unions. For example, during the lengthy reign of the Liberal Party/ National Party coalition governments from 1949 to 1972, the role of the arbitration system and the role of unions to represent employees was continually reaffirmed. Nevertheless, the Liberal government did occasionally attempt to gain electoral advantage by attacking the unions. During the 1980s and 1990s, however, relations between the trade union movement and conservative political parties deteriorated dramatically. Briefly, conservative parties in Australia, in common with their counterparts in other countries, became ardent converts to labour market deregulation, and came to view both unions and the existing centralized industrial relations system as major obstacles to the efficient working of labour markets. Consequently, when it won federal government in 1996, the Liberal/National Party coalition introduced legislation that mandated the dominance of enterprise agreements over awards (arbitrated decisions of the Australian Industrial Relations Commission). This Act also enshrined both individual contracts of employment and non-union-based collective agreements as alternative mechanisms of regulating the employment relationship. Subsequently, in both 1999 and 2000, the government attempted to pass further legislation that required secret ballots prior to strike action and would have imposed further restrictions on union access to workplaces. The legislation was defeated in the Upper House of Parliament, the Senate, where a small party controls the balance of power. Despite this defeat, in late 1999 a Ministerial Discussion Paper proposed further regulation of the internal affairs of trade unions (see Forsyth, 1999). The federal government has also sought to shape union behaviour by non-legislative means such as restricting payroll deductions to those unions that the government considers to be acting responsibly and forcing public sector unions to provide new written authorities from their members to continue payroll deductions. Overall, a high level of antagonism characterizes the relationship between trade unions and conservative political parties.

Links between trade unions and the ALP have always been very strong. Traditionally, the party and the unions have referred to themselves as the political wing and the industrial wing of the labour movement. The ALP grew out of the union movement and, over time, many parliamentarians, including prime ministers, started their careers as union officials. Unions formally affiliate to the ALP at state, rather than federal, level, pay fees on behalf of their affiliated members and control significant block votes at decision-making conferences. Despite these levers of power, the party is by no means the handmaiden of the unions. The capacity for unions to direct ALP policy is diffused by many factors, including the federal system, the frequent lack of an ALP majority in both chambers of Parliament, a lack of unity among trade unions, and the ability of Labor governments to interpret party policy in unusual ways (Cole, 1982). There are numerous examples of Labor governments failing to do what unions wanted or expected; for example, the Scullin government's failure in 1930 to end a lockout in the coal-mining industry, the Chifley government's use of troops as strike-breakers in the 1949 coal strike and aspects of the Keating government's Industrial Relations Reform Act of 1993.

The oscillating relationship between the unions and the ALP, particularly during the period 1983–96 when the party held federal government, set the framework for macro-level industrial relations and also, ultimately, for the decline of trade unionism. During these years, the ALP government, led for much of the time by a former President of the Australian Council of Trade Unions (ACTU), entered into a succession of eight agreements (known collectively as the Prices and Incomes Accord) with the ACTU. The Accord was meant to produce economic growth, lower inflation and reduced unemployment (Singleton, 1990). The major policy instrument to achieve these objectives was the reduction of labour costs. Wage growth was restricted initially through full wage indexation, followed by the reduction of real wages through partial indexation. Improved family allowance benefits were provided to offset the effects of lower wages on families. An interventionist industry policy was also promised. This involved reducing tariffs and increasing direct assistance to business. Industries such as steel and stevedoring were restructured to make them less labour intensive, and many thousands of jobs were shed. Optimists argued that such changes would pave the way for unions, workers and employers to cooperate in economic management and industrial restructuring and avoid a slide into decentralized bargaining (Frenkel, 1988). In effect, the Accord process was envisaged by its designers as an Antipodean social contract and as a means of achieving industrial relations consensus rather than conflict; a vision explicitly influenced by study tours to Europe, particularly Scandinavian countries (ACTU/TDC [Trade Development Council], 1987).

This vision was not achieved. Instead, in the latter part of the Accord period, the government and ACTU cooperated in the design and promotion of enterprise bargaining, albeit not without some tensions. Employer groups came increasingly to favour decentralization, while key members of Labor governments displayed a growing zeal for neo-liberal economic solutions. This was exhibited through policies like the deregulation of the financial system, taxation changes, fiscal restraint and tariff reductions (Griffin and Teicher, 1997).

Prior to 1993, changes to the federal industrial relations system had been made in a climate of relative harmony between the political and industrial wings of the labour movement. The Industrial Relations Reform Act of 1993, however, represented a major departure. It made significant changes to the general enterprise bargaining system and extended enterprise bargaining to encompass non-unionized employees. Among other outcomes, these developments led to an ALP Minister for Industrial Relations receiving a rowdy reception when he addressed the 1993 ACTU Congress (Gahan, 1993). In many ways, these legislative changes provided a framework for the then newly elected conservative government to introduce the more radical Workplace Relations Act of 1996. For its part, following its electoral defeat, the ALP announced that it did not envisage a future Labor government entering into an Accord-type arrangement with the union movement.

This new Act, which came into effect in 1997, was a landmark: for the first time in the federal system, the encouragement of representative organizations and their registration was not made an object of the Act (for detailed discussions of various aspects of the Act see Creighton, 1997; Ford, 1997; and McCarry, 1997). Instead, principal objects included the ensuring of 'freedom of association' and for wages and conditions to be determined as far as possible by the agreement of employers and employees at the workplace. While organizations could be registered, the object of the part of the Act dealing with registered organizations was not to encourage registration, but to encourage democratic control, member participation, and efficient management of those organizations. The Act was also a landmark in that it provided for the making of individual contracts for the first time in federal legislation. Equally important for unions, non-union collective agreements could be made and registered. Awards became residual in that they were to be stripped back to twenty allowable provisions within eighteen months. The Industrial Relations Court was abolished, and the role of the AIRC was downgraded, although not by as much as the government had originally planned.

The new Act made significant changes to the way in which unions could organize. The minimum membership size of unions was set at 50, and provision was made for enterprise unions. The entry of union officials to workplaces was made more difficult. Officials are required to hold permits, give 24-hours notice and are restricted in their activities. Permits can be revoked if the official obstructs employers or employees, or otherwise acts in a manner considered improper. The Act places significant restrictions on industrial action, with provision for fast-track sanctions against illegal strikes. Industrial action is permitted during bargaining periods subject to certain limitations, but action intended to protect or promote the broader social and economic interests of workers and unions is unlawful. Closed shops were outlawed. Cumulatively, the provisions of this 1996 legislation raise significant difficulties for trade unions with regard to both bargaining and organizing and, as noted earlier, the federal government has attempted to further amend the Act and foreshadowed further changes.

Apart from changing legislation and providing support for employers or unions, governments can also produce changes in industrial relations through the way they deal with their own employees. From the late 1980s onwards, the ALP government initiated a series of public sector changes which had the cumulative effect of replacing the traditional public administration model of the public service with the creation of a technocratic, managerial state, considered necessary to integrate Australia into an internationalizing economy (Fairbrother, Svensen and Teicher, 1997a). A major focus of this programme was increasing efficiency through the reduction of input costs and cost recovery through greater commercialization. In particular, government business enterprises were reshaped into corporations, and some were privatized. The number of public servants was reduced and increased use was made of contracting-out. Post-1996, these changes were accelerated by the Conservative government, which saw less need to negotiate changes with unions. The number of federal employees fell from 408,800 in 1991 to 347,600 in 1995, and to 285,600 in 1997 (Macdonald, 1998). Similar changes have been occurring at the state and local government levels, most dramatically in Victoria (Fairbrother, Svensen and Teicher, 1997b). These changes have had a serious adverse affect on the numerical strength of unions, and their capacity to represent their remaining members effectively.

So far we have focused on federal legislation. While the federal jurisdiction is the key arena – for example, federal law holds sway in any clash of jurisdictions – the combined employee coverage of state industrial relations jurisdictions is roughly equal to that of the federal jurisdiction. During the 1980s and 1990s, conservative parties held office in a number of states and frequently passed legislation with significant impact on trade unions. The first major legislative challenge to unions came in Western Australia, where a new Act introduced by the Liberal government in 1979 prohibited preference clauses (clauses granting preference in a wide area of employment conditions to unionists over non-unionists) in awards and agreements and discrimination against non-unionists by employers. These laws were later extended so that victimization or discrimination against non-unionists became a criminal offence. Union membership in the state fell 3.2 per cent in the two years after the introduction of the legislation, compared with a rise of 4.9 per cent elsewhere in Australia. Membership fell by 10.4 per cent among those unions which were registered under the state system. The heaviest falls occurred in industrially weaker unions, which relied most heavily on legally enforced preference arrangements to maintain membership levels. These were predominantly moderate, white-collar unions. Unions with stronger workplace organization, such as those covering mining, waterfront, construction and transport workers, did not suffer to the same degree. This latter group of unions openly and successfully flouted the laws.

Other legislation introduced by conservative state governments, notably the Tasmanian Industrial Relations Act (1984), the New South Wales Industrial Relations Act (1991), the Victorian Employee Relations Act (1992), the Western Australian Workplace Agreements Act (1993), and the South Australian Industrial and Employee Relations Act (1994), also attempted to end discrimination against non-unionists, with results broadly similar to those observed in the case of Western Australia. It has been estimated that the proportion of employees in compulsorily unionized jobs has declined from 34 per cent in 1976, to 23 per cent in 1988 and 11 per cent in 1995 (Peetz, 1997).

The Queensland government took a different approach to dealing with unions. In 1984, it passed legislation restricting the rights of unions to take industrial action. During an industrial dispute in the state-owned electricity utility in early 1985, approximately 1,000 employees were dismissed and their replacements hired under individual contracts. Anticipating that the state Industrial Relations Commission would order the reinstatement of the sacked workers, the government issued an Order in Council removing the Commission's power to make such an order. This was followed by legislation both legitimizing individual contracts and placing further restrictions on industrial action (Moore, 1986). Oddly, the Queensland government did not prohibit union preference until 1997 and, between 1990 and 1996, the state had the lowest rate of decline of union membership (Hamberger, 1998).

These legislative and strategic changes at the state level were, to a great extent, responses to demands by employer groups and advocates of neo-liberalism for a more market-oriented and enterprise-focused system of industrial relations, as opposed to the continuation of the traditional arbitral model. Inevitably, these same forces were at play in the federal system. From the mid-1980s, the federal arbitration system was lampooned as an inflexible, archaic system run for the benefit of an 'industrial relations club'

(Henderson, 1985). A key part of this club were trade unions, organizations fostered, according to these 'new right' supporters, by the centralized arbitration system. Clearly, the introduction of the federal arbitral model in 1904 granted the union movement some very significant concessions. Among the foundation stones of the arbitral model were:

- formal registration of organizations, including trade unions

- the granting of exclusive jurisdiction over specified segments of the workforce to registered organizations

- the ability to have claims for improved wages and working conditions arbitrated by a third-party external to the employment relationship

- the legal enforcement of awards, decisions of the tribunal establishing minimum wages and conditions.

There was, of course, some price to be paid for such benefits, including formal curtailment of industrial action and scrutiny of union rulebooks and internal affairs. To a union movement desperately trying to recover from the ravages of the 1890s, this was not a very high price to pay. The nature of the subsequent relationship between the union movement and the arbitral system, particularly the AIRC, has been the subject of some controversy. Howard, for example, claims that, because of its dependence on the state, Australian unionism 'is a labour movement in form and intention, rather than in tactic and achievement' (1977, p. 269), a claim disputed by Gahan (1996). Dabscheck argues that a 'bargaining/activist theory provides the clearest insight into gaining an understanding of the role of industrial tribunals in Australia' (1992, p. 353). Regardless of the validity of the contending claims, there is widespread agreement that the relatively unique Australasian system of industrial relations guaranteed a central role to trade unions. It is difficult to envisage the operation of a centralized system without trade unions, indeed without broadly representative trade unions. Over time, the union movement and its officials became skilled at utilizing the central system both to make initial gains in wages and conditions and to subsequently flow these gains on to the workforce at large. As we will argue later, union strategy revolved in large measure around the arbitral system. Decisions of the AIRC, termed awards, became large and complex documents, and lengthy hearings, interspersed with appeals to various courts, became standard practice. For many union officials, the floor of the Commission hearing rather than the shopfloor became their bailiwick. Many employers accepted the rigidity of the system, and tended to leave the management role within this macro-level industrial relations system to employer associations; associations which themselves held the status of registered organizations.

The first stirrings of possible change emerged during the 1970s following the oil-price shock of 1973/4. A Conservative government elected in 1975 quickly discarded its pre-election promise to support the existing system of automatic wage indexation linked to prices. Yet the system was such that this government had to argue a case for some discounting of Consumer-Price-Index-based wage increases before a hearing of the AIRC. Change was still some time off. During the 1980s, however, the pro-market, pro-deregulatory, anti-central wage-fixing forces gained supremacy, first within the ranks of employers and conservative politicians and ultimately within the ALP. The various state laws, detailed above, as well as the 1993 ALP federal legislation, reflected this supremacy. The arbitral model and the AIRC were relegated largely to providing a supportive role to the new, market-oriented enterprise bargaining system. The union movement faced the prospect of similar relegation. If a centralized system necessitated unionism, an enterprise bargaining system, particularly one with provision for individual contracts and non-union collective contracts, certainly did not. If unions were indeed creatures of the arbitration system, their time was now up and they faced decline. One key dimension and measurement of this possible decline is membership data.

Membership

Gross trends in Australian union membership and union density are shown in Table 2.1. There are two main sources of data on Australian union membership. The Australian Bureau of Statistics (ABS) series *Trade Union Statistics Australia* (Australian Bureau of Statistics 6323.0) and corresponding membership data in the earlier *Labour Report* are derived from a census of union returns. This series provides annual data for the period from 1907 to 1996 when the census was discontinued. The Bureau's other series, *Trade Union Members Australia* (Australian Bureau of Statistics 6325.0), *Working Arrangements* (Australian Bureau of Statistics 6342.0) and, since 1995, *Earnings, Benefits and Union Membership* (Australian Bureau of Statistics 6310.0) is based on a household survey conducted in 1976, 1982, 1986, 1990, and annually from 1992. Both series have significant potential for error, but, as indicated by the ABS decision to discontinue the census series, the survey series is regarded as a more reliable indicator of trends.

Table 2.1 *Union membership and density in Australia, 1901–99*

Year	Union membership ('000)		Union density	
	Census	Survey	Census	Survey
1901	97.2	n.a.	6.1	n.a.
1911	364.7	n.a.	27.9	n.a.
1921	703.0	n.a.	51.6	n.a.
1931	740.8	n.a.	47.4	n.a.
1941	1,075.6	n.a.	49.9	n.a.
1951	1,690.2	n.a.	60.0	n.a.
1961	1,894.6	n.a.	57.0	n.a.
1971	2,452.2	n.a.	51.0	n.a.
1976	2,800.0	2,512.8	55.0	51
1982	3,012.4	2,567.6	56	49.5
1986	3,186.2	2,593.9	55	45.6
	(2,870.5)[a]		(50)	
1990	3,422.2	2,659.6	54	40.5
	(3,053.2)		(48)	
1992	3,135.1	2,508.8	49	38.6
	(2,822.6)		(44)	
1993	3,000.1	2,376.9	47	37.6
	(2,715.2)		(43)	
1994	2,890.2	2,283.4	44	35.0
	(2,424.0)		(38)	
1995	2,756.3	2,251.8	40	32.7
	(2,439.7)		(35)	
1996	2,800.5	2,194.3	43	31.1
	(2,450.5)		(36)	
1997	n.a.	2,110.3	n.a.	30.3
1998	n.a.	2,037.5	n.a.	28.1
1999	n.a.	1,878.2	n.a.	25.7

a. ABS estimates of financial members in brackets.

Sources: Deery and Plowman (1991); ABS 6325.0 *Trade Union Members* (1976–92, 1994, 1996); 6342.0 *Working Arrangements Australia* (1993); 6310.0 *Weekly Earnings of Employees* (1995, 1997) retitled *Earnings, Benefits and Union Members* (1998 and 1999).

According to the census-based series, union density increased dramatically between 1901 and 1911, and nearly doubled again between 1911 and 1921 when the 50 per cent density rate was breached. The 1930s depression caused a fall in density rates back into the 40–50 per cent decile with a steady climb thereafter to a peak of 61 per cent in 1954. Density declined gradually during the remainder of the 1950s and the 1960s as unions struggled to make inroads into the growing white-collar workforce. Success in these endeavours saw the low-point of 49 per cent in 1970 climb to the mid-50s for most of the 1970s, rise to a peak of 57 per cent in 1985 and decline steadily thereafter.

Each of the surveys since 1976 has recorded a decline in union density. In the 1980s, density decline occurred chiefly through an increase in the workforce and the inability of unions to maintain their share of this expanding workforce. In the 1990s, not only has density declined but so has absolute membership from 2.66 million in 1990 to 1.88 million in 1999. These survey figures increasingly diverged from the census data. Commencing in 1985, the ABS, in an attempt to explain the divergence, differentiated between total and financial membership of unions. This practice continued for a decade; ultimately, the ABS decided to drop its census series completely.

Regardless of which series is used, union membership during the 1990s declined rapidly. Tables 2.2 to 2.4 show fluctuations in union density by various characteristics since 1990. A number of trends can be discerned. Density has fallen more slowly among females than males, leading to a reduction in the different density rates between the sexes. Density is declining faster in the private than in the public sector, although there was a rapid density decline in the central public service areas in the period 1994–6. Employment in the public sector is also shrinking, with increasing privatization, outsourcing and other reductions in the public sector. While

Table 2.2 *Union density, Australia, by selected characteristics, 1990–9*

	Sex		Sector		Hours		Engagement		
Year	Male	Female	Public	Private	Full-time	Part-time	Permanent	Casual	Overall
1990	45.1	34.7	66.8	30.8	44.7	25.1	45.7	18.8	40.5
1991	n.a.	n.a.	n.a.	n.a.	n.a.	n.a.	n.a.	n.a.	n.a.
1992	43.4	34.8	67.1	29.4	44.3	25.2	46.1	17.2	38.6
1993	40.9	33.5	64.4	27.5	42.1	23.6	43.9	16.0	37.6
1994	37.9	31.3	62.3	26.0	39.1	22.9	41.3	14.7	35.0
1995	35.7	29.1	56.4	25.1	36.3	22.4	n.a.	n.a.	32.7
1996	33.5	28.1	55.4	24.0	34.5	21.6	37.4	13.1	31.1
1997	33.0	26.9	54.7	23.3	33.7	21.3	36.0	13.8	30.3
1998	30.0	25.8	52.9	21.4	31.2	20.2	34.2	11.6	28.1
1999	27.7	23.4	50.0	19.6	29.0	17.5	31.1	10.7	25.7

Sources: ABS 6325.0 *Trade Union Members* (1976–92, 1994, 1996); 6342.0 *Working Arrangements Australia* (1993); 6310.0 *Weekly Earnings of Employees (Distribution)* (1995, 1997–9).

Table 2.3 *Union density, Australia, by age, 1990–9*

Year	Age Group						
	15–19	20–24	25–34	35–44	45–54	55–59	60+
1990	25.0	33.5	42.3	43.5	45.6	49.6	43.4
1991	n.a.	n.a.	n.a.	n.a.	n.a.	n.a.	n.a.
1992	22.6	31.5	40.5	43.0	46.5	45.7	37.9
1993	21.5	30.0	37.2	42.6	42.7	42.9	37.0
1994	19.3	26.7	34.4	40.5	40.2	42.9	31.6
1995	19.0	24.6	32.3	36.8	38.4	38.8	30.4
1996	18.5	24.0	29.5	35.9	36.1	38.6	25.3
1997	18.6	21.8	28.4	35.2	35.9	34.8	27.0
1998	17.3	20.3	25.4	32.5	34.4	32.1	26.6
1999	14.2	16.6	23.2	32.4	31.4	28.8	26.0

Sources: ABS 6325.0 *Trade Union Members* (1976–92, 1994, 1996); 6342.0 *Working Arrangements Australia* (1993); 6310.0 *Weekly Earnings of Employees (Distribution)* (1995, 1997–9).

Table 2.4 *Union density, Australia, by number of employees, 1990–9*

Year	Size			
	1–9	10–19	20–99	100+
1990	16.4	30.3	46.0	58.2
1991	n.a.	n.a.	n.a.	n.a.
1992	16.3	29.8	46.1	57.6
1993	14.0	28.6	44.9	55.0
1994	12.6	25.3	42.0	53.4
1995	11.8	22.6	38.8	50.5
1996	n.a.	n.a.	n.a.	n.a.
1997	10.3	20.0	33.8	46.3
1998	9.4	18.2	32.4	43.9
1999	9.3	15.6	28.5	40.5

Sources: ABS 6325.0 *Trade Union Members* (1976–92, 1994, 1996); 6342.0 *Working Arrangements Australia* (1993); 6310.0 *Weekly Earnings of Employees (Distribution)* (1995, 1997–9).

density is lower among part-time employees, reduction in density has been faster among full-time employees. Density is much lower among casual employees, and has been falling at a steeper rate than for permanent employees. Density decline has been slower among workers aged 35 to 54

Table 2.5 *Membership changes in the ten largest Australian unions, 1995–2000*

Union	1995	1997	2000
Shop Distributive and Allied Employees Association	208,925	227,656	210,974
Australian Education Union	156,195	164,343	151,767
Construction Forestry Mining and Energy Union	120,000	120,000	120,000
Communications, Electrical and Plumbing Union	195,322	189,523	166,576
Communications and Public Sector Union	110,520	106,080	72,497
Australian Manufacturing Workers Union	200,000	191,750	172,112
Australian Services Union	182,312	169,903	129,888
Finance Sector Union	119,081	109,771	83,073
Australian Workers Union	161,000	145,000	90,967
Australian Liquor, Hospitality and Miscellaneous Workers Union	201,740	160,266	150,413

Source: Davis (1997) for 1995 and 1997; reported by unions for 2000.

than for other age groups. Overall, however, these differences are merely variations of a theme and that theme is very clear: all categories of employees have significantly lower density rates in 1999 than they had in 1990. Based on membership data, the union movement has had a horrendous decade.

Table 2.5 shows membership fluctuations in Australia's ten largest unions over the period 1995–2000. These figures show that unions are holding the line in education and retailing but are doing poorly in other areas. Over the five-year period, the combined membership of these ten unions dropped by 19 per cent. The merger process, discussed later, has led to a very high concentration of union members in a small number of key unions: the combined membership of these ten unions accounted for 71 per cent of all unionists in 2000. This was a slight decrease from the equivalent 75 per cent figure for 1997 and the 73 per cent figure for 1995 but was a huge increase on the 36 per cent figure for 1983.

The dramatic decline in union membership has been caused by a number of factors (for a review of the literature, see Griffin and Svensen, 1996). Briefly, the pattern of membership decline does not appear to be explicable by wage movements. Real wages declined from 1984 to 1990, but subsequently rose. The wage rises of the 1990s, though, have generally been achieved through the erosion of working conditions, especially variations of working hours. The union movement thus has not been able to achieve significant gains for workers for two decades, and this is likely to have affected the union-joining decision. Another important factor in the decline is the reduction of the incidence of closed-shop arrangements which, as noted earlier, has had an adverse impact on membership, especially in industrially weaker unions (Weeks, 1995). Changes in industry structure have also been implicated in the decline in union density, particularly in the 1980s (Peetz, 1998a). These industry effects, however, may have been overestimated (Griffin and Svensen, 1996). Finally, the changed attitude of employers has probably played a significant role in influencing levels of unionization. The best example of this change was the 1999 decision by BHP, Australia's largest company, to offer individual contracts of employment to its workers in the iron ore mining industry in Western Australia.

Structure and Governance

The organizational model for nineteenth-century unionism was the British horizontal, occupational-based union structure. This was not unexpected given that the vast majority of workers were British migrants who brought with them the mores and values of their homeland. Indeed, a number of the craft unions established in the 1850s were established as overseas branches of the 'parent' British union (for one example, see Sheridan, 1975). Importantly, following the introduction of the conciliation and arbitration system in 1904, the then Commonwealth Court of Conciliation and Arbitration, now the Australian Industrial Relations Commission, adopted the entrenched, traditional occupational structure of unionism as the basis for granting membership jurisdiction. Indeed, by giving legal force to exclusive occupational jurisdiction, the AIRC enshrined this horizontal union structure for much of the twentieth century.

In the decade following the 1904 legislation, the number of unions jumped significantly, increasing from a figure of 198 in 1901 to over 600 in the 1910s. However, many of these unions disappeared in the post-First World War rationalization and, by the early 1920s, the total number of trade unions had settled in the 350–400 range. Over the next six decades, this total number of unions slowly decreased, but did not finally drop below 300 until 1989. Unions continued to be mainly occupationally based and no true industry unions were formed in this period. Enterprise unions were not common, although they were permitted in New South Wales (Rimmer, 1981). The relative stability in numbers and type of unions until the 1980s obscured some significant structural change. For example, the average membership size of unions grew from 620 in 1907 to 9,800 in 1986 (Dabscheck, 1995, p. 124) and the number of unions covering skilled workers decreased while the number of white-collar unions increased (Griffin and Scarcebrook, 1989).

Throughout these decades, trade union structure was characterized by, first, a skewed distribution of union membership; second, multi-unionism at both the industry and enterprise level; and third, well-developed inter-union structures at the national and state level but not at the enterprise level. Table 2.6 details the number and membership size of trade unions between 1968 and 1996; the Australian Bureau of Statistics ceased collecting data on the numbers of unions after 1996.

Table 2.6 *Size distribution of Australian trade unions, 1968–96*

Number of members	Number of trade unions				Proportion of total members	
	1968	1976	1992	1996	1992	1996
Under 100	57	37	32	21	0.0	0.0
100–under 250	42	36	26	12	0.1	0.1
250–under 500	49	35	18	18	0.2	0.2
500–under 1,000	44	49	28	11	0.6	0.3
1,000–under 2,000	46	38	21	14	0.8	0.7
2,000–under 5,000	47	44	30	16	3.0	1.8
5,000–under 10,000	21	24	19	6	4.0	1.6
10,000–under 20,000	24	20	15	10	6.8	5.1
20,000–under 30,000	8	10	7	2	5.5	1.8
30,000–under 40,000	8	9	6	5	6.7	6.3
40,000–under 50,000	5	6	5	2	7.0	3.2
50,000–under 80,000	–	7	5	3	10.6	7.7
80,000 and over	10	7	15	12	54.7	71.2
TOTAL	**361**	**322**	**227**	**132**	**100.0**	**100.0**

Source: Australian Bureau of Statistics, *Trade Union Statistics*, Catalogue No. 6323.0.

Since the early twentieth century, there has been a large number of unions with very small memberships. Indeed, as late as 1996, some 21 unions each had less than 100 members. Not unexpectedly, few of the smaller unions operated outside the confines of more than one state. In 1996, there were 132 unions of which only 46 unions operated in two or more states but covered 86 per cent of total membership.

The large number of unions inevitably resulted in multi-unionism at the industry level. In 1981, Plowman calculated the number of unions operating in fourteen industries; these data ranged from six in the entertainment industry through 26 in manufacturing to 55 in the transport industry (Plowman, 1981, p. 32). This multiplicity at the industry level need not necessarily translate into multi-unionism in the enterprise. It is not unusual for unions with coverage of similar workers to have negotiated demarcation lines, frequently along state boundary lines. The first Australian Workplace Industrial Relations Survey (AWIRS) provided detailed data for 1989 on the number of unions in individual workplaces and showed that the average number of unions in enterprises with more than five employees was just under two. Not surprisingly, the larger the number of employees in the enterprise the greater the number of unions. For example, while only 5 per cent of workplaces with twenty or more employees had six or more unions, 43 per cent of workplaces with 500 or more employees were covered by six or more unions (Callus et al., 1991, p. 118). Inevitably, some large enterprises had to deal with a large number of unions; for example, Benson (1991) found that, for most of the 1980s, 24 unions had members within the State Electricity Commission of Victoria. Arguably, multi-unionism and its attendant potential problems was an issue largely restricted to large enterprises.

With the exception of a limited number of industries, trade union structures at the workplace level have traditionally been relatively poorly developed. AWIRS found a low level of joint union organization: only 11 per cent of managers at workplaces with more than one union reported the existence of a joint union committee. Even in manufacturing, such committees existed in only 18 per cent of workplaces. Of course, in small enterprises with relatively few unions, union and employee coordination can be organized relatively quickly and easily through forums less formal than joint committees. However, the survey highlighted the relative paucity of such committees even in large enterprises with only 35 per cent of multi-union workplaces with 500 or more employers having reported a joint union committee (Callus et al., 1991, p. 119). Focusing on shop stewards, just over half of workplaces with 20 or more employees had a union delegate presence in the AWIRS surveys of 1989 and 1995. This was much more likely in public sector workplaces (84 per cent in 1995) compared to the private sector (39 per cent in 1995) (Morehead et al., 1997).

The existence of one unified broadly-based confederation (usually termed a peak council in Australia) stands in sharp contrast to this lack of structure at the workplace level. This unity, however, is a relatively recent development. When the ACTU was established in 1927 a 'rival' organization was already in existence. The Australian Workers Union, by far the largest trade union, had, for some years prior to 1927, regarded itself as the logical organizational base for an all-Australian union federation. In addition, as early as 1915 a peak council covering associations of federal public sector employees had been established. After the founding of the ACTU, a number of other peak councils, such as the Australian Council of Salaried and Professional Associations, were also established.

During the 1970s and 1980s, however, the ACTU has absorbed most of these sectional union groups. In 1967, the Australian Workers Union chose to end its self-imposed exile and affiliated to the ACTU. In 1979, following a lengthy courtship, the Australian Council of Salaried and Professional Associations disbanded and most of its affiliates transferred to the ACTU. The small number of affiliates that decided not to join the ACTU at this time did so during the 1980s. In 1981, the Council of Australian Government Employee Organisations, the federal public sector peak council, disbanded and all its affiliates transferred allegiances to the ACTU. In 1985, the Australian Public Service Federation, the grouping of the state-based public service associations, joined the ACTU. By 1990, 167 unions were affiliated to the ACTU and, although this figure was not much more than half the then total number of unions, these unions contained within their ranks over 90 per cent of all unionists. As a result of all of these mergers, the ACTU can legitimately claim to be the collective voice of organized labour and to speak with authority on its behalf.

Between the two extremes of enterprise and national union structures lie two intermediate levels: industry federations and state-based Trades and Labor councils. Industry federations have played a not unimportant role in a limited number of industries. The rationale for these federations is to provide a forum for unions in the industry to both resolve inter-union problems, such as demarcation disputes, and to provide a mechanism for negotiations with employers at the industry level. The Metal Trades Federation has been the most prominent federation but similar groupings exist in industries such as mining and building. Trades and Labor councils, although predating the formation of the ACTU, are now formally the state-based branches of the peak council. Given that, historically, a majority of unions operated only in one state, these councils played an important linking mechanism in trade union structures. Generally, most unions operating in each state, with the exception of the very small unions, are affiliated to the appropriate council. Consequently, the level of influence and degree of importance of these state-based bodies has been not insignificant, particularly when the Labor Party forms the state government.

Overall, prior to the 1980s, changes to union structure were gradual and evolutionary. These decades of stability were, however, followed by a wave of union mergers initiated largely at the behest of the increasingly powerful ACTU. The ACTU had been advocating large industry-based unions since its inception, but it was not until the late 1980s that substantial progress commenced. The ACTU/Trade Development Council document *Australia Reconstructed* (ACTU/TDC, 1987), formulated after a fact-finding mission to Sweden, Norway, Austria, West Germany and the United Kingdom, recommended that the Australian union movement adopt a paradigm of 'strategic unionism'. This approach was aimed at extending the influence of unions through the development of integrated strategies for full employment, a greater focus on ways to improve wealth creation, and related policies. This ambitious corporatist project was never implemented, and probably had little chance of success in any case (Beeson, 1997; Frenkel, 1993).

At the 1987 ACTU Congress, drawing on both ABS survey statistics and the concept of strategic unionism, Secretary Bill Kelty attempted to instill a sense of crisis, warning delegates that unionism would decay and decline to the point of irrelevancy unless drastic action was taken to restructure the union movement. Congress endorsed the ACTU restructuring plan outlined in *Future Strategies for the Trade Union Movement* (ACTU, 1987), which recommended the absorption of most of Australia's unionists into 20 mainly industry-based 'super' unions, through amalgamations.

Based on historical data, this ACTU policy appeared unlikely to be implemented. In the period 1951 to 1985, there had been only 23 mergers between federally registered unions. Indeed, prior to 1972 there were no formal merger procedures. In that year, three unions merged to form the militant Amalgamated Metal Workers Union, and the federal government legislated to make union mergers more difficult through ballot and voter-turnout requirements. Over the next decade, however, spurred by a combination of factors, such as declining membership, changed legislation and leadership drive (see Griffin, 1992; Griffin and Scarcebrook, 1989), a relative tidal wave of unions mergers occurred and the total number of unions decreased from 316 in 1987 to 132 in 1996 (see Table 2.7). In an a priori sense, it could have been logically hypothesized that most of this reduction would have come from among the ranks of the large number of state-based unions with low membership. However, almost half of the total of 184 unions that disappeared were federally registered unions. In total, of the 172 mergers, 79 were between federally registered unions. The main concentration of mergers took place in the early 1990s. During the period 1991–4, some 61 federal mergers occurred; an average of over fifteen each year. In a very real sense, the ACTU thrust to restructure the Australian union movement has been largely achieved. Currently, trade unionism is dominated, both in terms of membership and power, by a small number of relatively large, leading unions.

Table 2.7 *Number of union mergers, Australia, 1987–99*

Years	No. of unions		No. of mergers	
	Total	Federal	Total	Federal
1987	316	144	8	2
1988	308	146	8	6
1989	299	140	7	1
1990	295	134	4	4
1991	275	125	22	21
1992	227	94	44	18
1993	188	66	35	14
1994	157	54	27	8
1995	142	47	10	3
1996	132	47	7	0
1997	n.a.	46	n.a.	1
1998	n.a.	46	n.a.	1
1999	n.a.	45	n.a.	0

Source: Australian Bureau of Statistics, *Trade Union Statistics*, Catalogue No. 6323.0; data from the Industrial Registrar's Office.

From the organizational structure and governance perspective, an important feature of the amalgamation process was that the mergers tended to be motivated more by occupational, ideological and factional convenience than by industry considerations. The 1991 ACTU Congress endorsed the formation of both occupational and industry-based unions. The result was the formation of conglomerate as well as industry unions. A number of craft unions remained; some of these affiliated into super craft unions, such as the plumbers and electricians, retaining their autonomy through branch structures (Yates and Ewer, 1997). Some reduction of multi-unionism was achieved by the designation of a hierarchical order within industries of 'principal', 'significant' and 'other' unions with specified rights to provide representation (Griffin, 1992). In general, however, the governance of these organizations is frequently very complex, with the degree of complexity related to factors such as the extent of 'membership fit' of the merging partners, historical power relationships and the organizational structures agreed to at the time of the merger. In brief, it has been easier to integrate organizational structures where some commonality of membership was present; conversely, little integration has occurred where the memberships had little in common. The historical distribution of power between the state and federal levels of the antecedent unions has also influenced integration:

similar loci of power facilitated integration. Finally, some mergers were consummated on terms that militate strongly against full integration; in some cases these terms were formalized in the rules of the new, merged organization.

Turning to the issue of governance, the dominant feature in the twentieth century has been the centralization of power and authority, initially at the individual union level, then at the federation level during the 1980s and much of the 1990s, and more lately again at the individual union level. This centralization is linked to, and arguably caused by, the traditional dominance of the arbitral model of industrial relations with its centralized wage determination system. As in other countries, unions concentrated their resources at the organizational level that determined wages and working conditions; in Australia this was largely at the industry or national level. In short, improved wages were won most often through argument and advocacy in the Industrial Relations Commission, not through industrial action in the factories and offices. The key negotiations were mainly with officials of the relevant employer association, not with the managers at the workplace level. There were, of course, exceptions to this generality so that a history of shop-steward activism can be found in industries such as mining, meat and railways. Equally, at certain times, such as the late 1960s and early 1970s, collective bargaining assumed a much higher status. Overall, however, full-time officials, not lay officials, were the source of wage increases. Inevitably, they accumulated and wielded power and authority.

Figure 2.1 outlines a standard, basic union governance structure that can be applied to most unions despite the added complexity introduced by mergers. In theory, the membership dominates the decision-making processes. Members select the shop stewards and sub-state branch officials,

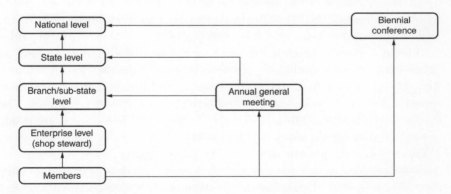

Figure 2.1 *Flow of authority in Australian unions*

vote for the full-time officials at state and federal level (usually through secret postal ballots), can attend and vote at Annual General meetings at the state level, and elect delegates to the supreme decision-making body, usually the annual or biennial conference. When this structure is linked with the extensive, legally based, external regulation by the Industrial Registrar of the internal affairs of trade unions, noted earlier, it is difficult to conceive of a more democratically mandated governance structure. The 'problem', of course, is that, in common with union movements everywhere, a majority of union members chose to not exercise their participation rights. It is extremely unusual, even in plebiscites involving mergers, to secure more than a 50 per cent membership participation rate; rather, the usual turnout is less than one-third of eligible members. Inevitably, as with union movements in other countries, the activist members, usually the source of future full-time officials, dominate. Overall, in many unions, a self-perpetuating group of officials maintain power and control and, while contests for official positions are not unusual and challenges to incumbents are sometimes successful, the handover of authority more frequently occurs within the existing power elite.

One difference between unions is the level of full-time official at which power resides – the state or the federal level. In some cases, the federal union is merely a conglomeration of independent state fiefdoms; in others, the federal officials dominate. The history of the union and the legal coverage of the union members as between state and federal tribunals often help explain this differing location of power.

Traditionally, the peak council, the ACTU, wielded little authority as noted above. Commencing in the early 1980s, however, a range of factors combined to thrust the ACTU into a major position of authority among trade unions. These included the greater inclusiveness achieved through the affiliation of the AWU in 1967 and the absorption of the three, white-collar and public sector peak bodies. ACTU affiliates represented 45 per cent of unionists in 1945, 65 per cent in 1961, and at least 90 per cent in 1993. The ACTU gained additional authority through the need for the ALP government to have an authoritative representative organization to enter into the Accord relationship. Other factors reinforcing the growing influence of the ACTU were reduced factionalism, changes in leadership and policy development, and the increased use of a willing ACTU by the Industrial Relations Commission to help enforce its decisions (Griffin, 1994).

This newfound authority of the ACTU had a number of major impacts on trade union governance. First, it relegated individual unions to a supporting role, effectively that of carrying out the dictates of the peak council. Unlike a country such as Ireland, national wage negotiations and agreements were sanctioned not by individual union members but by peak body officials. Second, it concentrated decision-making in the hands of the ACTU Executive. For example, the 1987 ACTU Congress increased the size and authority of the ACTU executive, and there was a concomitant reduction in the power of the Congress itself. The number of voting delegates was reduced, and Congresses became increasingly stage-managed. Each delegate was given a satchel containing conference resolutions and reports, which were generally endorsed with a minimum of debate (Davis, 1988). Following criticism of the anti-democratic way congresses were run, 'syndicate' sessions were organized at the 1993 Congress. Ostensibly, these were to provide debating forums, but they were well-orchestrated showpieces that served merely to diffuse dissent (Gahan, 1993). Third, because of the dominance of the centralized ACTU strategy, few affiliates considered the post-Accord alternatives. In short, the ACTU set the course for the whole union movement.

Consequently, the move towards an enterprise bargaining focus from around 1993 onwards caught many unions unprepared. In the main, they attempted to revert to the system that operated in pre-Accord days – the dominance of full-time state and national officials. The spread of enterprise agreements (approximately 6,000–7,000 agreements signed annually during the late 1990s) caused tensions within a number of unions. Quite simply, strong, centralized governance is not necessarily the most appropriate system in a deregulated, bargaining environment. A number of unions are attempting to resolve, somewhat tentatively, this tension by devolving some authority to the shop floor. Most are encouraging shop-steward involvement in negotiations; few are giving stewards the authority to conclude agreements. This tension is reminiscent of similar situations in Britain in the 1960s. Australian unions, in the main, have not yet varied their method of governance to reflect the changing locus of decision-making in wage negotiations, a factor contributing to the growth of non-union-based collective agreements. Such a change may prove necessary in the future.

Orientation and Strategies

The Australian union movement has traversed several evolutionary stages including its British craft origins, the parliamentary response to the defeats of the 1890s, the changes resulting from the adaptation to arbitration and the contemporary responses to challenges such as globalization and the transition to enterprise and individual agreement-making. For most of the twentieth century, however, the arbitration system has been the dominant influence on both the orientation and strategy of the Australian union movement. In effect, the arbitration system revived a dormant trade union movement and gave it extensive succour through the series of valuable, legally enforceable rights detailed earlier. Crucially, over time, and in marked contrast to other countries where unions regarded legal intervention in the employment relationship with a high degree of suspicion, the vast majority of Australian unions and union officials came to view this system as being the best mechanism to achieve their goals. Thus, rather than the industrial strategy complemented by a political strategy found more traditionally in other countries, Australian unions increasingly followed a hierarchy of, in descending order, arbitral, political and industrial strategies. This meant that, in many cases, wage increases were won not on the industrial battleground but rather through tactics such as arbitrated National Wage Cases or applying, on the grounds of traditional relativities, in the AIRC for flow-ons of increases granted to other groups of workers. Equally, rather than visit the workplaces and sign up non-organized employees, membership was achieved and retained through strategies such as *de facto* closed shops, government policies, employer support and the insertion of preference clauses into legally binding decisions of the AIRC. In practice, a centralized, arbitral model of industrial relations that, arguably, necessitated and required an organized and representative union movement, offered a range of inducements to Australian unions to operate within this centralized system. The package of benefits proved irresistible to most unions. Most, accordingly, built their orientations, tactics and strategies around this model. Few unions chose to exit the arbitration system voluntarily. Those threatened with deregistration, usually the militants, fought long and hard to remain within the system regardless of radical leaderships or strategic positions in the chain of production. In brief, the vast majority of unions, pragmatists all, played the arbitration game and used the avenues and mechanisms of that system to win higher wages and conditions.

Inevitably, this orientation had a large impact on the structures, power and operations of the union movement. We have already discussed one element – the growth, development and survival of a large number of small trade unions. Other elements include a largely bureaucratic, centralized union movement, often more concerned with tribunal cases than with the immediate concerns of members, limited union activity and structures at the workplace, and extensive regulation of union internal affairs. As noted above, it has been argued that, because of their dependence on the arbitration system, Australian unions during much of the twentieth century cannot be regarded as independent trade union organizations (Howard, 1977). Rather, as organizations established under an Act of parliament to carry out the purposes of that Act, they should be regarded as government agencies (Scherer, 1985, p. 91). Such broad assertions, however, need to be treated with some caution. As Scherer (1985, pp. 92–4) himself notes, Australian unions behave like independent trade unions in that they often oppose government policies and tribunal decisions. When governments attempt to enforce their policies on a recalcitrant union, they normally only succeed when the union can be isolated from the support of the broad trade union movement. Further, these arbitral tendencies vary from union to union. Coexisting with the arbitral system, particularly in industries such as mining and railways, there has always been an 'informal' industrial relations system in which unions organized and settled problems at the workplace level. Finally, of course, Australian unions have a history of engaging in industrial action, and traditionally ranked at least mid-table in any international comparisons of working days lost through strikes. Overall, the Australian union movement has generally comprised a pragmatic majority and a more radical, left-wing minority. Industrial action and 'extra-arbitral' activities occurred when appropriate, particularly in good economic times. Less propitious times saw a return to the order and protection of the arbitral model.

This orientation to arbitration, along with other tenets such as affiliation to the ALP and a focus on the wages of the full-time, blue-collar, male breadwinner, are parts of what has historically been referred to as the 'laborist' tradition in Australia (see Beilharz, 1994). The demise of this tradition (Hall and Harley, 1996), linked to the opening up of the Australian economy to international forces, led to a search for a replacement mechanism. Initially, the promise of the Accord process beckoned brightly. The effective demise of this neo-corporatist approach in the late 1980s and the concurrent rapidly declining membership convinced the union leadership, heavily influenced by the ACTU, to reposition their strategies. The two key elements of this repositioning were restructuring the union movement to create 20 large 'super-unions' and the development of an organizing culture within unions, particularly through a flagship programme named Organising Works.

It is not yet clear how the creation of large, conglomerate unions, detailed earlier, will alter the nature and strategy of Australian unionism. Inevitably, a number of the amalgamated unions were marriages of factional, political convenience (Yates and Ewer, 1997) while some unions were amalgamated in name only, retaining duplicated executives and infrastructure. Equally, the amalgamations had their share of tensions and problems (see Dabscheck, 1995). This has meant that some of the traditional facets of unionism, such as its occupational character and centralized bureaucratic tendencies, have not been eliminated in the merger process. The amalgamation strategy has been criticized from the right and left, but the most influential and coherent critiques have emanated from the right, especially from persons associated with the New South Wales Trades and Labor Council (Costa and Duffy, 1991; Ellem, 1991). According to this analysis, the centralization of trade union structures and power is discrepant with the trend towards decentralized bargaining in neo-Fordist workplaces. In the new environment, it is argued, 'niche strategies' are to be preferred to large, unresponsive bureaucracies imposed from above. Echoing the policies of business organizations (Business Council of Australia, 1989), Costa (1992) has called for a more market-oriented system of unionism. Other critiques of the amalgamation strategy have concentrated largely on what is seen as poor timing and implementation. It is argued that amalgamations have drained union resources and energy at a time when unions were under threat from increasingly aggressive employers, and highly activist neo-liberal state governments (Dabscheck, 1995; Yates and Ewer, 1997).

Despite such critiques, the failure to create true industry unions, and problems in implementation in some cases, it could be argued that the amalgamation strategy 'worked' in that most of the new entities do not look like unravelling in the near future. The 1995 Australian Workplace Industrial Relations Survey data indicate that members of amalgamated unions are no more likely, in aggregate, to have left their unions than other union members (Griffin and Svensen, 1998). In an analysis of panel data from the same survey, Peetz (1998b) found that the effect of amalgamation on workplace union collapse was conditional on the extent to which the amalgamation reduced multi-unionism and, hence, friction between unions.

Overall, what is clear is that amalgamations did not prove to be the hoped-for mechanism to reverse declining unionization. While the ACTU 'top-down' approach succeeded at effecting a large number of amalgamations in a relatively short span of time, the process must be judged unsuccessful on the membership criterion. This conclusion led to some rethinking within the ACTU and a number of key individual unions. Analysis focused around the need to recruit unorganized workers. Ultimately, heavily influenced by the report of a study tour of the USA in August 1993, ACTU Executive determined on a programme to:

- select and train young persons for recruitment and organizing

- devote more resources to recruitment and organizing activities more generally

- ensure that organizers appropriately reflect union membership and potential membership in terms of gender, age and ethnicity.

The approach underlying this programme became known as the organizing model. Adherents and supporters of this model contrasted it with the servicing model, which they characterized as an approach that situates the union as a reactive third party that attempts to solve problems and can be blamed when results are unsatisfactory. In contrast, the organizing model was viewed as a more inclusive, empowering approach, where members see themselves as the union and establish their own agendas (ACTU, 1995). Organizers employed by the union provide assistance as required, especially in specialized areas, but the focus is on members becoming active, organizing themselves, and establishing a culture of unionization in the workplace. The role of participating unions should be stressed here. While the Organising Works structure was established by the Executive and operated under the aegis of the ACTU, in practice, the new organizers spent on average four days each week working in and for their employing union and one day in training.

Organising Works no doubt had a number of beneficial effects. However, as detailed in Table 2.1, the total number of union members clearly continued to decline during the last five years of the 1990s. On this criterion, as with the union mergers, Organising Works has failed in its primary objective.

Overall, whatever may be said of both the ACTU and individual union responses to the membership crisis, neither have been guilty of strategic inertia. Commencing in the 1980s, the union movement has initiated three major strategic changes. The Accord, union mergers and inculcating an organizing culture were not the only strategies pursued by the union movement. Additional approaches include

- the provision of a wide range of discounted services to members, ranging from cheap telecommunications and housing loans to legal and shopping services

- promotion of female union officials (half of the ACTU Executive must now be comprised of female officials)

- forging stronger links with progressive community organizations and progressive academics and research organizations

- the latest ACTU initiative to reinvigorate the union movement, *unions@-*

work, which attempts to link workplace organization, particularly in growing areas of employment, with enhanced communication and the use of information technology (ACTU, 1999).

To date, however, these policies have not prevented declines in union membership, power or influence.

The State of the Unions

It is difficult not to offer a pessimistic assessment of the state of trade unions in Australia. Until the 1980s, trade union membership density was high, the legitimacy of unionism was widely accepted among employers and political parties, and long-standing legislation conferred a range of rights and privileges on unions. In short, unions were a central, core part of the industrial relations system. Within the space of a decade and a half, this comfortable, entrenched position changed dramatically. This section scores Australian unions with respect to membership, legislation, political influence, and the broad industrial relations and wage-fixing system.

Earlier, we presented tables detailing the decline in density during the 1980s and 1990s. Briefly, density declined sharply between 1982 and 1988. The next four years saw a reduction in the rate of decline and many union officials started to allow themselves the belief that the worst was over. The experience from 1992 onward, however, was a repeat of the 1982–8 pattern leading to an overall density rate of 26 per cent in 1999. Particularly noteworthy is the 20 per cent density rate in the private sector, the growing sector of the economy. For a union movement that, for much of the previous 60 years, had a density rate of over 50 per cent, the current figures are depressing. Further, there is no evidence that the decline may slow in the near future: the decline of 2.4 percentage points in overall density between 1998 and 1999 was above the average decline for the 1994–9 period.

Unions, of course, have attempted to halt this decline. The previous section detailed the various strategies pursued. While the union movement has been comprehensively restructured and while some recruiting successes have been achieved, these have been far outweighed by the numbers of departing members, the result of factors such as high labour turnover and the demise of the closed shop. In common with most other union movements, Australian unions have to recruit significant numbers of new members merely to replace exiting members. Over the last few years, unions have not achieved this breakeven recruitment figure. By this measure none of the union strategies has been successful, although some concession must be made to the hypothetical case of a 'worse state of the unions' without the implementation of these strategies.

Between 1983 and 1996 the ALP, the political wing of the labour movement, was in government at the federal level. Through both the Accord mechanism and personal contacts, the views and opinions of unions and union officials were expressed and heard in a broad range of fora. In brief, these were years when the union movement, particularly senior officials of the ACTU, had unparalleled access to legislators and policy-makers, and there can be little doubt that such officials were very influential in determining a range of government policies. Obviously, not all government policies were supported by the union movement. For example, the provisions of the Industrial Relations Reform Act (1993) that introduced enterprise flexibility agreements – the so-called non-union agreements – were opposed vehemently by the ACTU. Overall, however, as exemplified by the continued support for the various Accords, the union movement as a whole achieved significant political influence under the ALP government. This influence ended dramatically with the election of a Conservative government in 1996. Access to Ministers ceased, appointments to various boards and committees were terminated and a flow of funds for activities such as union migrant liaison officers halted. The insider quickly became the outsider. Will this exclusion adversely affect the union movement? A number of commentators, including union officials, have recently advanced the argument that being an insider under Labour had adverse effects because, under the Accord process, all employees, regardless of union status, were awarded similar wage increases. Thus, the argument goes, being an outsider may actually contribute to union membership in that the free-rider effect will no longer occur. Regardless of the validity of this argument – a case of looking on the bright side of life – the political influence of the union movement in the early 2000s is at a very low level.

One very important, practical outcome of this low level of influence is the Workplace Relations Act introduced by the new government in 1996. In a number of ways, this new legislation provides a much tougher legislative environment within which unions must operate. For example, the Act facilitates de-mergers of existing unions and the creation of enterprise unions while access to workplaces for organizing purposes is restricted. More broadly, the introduction of individual contracts, the paring back of awards to 20 core matters and the general encouragement of an individual as opposed to the traditional collective ethos, threaten the role of unions. Again, this new legislation is a negative on the union scorecard.

Linked with this legislative development, a significant move away from the long-dominant arbitral model of industrial relations and wage-fixing has occurred. The new system of enterprise bargaining, though a misnomer in many ways, indicates the direction of change. This change both poses challenges and offers opportunities to trade unions; challenges that unions may become increasingly irrelevant to many employees, and opportunities to show how they can improve the lives of employees. So far, the influence of the union movement on enterprise bargaining has been mixed. In some industries, such as construction, unions have been very successful in winning increases in real wages and improved working conditions. In most cases, however, there has been a significant deterioration in members' working conditions, particularly in areas such as hours of work, overtime and penalty rates. Simply stated, unions are now much less influential and central to the determination of wages and conditions than they were under the arbitral model, and in many cases where unions are involved in negotiations, their role is overwhelmingly reactive and the outcome usually linked to employee concessions.

The Future

On balance, the 1990s witnessed a very severe deterioration in the power, status and standing of the union movement. Can the unions reverse this state of affairs in the near to medium future? During the second half of the nineteenth century, Australian unions followed the traditional industrial strategy found in other industrializing economies: bottom-up organization with bargaining outcomes related to industrial power. The events of the 1890s resulted in the growth of the ALP and the introduction of the arbitral system. Unions could now draw from a mix of industrial, arbitral and political strategies. For most of the twentieth century, the mainstream of unionism followed a combination of arbitral and political strategy, for the very simple and good reason that these laborist strategies were perceived as being successful. These strategies evolved into the Accord in 1983. However, even with the continuation of a form of the Accord into the 1990s, union strategic choice in this decade was much reduced. Economic changes during the 1980s, such as the floating of the Australian dollar and the commitment to open up the economy to external competition, together with the increasing globalization of the 1990s, meant that the traditional strategic mix was no longer possible. An ALP government, even if it had wished, was not going to be able to protect trade unionism while the role of the Industrial Relations

Commission was inevitably going to diminish with the introduction of enterprise bargaining. In practice, the industrial strategy has become the only option open to unions, and the changeover to this strategy is being made in an atmosphere not dissimilar to that of the 1890s, including hostile employers, hostile governments and deteriorating overseas markets for our exports.

Given this context it is perhaps not surprising that the extensive union responses to these changes have not been successful. At the macro-level, there seems little prospect of an immediate reversal in fortune. Clearly, unions will survive. After all, if unions can survive in such a hostile environment as the USA then they should similarly be able to continue to function in Australia. However, it is looking increasingly likely that the USA model of business unionism – with concentrations of members in larger organizations, among skilled workers and in the public sector – is the likely future scenario for Australian unions. This limiting situation, should it occur, will be a major change for a union movement long accustomed to playing a major role in political and industrial life and with a federation that regarded itself as the parliament of workers. The key issue to the future character of trade unions is the size and level of membership.

The latest ACTU response to the crisis in membership involves three main approaches. The first is for unions more effectively to represent members at the workplace through better workplace organization. The second is to link work issues with community concerns, such as government funding cuts to childcare, and the exploitation of outworkers or piece-rate workers in industries such as clothing and textiles. Third, the ACTU intends to provide a more sophisticated package of financial, legal and buying services (Pallas, 1998). To our minds, the first approach is the key issue, and is related to the core question of why employees join unions. Particularly in the face of increased employer opposition, unions must ensure that they are doing the bidding of members and delivering on their wages and conditions. The other two approaches are subsidiary policies. At the micro-level, there have been some success stories for trade unions, particularly in education and health. Lyons (1998) argues the more general case that professional employees may prove fertile ground for unions. Two government-funded surveys also offer hope. First, the 1995 AWIRS (Morehead et al., 1997) found that, given a totally free choice, 38 per cent of employees said they would rather be in a union than not, 21 per cent were ambivalent, and 33 per cent said they would rather not be in a union. The second survey, commissioned by the Office of the Employment Advocate, which oversees the administration of individual contracts of employment, covered only union members and had as its central focus an analysis of the extent of now-illegal compulsory unionism (Wallis Group, 1999). The responses indicate that only 20 per cent of employees would consider leaving their union if they had a choice. The basis for a union revival exists. The challenge for unions is to attract that latent support and transform it into actual membership. It is a major challenge but the price of failure will be a future as a niche player, albeit a significant niche player, and a public perception of unions as just another self-interested subgroup in society.

References

ACTU (1987) *Future Strategies for the Trade Union Movement*, Melbourne: ACTU.

ACTU (1995) *Organising Works*, No. 2, Melbourne: ACTU.

ACTU (1999) *unions@work*, Report of the ACTU Overseas Delegation, Melbourne: ACTU.

ACTU/TDC (1987) *Australia Reconstructed*, Canberra: AGPS.

Beeson, M. (1997) 'Organised labour in an era of global transformation: *Australia Reconstructed* revisited', *Journal of Australian Political Economy*, **39**, 55–71.

Beilharz, P. (1994) *Transforming Labor: Labor Tradition and the Labor Decade in Australia*, Melbourne: Cambridge University Press.

Benson, J. (1991) *Unions at the Workplace: Shop Steward Leadership and Ideology*, Melbourne: Oxford University Press.

Business Council of Australia (1989) *Enterprise-based Bargaining Units: A Better Way of Working*, Melbourne: BCA.

Callus, R., Morehead, A., Cully, M. and Buchanan, J. (1991) *Industrial Relations at Work: The Australian Workplace Industrial Relations Survey*, Canberra: AGPS.

Cole, K. (1982) 'Unions and the Labor Party', in K. Cole (ed.) *Power, Conflict and Control in Australian Trade Unions*, Ringwood: Penguin, pp. 85–101.

Costa, M. (1992) 'Mythology, marketing and competition: a heretical view of the future of unions', in M. Crosby and M. Easson (eds) *What Should Unions Do?*, Leichhardt, NSW: Pluto Press, in association with the Lloyd Ross Forum and Labor Council of New South Wales, pp. 316–31.

Costa, M. and Duffy, M. (1991) 'The decline of trade unions and the amalgamation quick fix', in M. Costa and M. Duffy, *Labor, Prosperity and the Nineties: Beyond the Bonsai Economy*, Leichhardt: Federation Press, pp. 100–32.

Creighton, B. (1997) 'The Workplace Relations Act in international perspective', *Australian Journal of Labour Law*, **10**, 31–61.

Dabscheck, B. (1992) 'Industrial tribunals and theories of regulation', in B. Dabscheck, G. Griffin and J. Teicher (eds) *Contemporary Australian Industrial Relations*. Melbourne: Longman Cheshire.

Dabscheck, B. (1995) *The Struggle for Australian Industrial Relations*, Melbourne: Oxford University Press.

Davis, E. (1988) 'The 1987 ACTU Congress: Reconstructing Australia?', *Journal of Industrial Relations*, **30** (1), 118–29.

Davis, M. (1997) 'Crisis as union membership falls', *Australian Financial Review*, 4 August.

Deery, S. and Plowman, D. (1991) *Australian Industrial Relations*, Sydney: McGraw Hill.

Ellem, B. (1991) 'Solidarity in the nineties? An analysis of the ACTU blueprint and the Costa Duffy critique', *Economic and Labour Relations Review*, **2** (2), 90–113.

Fairbrother, P., Svensen, S. and Teicher, J. (1997a) 'The ascendancy of neo-Liberalism in Australia', *Capital & Class*, **63**, 1–12.

Fairbrother, P., Svensen, S. and Teicher, J. (1997b) 'The withering away of the Australian state: privatisation and its implications for labour', *Labour & Industry*, **8** (2), 1–29.

Ford, W. J. (1997) 'Reconstructing Australian labour law: a constitutional perspective', *Australian Journal of Labour Law*, **10**, 1–30.

Forsyth, A. (1999) 'Ministerial Discussion Paper – accountability and democratic control of registered industrial organisation', *Australian Journal of Labour Law*, **12** (3), 193–8.

Frenkel, S. (1988) 'Australian employers in the shadow of the Labor Accords', *Industrial Relations*, **27** (2), 166–79.

Frenkel, S. (1993) 'Australian trade unionism and the new social structure of accumulation', in S. Frenkel (ed.) *Organized Labor in the Asia-Pacific Region: A Comparative Study of Trade Unionism in Nine Countries*, Ithaca: ILR Press, pp. 249–81.

Gahan, P. (1993) 'Solidarity forever? The 1993 ACTU Congress', *Journal of Industrial Relations*, **35** (4), 606–25.

Gahan, P. (1996) 'Did arbitration make for dependent unionism? Evidence from historical case studies', *Journal of Industrial Relations*, **38** (4), 648–98.

Griffin G. (1992) 'Changing trade union structure', in B. Dabscheck, G. Griffin and J. Teicher (eds) *Contemporary Australian Industrial Relations*, Melbourne: Longman Cheshire, 211–22.

Griffin, G. (1994) 'The authority of the ACTU', *Economic and Labour Relations Review*, **5** (1), 81–103.

Griffin, G. and Scarcebrook, V. (1989) 'Trends in mergers of federally registered unions, 1904–1986', *Journal of Industrial Relations*, **31** (2), 257–62.

Griffin, G. and Svensen, S. (1996) 'The decline of Australian union density – a survey of the literature', *Journal of Industrial Relations*, **38** (4), 505–47.

Griffin, G. and Svensen, S. (1998) 'Determinants of same-workplace union exit: evidence from AWIRS II', in R. Harbridge, C. Gadd and A. Crawford (eds) *Current Research in Industrial Relations: Proceedings of the 12th AIRAANZ Conference*, Wellington, 3–5 February 1998, 150–8.

Griffin, G. and Teicher, J. (1997) 'Workplace flexibility: changing industrial relations', in P. James, W. F. Veit and S. Wright (eds) *Work of the Future: Global Perspectives*, St Leonards: Allen & Unwin.

Hall, R. and Harley, B. (1996) 'Australian trade unionism and the interpretation of change', in G. Griffin (ed.) *Contemporary Research on Unions: Theory, Membership, Organisation and Non Standard Employment*, NKCIR Monograph No. 7, Melbourne: National Key Centre in Industrial Relations, 32–62.

Hamberger, J. (1998) 'Freedom of association', in J. Teicher (ed.) *The Workplace Relations Act: Where Are We Now?*, NKCIR Monograph No. 10, Melbourne: National Key Centre in Industrial Relations.

Henderson, G. (1985) 'The industrial relations club', in J. Hyde and J. Nurick (eds) *Wages Wasteland: A Radical Examination of the Australian Wage Fixing System*, Sydney: Hale and Iremonger, 41–58.

Howard, W. A. (1977) 'Australian trade unions in the context of union theory', *Journal of Industrial Relations*, **19** (3), 255–73.

Lyons, M. (1998) 'The professional work ethic and trade union membership', in G. Griffin (ed.) *The State of the Unions*, NKCIR Monograph No. 11, Melbourne: National Key Centre in Industrial Relations, 178–200.

Macdonald, D. (1998) 'Public Sector Industrial Relations under the Howard Government', Paper presented to Unions in Crisis Conference, Monash University, 14–15 July.

Markey, R. (1988) *The Making of the Labor Party in New South Wales 1880–1900*, Kensington: University of New South Wales Press.

Markey, R. (1989) 'Trade unions, the Labor Party and the introduction of arbitration in New South Wales and the Commonwealth', in S. Macintyre and R. Mitchell (eds) *Foundations of Arbitration: The Origins and Effects of State Compulsory Arbitration 1890–1914*, Melbourne: Oxford University Press, pp. 156–77.

McCarry, G. (1997) 'Industrial action under the Workplace Relations Act 1996 (Cth)', *Australian Journal of Labour Law*, **10**, 133–57.

Mitchell, R. (1989) 'State systems of conciliation and arbitration: the legal origins of the Australasian model', in S. Macintyre and R. Mitchell (eds) *Foundations of Arbitration. The Origins and Effects of State Compulsory Arbitration 1890–1914*, Melbourne: Oxford University Press, pp. 74–103.

Moore. T. (1986) 'Industrial relations legislation in 1985', *Journal of Industrial Relations*, **28** (1), 109–15.

Morehead, A., Steele, M., Alexander, M., Stephen, K. and Duffin, L. (1997) *Changes at Work: The 1995 Australian Workplace Industrial Relations Survey*, South Melbourne: Addison-Wesley Longman.

Pallas, T. (1998) 'The role of unions in the new legislative environment', in J. Teicher (ed.) *The Workplace Relations Act: Where Are We Now?*, NKCIR Monograph No. 10, Melbourne: National Key Centre in Industrial Relations.

Peetz, D. (1997) 'The Accord, Compulsory Unionism and the Paradigm Shift in Australian Union Membership', Discussion Paper 358, ANU Centre for Economic Policy Research.

Peetz, D. (1998a) *Unions in a Contrary World: The Future of the Australian Trade Union Movement*, Melbourne: Cambridge University Press.

Peetz, D. (1998b) 'Workplace effects of union amalgamations', in R. Harbridge, C. Gadd and A. Crawford (eds) *Current Research in Industrial Relations: Proceedings of the 12th AIRAANZ Conference*, Wellington, 3–5 February, 1998, 512–20.

Plowman, D. (1981) *Australian Trade Union Statistics*, Sydney: Industrial Relations Research Centre, University of NSW.

Quinlan, M. and Gardner, M. (1995) 'Researching industrial relations history: the development of a database on Australian trade unions 1825–1900', *Labour History*, **66**, 90–113.

Rimmer, M. (1981) 'Long-run structural change in Australian trade unionism', *Journal of Industrial Relations*, **23** (3), 323–43.

Scherer, P. (1985) 'State syndicalism?', in J. Hyde and J. Nurick (eds) *Wages Wasteland: A Radical Examination of the Australian Wage Fixing System*, Sydney: Hale and Iremonger, 75–94.

Sheridan, T. (1975) *Mindful Militants*, Cambridge: Cambridge University Press.

Singleton, G. (1990) *The Accord and the Australian Labour Movement*, Melbourne: Melbourne University Press.

Turner, I. (1978) *In Union Is Strength: A History of Trade Unions in Australia*, Melbourne: Nelson.

Wallis Group (1999) 'De facto compulsory unionisation in Australia', www.dewrsb.gov. au.

Weeks, P. (1995) *Trade Union Security Law: A Study of Preference and Compulsory Unionism*, Annandale: Federation Press.

Yates, C. and Ewer, P. (1997) 'Changing strategic capacities: union almagamations in Canada and Australia', in M. Sverke (ed.) *The Future of Trade Unionism: International Perspectives on Emerging Union Structures*, Brookfield, USA: Ashgate, pp. 131–48.

3 UNIONS IN BRITAIN: TOWARDS A NEW UNIONISM?

Peter Fairbrother

Introduction and Context

Unions in Britain have long occupied an established and central position in the industrial and political landscape of the country. Established in the nineteenth century, unions went on to play an influential part in the establishment of the Labour Party and subsequent politics. However, the pattern of union recognition was not straightforward and unions developed out of the manufacturing, transport, and extractive industries, principally amongst manual workers, extending into other sectors, such as public sector, and non-manual workers, in the twentieth century. The highpoint of unionism occurred in the period following the Second World War, when trade unions became an integral part of the polity, when unions were recognized, membership expanded and union leaders were involved in the formulation of social and economic policy. It was only in the 1980s that this pattern of development and growth was ended, and British trade unions found themselves excluded from policy-formulation.

Thus, the history of British trade unionism was one of seeming progress during the major part of the twentieth century. Clearly, there were setbacks and uncertainties, particularly in the period after the First World War, when sections of the union movement sought to establish active and participative forms of unionism, building on syndicalist traditions and emerging Communist politics. Equally, during the Second World War, many unions were able to lay the foundation for the growth and expansion of the early post-war period through active participation in joint consultative committees. In these various ways, the union movement, particularly in the manual occupations in engineering and related industries, developed a tradition of shop-steward forms of organization and activity. There was a growing interrelationship between the Labour Party and the trade union movement, particularly via the Trades Union Congress (TUC) and involving national leaderships. These relations characterized the form and pattern of trade unionism. There was a relatively well-organized and active trade union base within industry and fruitful, if occasionally contentious, relations between the trade union movement, on the one hand, and the Labour Party, on the other (Minkin, 1991).

These patterns were reversed in the 1980s and into the 1990s, in the harsh political climate of the period, when union membership declined massively and union leaderships and their memberships lost their former public eminence and place in the political arena. Many unions saw their membership disappear as a major industrial restructuring was initiated. Accompanying these developments, Conservative governments of the period put in place a comprehensive array of legislation which further constrained unions. A more assertive private and public sector management drew back from the accommodations of the 1960s and 1970s. Taken together, these changes amounted to a massive reversal of union fortunes in the United Kingdom.

It is now no longer clear whether unions will be able to re-establish their past eminence both within the bargaining arena as well as within the polity. The emergence of 'New Labour' has altered the terrain of unions and politics in Britain. This term is used to identify the Labour Party of the mid-1990s under the leadership of Tony Blair, suggesting the Party has been renewed with a distinctive modernization programme that includes a distancing from trade unions. The origins of the shift in focus lie in the mid-1980s when the Labour Party initiated a reassessment of programmes, commitments and organizational relationships. Unions are now faced with the prospect of rebuilding their organizational bases, so as to represent their members within the industrial arena as well as the polity. To add to these problems, union memberships increasingly experience the uncertainties of internationalized economies and states, further adding to their problems they face. British unions thus face a very uncertain future.

Despite this gloomy context, I argue that, while it may appear that trade unions are on a downward spiral, towards marginalization and political irrelevance, this is a mistaken assessment. Unions face a number of distinctive challenges, which suggest that unions are at a watershed, where the certainties of the past no longer suffice but where it is unclear what form of unionism is emerging. There has been a shift in the locus of power within and between unions and it is unclear how unions will respond to the challenges they now face. What is clear is that the union form of organization is changing, in the context of the changing social relations of production and service. The result is a shift from the routinized and established relations of the past to one where there is uncertainty and opportunity. In these circumstances, I argue that unions are likely to remain a central feature of the unfolding political economy (see also Fairbrother, 2000a).

There are four stages to the argument. First, in section two, I briefly review the changing relations between unions, the state and political parties, focusing on the end of the voluntarist period of legal regulation and its succession by a more overt pattern of legal regulation. This shift has occurred at a time when there has been a distancing between the Labour Party and the trade unions, reinforcing the view that unions are now at a watershed in their relations with political parties and the state. Second, in section three, these developments are located in the context of membership patterns. One influential argument that has been advanced is that unions are in a state of irreversible decline. This assessment, however, ignores the way unions are part of a changing political economy. Pointing to the ways that workers continue to organize collectively in these circumstances, further develops the argument. Third, in sections four and five, the changing structure and governance of unions is examined, drawing attention to the redefinition of union objectives that has begun to take place during the 1980s and 1990s. Fourth, in section six, I review the patterns of continuity by trade unions and the major confederation. Finally, in section seven, I conclude that unions face a vibrant and contestable future.

Unions, the State and Political Parties

The development of British unions has taken a distinct form. There are two noteworthy features to this history: first, the state has played a non-interventionist role in the legal regulation of unions for most of the twentieth century and, second, the focus of union organization and activity outside the state sector and sections of the private services, such as retail, was on the workplace. The role of the state was predicated on an assumption that trade unions should seek to pursue their industrial goals via collective bargaining, without direct state intervention. Broadly, and particularly in the engineering sector, unions negotiated with managements at a local level.

The Voluntarist Tradition

A voluntarist approach to industrial relations was one where there was limited state intervention in the process of regulating relations between unions and employers. The origins of this social formation lay in the nineteenth century, which saw laws developed on the assumption that, while worker organization was a potential threat to the stability of the employment relations, such organization was best contained rather than suppressed (Fox, 1985). The outcome was a sequence of legislation that provided for immunity from prosecution in the event of industrial action and union organization. The state became the guarantor of the rule of law providing a legal framework that defined the relationships between employers and unions (Kahn-Freund, 1983). The philosophy was that industrial relations was organized by a process of voluntary regulation of employment, involving both employers and workers. The role of the state was confined to the maintenance of law, rather than to legal prescription, with limited involvement of the judiciary in employment regulation, although the emphasis on the absence of the state from the process of industrial relations is an overstatement (McIlroy, 1995, pp. 67–8). There was not a positive right to strike, rather a negative immunity from legal redress; employers were not obliged to bargain with unions and collective agreements were not legally enforceable.

One of the key characteristics of unionism associated with these developments was the shop steward. The steward is the work-group representative and embodies the union at the workplaces, speaking on behalf of workplace members and negotiating work rules with local management. The key area for this type of representation was in the engineering industry, where this form of organization emerged out of disputes in the late nineteenth century. Nonetheless, this was a relatively unusual and restricted form of organization in the economy as a whole, until the 1960s. It was in this period that the steward form of organization was extended, beyond craft workers and into the large factories in manufacturing. The result was a form of union organization where steward organization in many unions acquired an independence of official union hierarchies and where national union leaderships began to develop ways of incorporating these representatives formally into union structures (Terry, 1995).

A Tentative Corporatism

A key dimension of the voluntarist set of relations was the inability of governments to address the emerging structural problems of the British economy after the Second World War. The difficulties faced by governments had their roots in the long-term decline of the British economy, which saw a shift from a major exporting economy in the early 1950s to a net importer of manufactured goods by the mid-1980s. This was an economy characterized by low rates of growth, rising unit labour costs and low productivity. In order to deal with the recurring economic crises during this period, a succession of governments embraced corporatist-type policies. Shortly after the Second World War, attempts were made to regulate the wage-bargaining system via incomes policies (Clegg, 1979). While in part these policies rested on the compliance of union leaders in limiting union demands for wage increases, the political accommodation required, particularly from the unions, was often costly, both economically and socially.

The highpoint of these types of policies came in the 1970s with the initiation of the 'Social Contract' from 1975 to 1979. This programme was an agreement between the Labour Government and the TUC, formalizing the long-standing partnership between the Labour Party and the trade union confederation (Flanders, 1970). Briefly this 'quasi-contractural exchange' (Edwards *et al.*, 1998, p. 7) was a political accommodation where 'wage moderation was exchanged for tax concessions and other benefits in the field of labour legislation' (Edwards *et al.*, 1998, p. 7). This was very much an alliance between a number of national union leaders and the Labour government, and in this respect was a corporatist settlement in a very partial sense. It was part of an attempt by key labour leaders to lay the foundation for social legislation and wage restraint. However, it was also partial in another sense, in that the burden of wage restraint was borne by the public sector and in 1978/9 a number of public sector unions became involved in strikes (along with some private sector unions) as part of the 'winter of discontent'.

For the public sector unions this period was an important coming of age. Most of these unions (in the public services) had a history of quiescence and compliance with government policy. Historically, these unions had turned to negotiation and bargaining, often within the framework of consensual arrangements that had been established for a number of decades. In the 1970s, these arrangements were found wanting and these unions began to turn to more active forms of representation to pursue their interests (Fairbrother, 1989). The result was a challenge of government policy and a questioning of the broad thrust of a Labour Government's economic programme. It was the beginning of a shift in the locus and focus of union relations with the Labour Party that came to fruition in the 1980s.

The Neo-Liberal Interventionist State

With the election of a Conservative Government in 1979 there was a rejection of the politics of accommodation. The government was committed to an emerging neo-liberal agenda of economic management and pursued a policy of legislative intervention that ended the voluntarist tradition of British industrial relations in decisive ways. The 1980s and 1990s was a period where legislative changes had a noticeable impact on the incidence and conduct of industrial action. This legislation included the Trade Union Act 1984, Employment Act 1988, Employment Act 1990 and the Trade Union Reform and Employment Rights Act 1993 requiring unions to hold ballots before conducting industrial action, placing restrictions on unofficial action, and giving notice of industrial action. More generally, the import of the legislation during this period was that unions found themselves in sets of relations that were juridically defined and restricted.

This legislation was introduced cumulatively, in large part as a reaction to the corporatist compromise between the state and unions in the 1970s. Conservative governments aimed to reverse the seeming success that many union leaderships had in prosecuting their aims and objectives. This neo-liberal agenda of deregulation was buttressed by legislation that defined unions as a problem (McIlroy, 1995, pp. 245–50; Dickens and Hall, 1995). Increasingly, the focus of the legislation was on the replacement of collective bargaining with the individual contract of employment. In this world, there was little formalized role for trade unions. A feature of these policies was the attempt to lay the conditions for the marginalization of union organization and action (Davies and Freedland, 1993). The form that this took was to create the legal conditions for and the encouragement of a climate whereby managements would be empowered to marginalize trade unions, narrowing their legitimate concerns and restricting union members' capacity to act collectively.

'Neo-Liberal Stakeholders

The election of a 'New' Labour Government in 1997 has not modified the broad thrust of these policies, although the adversarial relationship between government and union movement has been replaced by a policy of interest-group representation. From the mid-1980s onwards there was a distancing in the previously close relationship between the Labour Party and the trade union movement. This relationship took the form of formal involvement of affiliated trade unions in the policy formation, administration and finance of the Labour Party. While there had always been a robustness in this relationship, it was a relatively close and effective partnership between the two wings of labour (Flanders, 1970). During the 1970s, as indicated, this relationship came under strain. However, it was not until the 1980s that moderate elements within the trade union movement became willing to accept a looser (new realism) relationship as the cost they had to pay for a more 'electable' Labour Party. This assessment was accompanied by the beginnings of a Party acceptance of the broad contours of Conservative economic policy and industrial relations programme, although not explicitly stated at the time. The Party indicated that it would not reverse the labour legislation of the 1980s. It also took the first steps to formally distance itself from affiliated unions, by reducing the voting powers of the unions at the annual conference and related measures.

Trade unions, including the TUC, faced a contradictory situation, with the election of the Labour Government in 1997. The passage of the Fairness at Work legislation (Employment Relations Act 1999) and the introduction of a Statutory Minimum Wage gave some comfort to trade unions, which had long campaigned for such legislation. They represented the partial achievement of union aspirations relating to worker and trade union rights, although the detail was much less than had been hoped for prior to the election. At the same time, the labour government made it clear that the trade union movement, including the TUC, would not have privileged access to the government and that the old notion of labour-movement partnership no longer applied (McIlroy, 1995, pp. 299–304, 410–11).

Even so, unions increasingly looked to legislation and state regulation as a solution to the problems they faced in representing the concerns and interests of their members. Such a strategy assumes that governments will be responsive to these requests. The problem for British unions is that the traditional ally of the trade unions, the Labour Party, has distanced itself from them and seems unlikely to reverse this stance, at least in the short to medium term. Where the Labour Government has taken steps to implement legislation in support of union rights – union recognition, minimum wages, and the acceptance of European Union (EU) directives – this has usually been in terms of providing specific rights at a minimal level. It has not been in terms of the broad range of concerns facing members, irrespective of government in office.

Membership

What became apparent is that, compared with the 1960s and 1970s, trade unions no longer had a marked presence, either with respect to the economy or the polity. In the economic arena, unions faced more confident managements, implementing policies of restructuring where unions had a much reduced part to play. No longer were trade union leaderships party to the formulation of policy and programmes that took into account the specific concerns and interests of their memberships. In other words, the place and position of trade unionism over the previous two decades suffered a decisive reversal.

While unions have had a long history in Britain, the right to belong to a union is of relatively recent origin. Until 1971, employers were free in law to obstruct union efforts to recruit, with the result that many unions were forced to secure recognition via organizing campaigns. The aim was to create the situation where employers had little alternative but to recognize unions. With the passage of the Industrial Relations Act 1971, by a Conservative Government, workers were granted the right to join a trade union, reaffirmed by a Labour Government in 1975. The peculiarity of the British situation is that this legislation granted rights to the individual worker, rather than rules relating to freedom of association. The result is that workers faced few restrictions to union membership, although unionism of military personnel is prohibited and there are restrictions on police-force activity. The implication of these arrangements is that union recognition was the result of active measures by workers rather than as of legal right.

There have been fluctuating patterns in British trade union membership profiles, indicated in Table 3.1. Unions effectively date from the mid-nineteenth century and both membership numbers and number of unions expanded until the 1920s. There was a decline in union members until the mid-1930s, after which there was a slow recovery. In the period following the Second World War, there have been three phases of membership development (Edwards *et al.*, 1998, pp. 26–7).

In the post-war period, from 1945 onwards, there was a period of membership stagnation when the proportion of eligible workers who were members of unions declined, albeit marginally. From 1965 to 1980, there was a massive expansion of union members, reflecting the expansion of public sector unionism, non-manual occupations and the increasing proportion of women in the workforce.

During the 1980s and 1990s, union membership declined, to less than a third of the workforce by 1995. From a peak of over 13.2 million union members in 1979, membership fell to 7.85 million by 1998 (Certification Office, 2000, p. 20). Trade union density declined from a high of 55.8 per cent in 1979 to 29.6 per cent in 1998 (Waddington, 2000). After 17 consecutive years of decline, the longest on record, union membership increased 0.6 per cent in 1998 (Certification Office, 2000, p. 20). However, it is unclear whether this will be maintained, in view of the extensive redundancies that have taken place in British manufacturing during 1999

Table 3.1 *Trade union membership in TUC unions, Great Britain, 1900–98*

	Total membership (000s)	Employment density (%)
1900	1,908	13.1
1910	2,605	16.0
1920	8,253	48.2
1930	4,783	25.7
1940	6,519	33.4
1950	9,003	44.3
1960	9,437	44.0
1970	10,672	48.5
1975	11,561	52.0
1979	12,639	55.8
1980	12,239	54.5
1985	10,285	49.0
1990	8,854	38.1
1995	7,275	32.1
1998	7,107	29.6

Note: The data is not a continuous series because of different calculations.
Bain and Price, 1980 (1900–40) include retired and unemployed workers who retain union membership, whereas Waddington, 2000 (1950–87) and the Labour Force (1989–98) exclude the retired and unemployed workers who retain union membership.
Source: Bain and Price (1980), p. 39 and Waddington (2000), p. 585.

and 2000. Among the TUC unions, the picture is no more encouraging. In the period 1974 to 1979, the TUC unions increased their membership by 1.5 million workers, but dropped from 8.4 million members in 1989 to 6.6 million in 1998 (TUC, 1998). A key feature of this decline was the increase in non-recognition and the decline of collective bargaining. Only a third of workers are union members and a minority of the workforce is covered by collective bargaining (McIlroy, 2000, p. 15).

It has long been the case that well over 50 per cent of union members were in the ten largest unions, although with mergers this proportion is increasing, shown in Table 3.2.

The data refers to all unions in Britain. The measure for each period is obtained using a concentration ratio 10. However, if concentration is measured using the Herfindahl Index, which takes into account all unions, concentration does not rise before 1987 (Waddington, 1993). In this respect, there is a long-standing continuity in the structure of British trade unionism.

However, this appearance obscures the changes that have taken place in sectoral organization, employment structures and occupational recomposition. As a result, the dominant unions in the immediate period after the Second World War – coalminers, railway workers, and the steel industry – have declined in major ways, while there has been a dramatic increase (in numbers and in gender composition) in the membership of public sector unions. Over the last two decades, there has been a major decline in trade union membership. This has not been uniform across all sectors and occupations, and reflects changing patterns in the composition of the workforce.

If the contrast is drawn between the public and private sectors, then the public sector has maintained a relatively high presence, despite the overall decline in union membership, as indicated in Table 3.3. Such figures should be placed in the context of the overall decline of public sector employment during the 1980s and into the 1990s, as a result of privatization and a more general restructuring of the public sector, through contracting-out and related measures. Between 1961 and 1981, public sector employment increased by 22.5 per cent, but fell by 9.5 per cent between 1981 and 1985 and a further 20 per cent from 1985 to 1995 (Hughes, 1996, p. 374). During the 1990s, there was some levelling out of these trends with increases in the health sector following the creation of National Health Service Trusts, as public corporations. In the decade from 1985 to 1995, the proportion of the total public sector male workforce declined from 50.8 per cent to 41.5 per cent and public sector employees working part time rose from 24 to 33 per cent.

While the manufacturing and public sector (public services and utilities) workforces were consistently more densely unionized during the 1980s and 1990s, there were differential patterns of decline. One feature of this decline was the recomposition of the economy, with a collapse of employment in heavy industry, where union density was traditionally high, and the growth of private services, where the figures remain correspondingly low. However, it is equally important to note that these figures mask the continuing relative strength of unionism in the public sector and its converse weakness in the private sector (Waddington, 1992; Fairbrother, 1996, 2000b). Nonetheless, it is necessary to note that within the public sector and the privatized utilities there has been a marked unevenness in membership patterns, with some unions increasing their membership (Association of Teachers and Lecturers and the Communication Workers Union) while others declined (UNISON) (Certification Office, 2000, p. 21). This unevenness suggests a progressive weakening of public sector unionism, related to the reforms to decentralize bargaining, the introduction of competition and the purchaser/provider split, which continue to test the abilities of unions to respond effectively

Table 3.2 *Membership patterns of the ten largest unions in 1975, 1990 and 1998*

Unions 1975	Membership 1975 (000s)	Unions 1990	Membership 1990 (000s)	Unions 1998	Membership 1998 (000s)
Transport and General Workers Union	1,856.2	Transport and General Workers Union	1,223.9	UNISON: The Public Service Union	1,272.3
Amalgamated Union of Engineering Workers[i]	1,434.5	GMB	865.4	Transport and General Workers Union	881.6
National Union of General and Municipal Workers[ii]	881.4	National and Local Government Officers Association[iii]	744.5	Amalgamated Engineering and Electrical Union[vi]	728.0
National and Local Government Officers Association[iii]	625.2	Amalgamated Engineering Union[iv]	702.2		
National Union of Public Employees[iii]	584.5	Manufacturing Science and Finance[v]	653.0	GMB	712.0
Electrical, Electronic, Telecommunications and Plumbing Union	426.8	National Union of Public Employees[iii]	579.0	Manufacturing, Science and Finance	416.0
Union of Shop Distributive and Allied Workers	377.3	Electrical, Electronic, Telecommunications and Plumbing Union	366.7	Royal College of Nursing	320.2
National Union of Mineworkers	374.2	Union of Shop Distributive and Allied Workers	361.8	Union of Shop Distributive and Allied Workers	303.1

Association of Scientific Technical and Managerial Staffs[iv] 351.0	Royal College of Nursing 289.0	Communication Workers Union 287.7
National Union of Teachers 284.9	National Union of Teachers 218.2	National Union of Teachers 286.5
		National Association of Schoolmasters and Union of Women Teachers 250.8
Total for listed unions 7196	6003.7	5458.2
(% of total) (61.7)	(61.2)	(69.5)
Total for all unions 11,656.4	9,810.0	7,852.0

Notes:

[i] A federated union comprising four sections: engineering, construction, foundry and a white-collar section.

[ii] Subsequently became part of UNISON.

[iii] Subsequently became part of GMB.

[iv] By 1990 the Amalgamated Engineering Union comprised three sections: engineering, construction and foundry, which merged to become a single organization.

[v] The result of a merger between Association Scientific Technical and Managerial Staffs and the former white-collar section of the Amalgamated Union of Engineering Workers.

[vi] The result of a merger between the Amalgamated Engineering Union and the Electrical, Electronic, Telecommunications and Plumbing Union.

Source: Certification Office (1976), p. 50; Certification Office (1991), p. 40; Certification Office (2000), p. 60.

Table 3.3   *Union membership density by sector, Great Britain, 1995–9*

Year	Private Sector	Public sector	All
1995	21	61	32
1999	19	60	30

Source: Cully and Woodland (1996), p. 220 and Hicks (2000), p. 334.

(Carter and Poynter, 1998; Waddington, 2000). In contrast, it would appear that the decline in the private sector is ongoing, at least for the time being, where there has been a continued decrease in union density, despite a relative upturn in the economy (TUC, 1997; Fairbrother, 2000b).

The second important development in union membership has been the change in the gender composition of trade union membership, shown in Table 3.4. The proportion of union members who are women is increasing, reflecting changing patterns of employment as well as increased openness on the part of male-focused and -dominated unions.

Table 3.4   *Union membership by gender, Great Britain, 1970–90*

	Union membership (000s)			
Year	Male	Female	All	% Female
1970	8,444	2,743	11,187	24.5
1975	8,729	3,464	12,193	28.4
1980	9,156	3,790	12,947	29.3
1985	n.a.	n.a.	n.a.	n.a.
1990	6,195	3,752	9,947	37.7

Note: The unreliability of the statistics during the 1980s means that there is no figure for 1985.

Source: Employment Gazette (1982), p. 54 and Bird *et al.* (1992), p. 188.

By the 1990s, more than 35 per cent of the membership of TUC affiliated unions were women, with the female membership of the largest union, UNISON, at 65 per cent. More than half the members in another twelve were women. However, there is still a gap between male union density (38 per cent) and female union density (31 per cent). The probable explanation for this lies in the fact that many women workers are employed on a part-time basis, and part-time workers are less likely to be in unions than full-time workers. Nonetheless, it is also the case that women part-time workers are much more likely to be in trade unions that their male counterparts.

The recruitment of women workers is against the background that a number of unions, such as the Amalgamated Engineering Union, only admitted women into membership in the 1940s. This, plus the continued dominance of males in union-officer positions, particularly at a national level, continues to underwrite a view that many unions remain patriarchal institutions, and that the recruitment of women members thus has an opportunistic side to it. However, it is also the case that many women union activists have increasingly challenged the male dominance of unions, leading to changes in policy and a slow expansion of the number of women in leadership positions within several unions.

Of equal importance is the position of black workers in trade unions. Black workers have a higher union density that white workers, with workers of an Afro-Caribbean background having the highest union density (mid-40 per cent) of any social group. This pattern of union membership is against a background where many unions had adopted exclusionary policies, in some cases formally and certainly informally until at least the 1970s. Historically, black workers were employed in low-paid and unskilled jobs, often grouped in particular industries, such as foundry work or passenger buses. These patterns of concentration underwrote the informal segregation within unions. In the 1970s, black workers were active participants in a number of notable strikes. Building on an emergent black consciousness and anti-racist campaigns during this period, union policy began to shift, and in the 1980s, the TUC abandoned its colour-blind ('we are all workers') policy and began to advocate more progressive policies. However, it remains the case that very few black members hold formal officer positions in unions, at local levels and nationally, although there are exceptions to this pattern, particularly in the public sector.

The pattern of union membership is changing in decisive ways, albeit slowly. Overall, the major development has been a shift in the locus of union membership from the manufacturing and extractive industries to the public sector, including the privatized utilities. More specifically, the composition of union members has been slowly changing, with the recruitment of female and black members. A feature of this changing composition is that public sector unions are now dominant players in the union movement – for example UNISON, the largest union in the country since its creation in 1993. By 1998, seven of the sixteen unions with 100,000 members or more organize predominantly in the public sector and related areas, while others have reasonably large clusters of members in these areas (Certification Office, 2000, p. 60).

Structure and Governance

The pattern of trade union organization in the UK is relatively simple, although, as noted by many commentators, there is no patterned basis to the structure of contemporary British trade unions (Edwards *et al.*, 1998, pp. 28–9). British trade unions have evolved over a long period of time, in some cases dating back nearly two centuries to the time of the Industrial Revolution. The result is that while individual unions will have experienced the vicissitudes of changing patterns of industrial and sectoral organization, employer assaults and challenges to trade unionism, and state restrictions on trade unionism, the trade union movement as a whole displays a continuity that is relatively unusual.

Patterns of Unionism

The broad structure of British unions is straightforward. The branch, often based on the workplace or a series of contiguous workplaces (geographically or employer-based), is the basic unit of the formal union organization. Members elect, directly or indirectly, representatives at district, area, divisional or regional levels. They also elect a national executive committee and chief officers, a general secretary and/or a president. The election of these representatives takes place every five years, by postal ballot (required by legislation). These relationships are depicted in Figure 3.1.

There are complicated relationships between the different levels of unions. In some cases, the District Committees of unions, such as the Amalgamated Engineering Union, exercised substantive authority. In others, the unions organized and operated as centralized unions, focused on the National Executive Council, as was the case until the 1990s in the civil service unions.

National Executives comprise lay members usually elected from branches. Theoretically, the General Secretary and/or President service them, although in practice these officials often exert a decisive influence over the operation of the National Executive Committee. Formally, the governing body of the union is the annual or biennial conference, although, in practice, there is often a complicated and sometimes antagonistic relationship between the national leaders and the conference, involving branch representatives and activists.

The lack of organizational logic is reflected in the large numbers of unions that characterized Britain throughout much of the twentieth century. However, this was a very uneven representative structure, with a few large

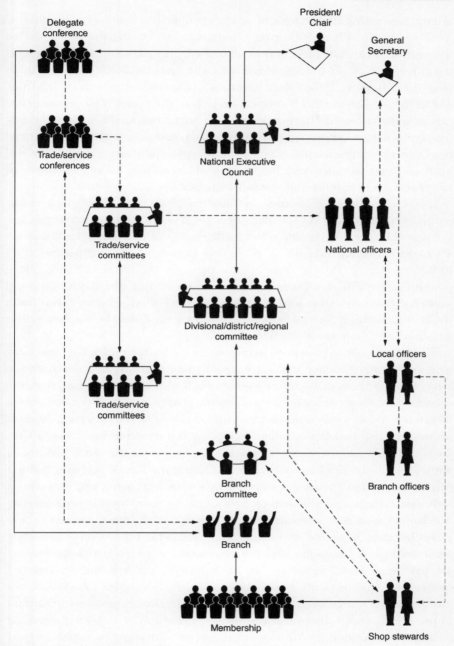

Figure 3.1 *The structure of trade unions in Britain*
Source: McIlroy (1995), p. 38.

unions accounting for the bulk of union membership and a large number of small occupationally or industrially based unions. During the latter part of the twentieth century, there was an extended 'merger wave' which has seen the absorption of 347 unions, 84 per cent with less than 5,000 members since 1966 (Waddington, 1995). More specifically, the number of unions fell from 454 in 1979 to 238 in 1998 (Certification Office, 1980 and 2000). In the main, this process reflected the non-viability of small unions in an increasingly internationalized economy undergoing major restructuring; however, there has been no inherent industrial logic underpinning these mergers. Rather, most of these mergers were based on political affinity or the ambition of larger unions to extend their recruitment bases.

The Trades Union Congress, founded in 1868, is the only peak union confederation in the UK. For many decades it comprised the major manual unions, although in the 1960s and 1970s, many of the non-manual unions who had stayed outside the TUC joined as part of the regularization of unionism during this period. Ninety per cent of trade unionists were members of the TUC-affiliated unions by the end of the 1970s, although there has been a decline in this proportion since then. In part, this reflects the membership growth of non-TUC unions such as the Police Federation and the Royal College of Nursing.

To understand the pattern of developments in trade unions, it is important to consider the changes that have taken place over the last two decades. However, the roots of these changes go back to changes that began in the nineteenth century. In both the public and private sectors, there has been a long-term trend, beginning at the turn of the twentieth century, towards industry or national pay settlements and related agreements (Clegg, 1976). This trend began in the engineering sector, with the 1898 Terms of Settlement of the Engineering Lockout. During the First World War this was further promoted by the government in the face of threats of widespread industrial action and the rise of syndicalist forms of union organization, which were seen as a threat to political stability (Aris, 1997). Related to this, the publication of the Whitley Committee (1917–18) reports recommending Joint Industrial Councils, and the development of collective bargaining arrangements and procedures at an industry level, resulted in national bargaining structures in the public and private sectors. Although the establishment of National Joint Industrial Councils became less important in the private sector, there was a continued extension of national formalized arrangements under the Whitley arrangements in the public sector.

While there is a long and complicated history relating to national and industry-level bargaining, the significance of the 1980s and 1990s is that this form of bargaining was severely compromised, particularly in the public sector. In part based on long-term trends involving ongoing struggles between sections of the trade union movement and employers, and in part as a feature of the extensive managerial restructuring and reorganization in the private and public sectors during the 1980s and 1990s, the balance of power was further tilted against unions as nationally-based and focused organizations. It was in these circumstances that unions began to look at the ways they organize and recruit, how leaderships represent membership, and the future role of trade unions (TUC, 1984, 1988a, 1988b, 1991, 1994a and 1994b).

Repositioning the TUC

Faced with the uncertainties and challenges of the 1980s, the TUC began to re-examine how it could play a part in some form of union recovery. Beginning in the early 1980s, it commissioned a series of reviews about trade unionism in Britain. The dominant argument was that unions were unlikely to regain the prominence they had in the 1970s. In these circumstances it was argued that the most promising future lay in the elaboration of service-model unionism. It was only in the mid-1990s that this was questioned.

The initial stimulus for a re-examination of unionism came with the election of the first Thatcher government, prepared to abandon the principal understanding between the TUC and successive governments in the 1960s and 1970s. The initial response by senior TUC leadership was to advocate a programme of criticism, campaigning and support for a return to the cooperative relations between union leaderships and Conservative governments of the past. This was not an activist-led approach from below; rather an orchestrated approach by senior TUC leaders, within the accepted parameters of Labourism (McIlroy, 1995, p. 209). In the meantime, TUC resources were directed towards economic and social policy development in anticipation of the re-election of a Labour government.

These initial responses took place against the background of a considerable expansion and development of the TUC as a service organization in the context of a developing partnership between the TUC and successive governments. The TUC had achieved a more prominent role as the voice of the trade union movement in three ways. First, TUC representatives were active participants in a range of tripartite bodies, including the National Economic Development Council and the Economic Development Committees. This involvement was complemented by policy statements and research on economic policy. Second, the TUC, with the support of the Labour governments of the 1970s, had overseen an expansion of educational activity, involving affiliated unions. Third, and related, the TUC had reorganized during the 1970s, broadening the representational base of its internal structure and developing the regional organization. While these initiatives did not represent new departures in the way the TUC organized and operated, they nevertheless were part of an increasingly prominent profile that was taken by the TUC leadership. These developments, however, did not qualify the continued dominance of affiliated unions and the subordination of the TUC as a union confederation; a position affirmed by the initial reviews in the early 1980s (Fairbrother and Waddington, 1990).

In 1983, when it became apparent that a more proactive approach was necessary if the TUC and lead affiliate unions were to play a more active part in the emergent political economy, the policy of 'new realism' was developed. The context in which the TUC Secretary, Len Murray, elaborated this approach was in opposition to a minority view that the TUC should formally break off relations with the government and develop more active campaigning against government policies. In effect, the Murray policy was one of acknowledging that the unions in general and the TUC in particular were a pressure group, whose leadership would deal with any government in office. These views were captured in the document, *TUC Strategy*, coauthored by Murray (TUC, 1984).

The argument for unions as a pressure group was clearly presented in this document: the TUC was willing to work with governments, irrespective of complexion, as it had done in the past. Such a stance was predicated on an acceptance of the view that unions represent and organize in the industrial arena, and that there is a self-limiting ordinance against union activity on political matters (TUC, 1984, p. 10, para. 28). Although the argument for cooperation and conciliation was turned down by the government, the sentiments expressed in the document became a motif for subsequent developments.

In the light of a further deteriorating position, and considerable in-fighting amongst unions about the appropriate strategies to be pursued (McIlroy, 1995, pp. 215–19), the TUC leadership established a Special Review Committee in 1987. While the reports from this Review addressed a range of issues, including labour market restructuring, union services, training, bargaining developments and inter-union relations, the thrust was to encourage and develop recruitment strategies as well as address the problems of union retention (TUC, 1988a, 1988b and 1989). It is also important to note (in view of later reference to the USA example) that the first report also contains reference to the American Federation of Labor–Congress of

Industrial Organizations' (AFL–CIO) formalization of procedures to avoid or settle inter-union recruitment disputes (TUC, 1988a: Appendix 4). To an important extent, these reports were side-tracked by the inter-union disputes of the time and the continuing collapse of union memberships, particularly in the manufacturing sector.

During the first part of the 1990s, the TUC began to consider the question of organization; in particular, focusing on representation (TUC, 1991, 1994b, 1995). These reports addressed a series of questions relating to union 'representation and recognition' (TUC, 1995, p. 5). The overall thrust was to promote the formal recognition of union representatives, supported by law, including European law and directives. The case was presented for a 'rights and standards' package, so as to create the conditions for bolstering and reinforcing the activity of unions. Not surprisingly, given this focus in the reports, there is almost no comment on the sociological and organizational conditions for representation within the workplace.

These developments were part of a relaunch of the TUC in 1994, as a modernized and improved trade union centre. The aim was to reposition the TUC in relation to its affiliates, so that they could be served in more effective ways as well as to develop more effective and focused campaigns. The emphasis was on service-type unionism, coupled with more effective lobbying and pressure-group approaches to employers, governments and the Labour Party, partly coinciding with the changes taking place in the Labour Party and the advent of New Labour.

This move to relaunch the TUC was succeeded by a more systematic and extensive review of the TUC in 1996/7. A Task Group was established in 1996 to research and make recommendations for re-designating the TUC and its affiliates under the label of New Unionism, making conscious parallels with the 'new Unionism' of the late nineteenth century as well as the reincarnation of the Labour Party in the 1990s. The focus of this programme of reform was on membership recruitment and retention, extending existing areas of membership as well as extending the representational basis into currently unorganized or lowly organized areas of employment. Reference was made to part-time workers, women (many of whom are employed on part-time bases) and young workers.

Increasingly, questions arose within unions in relation to union governance. In the large general unions, the Transport and General Workers' Union and the Amalgamated Engineering Union, the formerly semi-independent steward committees began to adopt defensive, pragmatic policies in relation to employers and rely on district and regional officials in the pursuit of their aims (MacInnes, 1987). In addition, these unions faced acute problems arising from falling union memberships and a seeming inability to extend recruitment into poorly organized areas, such as private services, or among particular social groups, such as the young. In contrast, the centralized public sector unions faced a situation where national-led negotiations and bargaining arrangements no longer had the relevance they had in the past. Unions such as the National Union of Civil and Public Servants (covering middle-grade civil servants and others) and UNISON (covering local authority, health workers and utility workers) faced problems relating to worker mobilization and representation at a local level. These unions began programmes of reform aimed at laying the foundation for steward-based structures, raising difficult questions about the relations between local and national leaderships (Fairbrother, 1996).

A key feature of this launch of New Unionism is the conscious reference to and modelling on exemplary trade union movements, elsewhere in the world. Specifically, the TUC made reference to the United States, Australia and the Netherlands, each of which has gone through a process of refocusing and rebuilding their trade union movement. The view taken by the New Unionism task force responsible for the research and visits to these countries is captured by the General Secretary of the TUC, John Monks, that:

> We can also learn from the experiences of sister unions throughout the world. And with the growth of globalization, multinational corporations and European Works Councils it is more important than ever that unions transcend national barriers not only to talk together but to work together too. (TUC, 1996, p. 3)

For the TUC there was an explicit choice between a revived social democracy, exemplified by Europe, and the more robust organizing strategies evident in the USA and Australia (Taylor, 2000, pp. 262–3).

Orientation and Strategies

A number of contradictory pressures are at work within trade unions, and the outcome is unclear. First, while the historical base of the unions was with manual workers in manufacturing, transport and extractive industries, the locus of power has increasingly shifted towards the manual and non-manual workforces in the public sector and the utilities. These developments pose difficulties for the institutionalized and established practices within the trade union movement, especially at the level of the TUC. Second, and as part of the structural shift in the industrial basis of trade unionism, the established patterns of organizing and operating within the industrial arena, have been found wanting. In general, there have been two modes of organizing, one based on a complex relationship between full-time officials and steward committees, particularly in the traditional areas of union representation, and another based on the pre-eminence and leadership of national officials, with relatively inactive local representative bodies, particularly in the public sector. Increasingly, the former mode of organization has been under pressure, as managements sought to assert their prerogatives during the 1980s. The latter mode of organization has been found wanting as national bargaining was rejected in all sectors, apart from the public sector, although even in the public sector such bargaining was severely curtailed by government policy as part of the devolution of managerial hierarchies in this sector. Third, the terrain of bargaining has shifted, partly with increased relevance of supra-state organization, via the European Union, but also with the internationalization of economies during the 1980s and 1990s. On the one hand, there is the possibility that these developments will open up new opportunities for unions, providing a broader platform for collective representation; on the other hand, it is unclear whether unions are prepared for these developments and in a position, as national organizations, to meet these challenges.

Trends and Emergent Patterns

The recent restructuring highlights different trends and patterns in union concerns. On the one hand, restructuring in manufacturing has generally meant a reaffirmation of an economistic remit. Unions have been concerned to address the issues and problems within the workplace rather than to look to the complex of relations that underpin and provide the opportunity for restructuring. The union response to these developments was largely defensive, concerned with securing the continued recognition of unions (MacInnes 1987; Gallie et al., 1996). In this context, the traditional steward forms of organization were maintained, although, in many instances, there was a greater reliance on regional and divisional levels of support than had been the case in the past. At a national level, the major unions in the manufacturing sector sought to extend their recruitment base, in some cases seeking single-union recognition agreements and in other instances attempting to recruit the poorly organized sectors.

In the 1980s, the trends in the public sector were clearer. There was a major restructuring of the public sector during the 1980s and into the 1990s, with a redefinition of management structures and the introduction of new work and employment practices (Fairbrother, 1989, 1994a, 1994b and 2000a). The evidence suggests lower levels of management have been given new and additional responsibilities for budgeting and that managerial lines of control and accountability have been recast. New work routines have been introduced, often in tandem with computerized technologies, and recruitment patterns have changed, with moves towards varied employment patterns. This recomposition of managerial hierarchies, accompanied by institutional fragmentation within the main sections that make up the public sector, has had a major impact on the way unions organize and operate. At the most general level, the unions representing public sector employees have found their established forms of membership representation and involvement wanting. There has been a restructuring of industrial relations arrangements with the result that there has been a dissonance with past procedures and practice. They were structured to pursue agreements at a national level, often involving direct relationships with senior levels of the government apparatus. These largely centralized unions have found it difficult to reorganize and operate at a more localized level, across a range of institutions. Alongside this, there has been a sequence of mergers that have resulted in a reconfiguration of unions in the public sector. The three largest unions in local government and health merged in 1993 to form UNISON, the largest union in Britain. Five years later, the two largest civil service unions merged, building on a sequence of earlier mergers in this sector. These developments are part of the reconstitution of union organization in these sectors.

Even where government policies can be seen to have a direct bearing and are detrimental to specific industries, such as telecommunications policies, unions have, perhaps because of the force of circumstance, pursued a narrow range of policies and concerns, particularly at the workplace level. Unions in the utilities, particularly during the privatization periods, and unions in the public services, have addressed state policies more directly and explicitly. This opens up opportunities for unions to broaden their remit beyond a narrow economistic one. While this does not necessarily mean such an outlook will be maintained, it may be the case that in forging workplace union practices in these conditions there is a greater likelihood that unions will be able to maintain this spectrum of concerns (Ferner and Colling, 1991).

One feature of the privatization process is that there has been an internationalization of ownership, particularly in the case of privatized utilities, which weighs heavily against labour. The reconfiguration of managerial hierarchies has involved both a devolution of operational responsibilities and an attenuation of financial and strategic relations. For unions, these developments provide opportunities for more discrete and localized bargaining, on the one hand, and increased difficulties, on the other, as the locus of power and decision-making shifts from the national to the international (cf. Colling and Ferner, 1995). A series of studies have addressed the question of the impact of the privatization process on industrial relations processes and institutions (Colling, 1991; Ogden, 1992; Pendleton and Winterton, 1993; Colling and Ferner, 1995). The feature of these analyses is that they identify processes of restructuring and reorganizing of the institutional arrangements relating to industrial relations. Generally, this reorganization takes the form of a devolution of bargaining fora, from a national to a more localized level. This devolution has involved a shift from national to company-level bargaining, evident in water and electricity supply (Ogden, 1992; Ferner and Colling, 1991) or from company to business unit sectors, as has been the case in steel and telecommunications (Blyton, 1993; Fairbrother, 1994b).

Transcending Boundaries

During the 1980s and 1990s, EU legislation and regulation began to have a growing impact on trade unionism. Increasingly, governments faced constraints that arose from British membership of the EU. The result was that governments were obliged to introduce legislation or recognize legislative rules that they were sceptical of or opposed. This gave rise to a tension between the labour market policies and programmes sought by these governments and the EU social agenda, which was rooted in the continental model of social regulation. The significance of these arrangements was that trade unions took steps to qualify government policy and objectives on the social agenda, in the context of restrictive national regulation towards trade unions.

Trade unions looked to European legislation and regulation as a way of countering conservative legislation and policies. On a range of topics, trade unions began to utilize European regulation as a way of challenging prevailing government policy. One of the clearest examples was on equal opportunities, where unions sought rulings from the European Court of Justice about unequal pay. In 1984, the European Court of Justice ruled that the Sex Discrimination Act of 1975 failed to comply with the EU equal treatment directive. The outcome was the passage of the Sex Discrimination Act of 1986, which explicitly made discriminatory clauses in collective agreements illegal.

Trade unions have used European regulation to open up and broaden issues. In a number of areas, trade unions have refocused their concerns to take account of the consultation procedures, redundancy regulations, equal opportunities and the establishment of Works Councils. The clearest example of this development involved the defence of employment conditions in those situations where there has been an externalization or contracting-out of public sector work. In 1977, the EU promulgated the 'transfer of undertakings' directive. The thrust of the directive is that when an undertaking is transferred from one operator to another then the existing contracts of employment remain in force. Some public sector unions were assiduous in their pursuit of these conditions, thereby shifting the campaigns against privatization from the public arena to legal defence and regulation.

As these aspects of the social relations of production became the province of supranational as well as the nation state, then unions began to broaden the scope of their concerns, beyond the British state. Increasingly, union leaderships began to identify with their European counterparts in ways that did not happen previously. One of the mechanisms of this involved the consideration of Works Councils and the possibility of developing a European rather than a specifically British approach. Another outcome was that a number of unions opened up offices in Brussels and began to focus aspects of their activity towards the European Union apparatus.

These developments became part of the ongoing redefinition of the relationship between unions and the Labour Party. Trade unions looked to European policy as a way of cementing their historic partnership with the Labour Party. At a time when successive Conservative governments were continuing to restrict the rights and opportunities of trade unions, union leaderships pressured the Labour Party to develop a European-focused set of policies. Initially, these policies centred on the Community Charter of the Fundamental Social Rights of Workers (the 'social charter'). When the Conservative Government negotiated an 'opt-out' from the social chapter to the Maastricht Treaty on European Union (Hall, 1994), such policies became the test of a future Labour government's commitment to recognize the difficulties faced by unions during this period as well as to take steps to lay the foundation for a more socially progressive period of social policy.

The outcome was a union movement that was more outward looking than it had been in the 1970s. Paradoxically, a period of increasingly restrictive legislation and anti-union policies stimulated a broadening of the concerns of trade unions. While there has been a long history of rhetorical commitments to international unionism, what marked out the 1980s and 1990s were the concrete steps that a number of unions took to rely on supra-state legislation to defend workers' conditions, as well as to develop policy approaches aimed at European employers.

Responses

The extent of the objective problems that unions face has forced the TUC to reflect upon the nature of contemporary trade unionism. Beginning in the early 1980s, as noted earlier, the TUC and its affiliated unions, faced with marginalization from the British polity, embraced a policy of 'new realism'. The orientation of the TUC appeared to be a reconciliation with employers based upon a recognition of its own weakness, together with the encouragement, if it were needed, for unions to sell themselves more effectively to members and potential members through the further development of services (Howard and Williams, 1995). In the mid-1990s, the TUC, building on this period of introspection and uncertainty, took steps to draw the threads of these developments together and lay the foundation for a 'New Unionism'. The precise nature of the New Unionism has not been delineated but contains a strong element of organizing. In some contexts, the term is synonymous with recruiting – a function that even the most conservative leader is happy with; in others, it is counterposed to the idea of the union as an external, servicing organization to indicate a model of more active and participative unionism. The former aspect is quite consistent with another feature within the 'New Unionism' perspective, which is an emphasis on the desire for partnership with employers. In this view, employers are divided into binary opposites: 'good' and 'bad'. It is assumed that the first type of employer will make an accommodation with unions while the second is likely to oppose union recognition. In the latter case the solution is to challenge such employers with a new muscular, 'in your face' unionism pioneered in the United States, particularly by the Service Employees International Union (SEIU, 1997).

Thus, three sets of responses to these developments are evident: a defensive strategy aimed at securing unions engaged in interest representation in terms of immediate terms and conditions of employment; a proactive policy where unions seek to redefine the basis of interest representation in the face of the restructuring of their sectors of representation; and finally, a strategy of affirming a centralized and coordinated response to the problems faced by unions, as part of an attempt to reposition unions in the polity.

The first type of response has been a defence of the established institutional arrangements, particularly at a workplace level, with limited attempts by unions to extend their representational base into poorly organized areas. Manufacturing unions, in particular, have developed pragmatic responses to the challenges they have faced, and adopted relatively reactive approaches. Where these unions have attempted to open up a more proactive policy, it has been in the extension of recruitment activity, although this has not been notably successful.

The second type of response reflects the shift in the locus of unionism in Britain and involves the former public sector unions. Here there has been a more proactive response to the developments that have taken place. At both a workplace level as well as nationally, unions have begun to look at the way they organize and operate. This has not been an easy process and there has been considerable debate within unions as they wrestle with the changes that are taking place.

In the case of the third type of response, there has been a hesitant process of institutional consideration of the way in which unions organize and operate. This initiative has focused on the TUC as it tries to redefine a role for itself in the context of its removal from direct political debate and involvement, increasingly within the Labour Party as well as within state structures. The result has been a debate about models of unionism, as well as an encouragement to refocus union objectives beyond state boundaries toward Europe.

Inevitably, emergent forms of unionism appear in the context of changes in management, the organization of work, different negotiating and bargaining arrangements, and a disaffection with past union forms (cf. Kelly, 1996, p. 102, n. 2). The logic of the argument is that a rearticulation of class relations in each sector is taking place, with implications for both managerial organization and activity as well as unionism in these sectors. The restructuring associated with privatization, the fragmentation of the state sector, market testing, competitive compulsory tendering, appraisal, and performance-related pay is part of a repositioning of management (Fairbrother, 1996). In its starkest form, a 'new' management is in place. It is concerned with reshaping the state sector in a devolved and decentralized way so as to secure the compliance of workforces. The stress is on individualism and individualized social relations. However, this is not a straightforward process, as established managers often require convincing of the need to change. Intractable traditional managers are often replaced by more committed managers. Further, these initiatives do not involve the individualization of the social relations of production as such but the attempt to reorganize collective workforces on an individualistic basis. This has involved the introduction of employment and work arrangements aimed at defining workers as individuals rather than as part of a collective. It is thus a complicated and uneven process of change.

The decline in the numbers in, and density of, trade unions has already been noted, indicating that unions have not been particularly effective in resisting changes or in adopting new and more effective organizational forms. They have not, however, simply been passive recipients of change (Martinez-Lucio and Weston, 1992; Fairbrother, 1996; Kelly, 1996; Carter, 1997). The TUC's response to labour market trends and its change of direction (whatever its limitations) is a further indication that trade unions can influence the shape of their own futures. Indeed, much of the debate about the nature of trade unionism in the 1980s and 1990s centred around the question of possible strategic directions. Sharp differences emerged. Should unions now reflect what was held to be the individualization of society, and of members and potential members, by offering services to members constituted as consumers or customers (Bassett and Cave, 1993)? Alternatively, given the worsening conditions of large sections of their members through privatizations, increased work intensity, longer hours and growing insecurity (Fairbrother 1994b; Nichols 1986), should unions attempt to mobilize members through increased calls for militancy (Fairbrother and Waddington 1990; Kelly, 1996)?

These developments occur within the context of the changing relation between unions and politics, particularly the larger manual unions and the Labour Party. The 'break' in relations between New Labour and the trade union movement is not surprising, because there are two processes at work. On the one hand, the impetus for the rupture comes from New Labour as the Party attempts to redefine the basis of social democracy. On the other hand, the shift in the material basis for trade unionism means that there are no longer grounds for the past accommodations between Party and unions. Thus, the fracturing of these relations has as much to do with the basis and form of trade unionism that is emerging, as with Labour Party policy. Unions are beginning to pursue their own agendas in the context of changing economic and political relations. In these respects, unions are active participants in their own fate with a future that is in the process of unfolding.

The State of Unions

Against this background, the prospects for unions in the United Kingdom are uncertain. There has been a decline in union membership, both absolutely and relatively, prompting some commentators to be very sceptical about the long-term future of unions. One strand of argument has begun to emphasize the importance of centralized union structures, and a devaluation of locally based trade unionism (Undy *et al.*, 1996; Willman *et al.*, 1993). A second strand of argument is that unions no longer have the salience they once had in the polity, reflecting the adverse legislative and political environment in which trade unions now operate. The implication is that unions can no longer rely on the Labour Party in office to provide the conditions for a return to the political prominence that was evident in the 1970s (McIlroy, 1995 and 1997). In this perspective, the future for unions is clear; it emphasizes the importance of centralized, effective union organization, achieving a fruitful and productive balance between active workplace unionism and forward-thinking centralized leaderships (arguably Heery and Kelly, 1994; McIlroy, 1997; Terry, 1996).

These assessments are overly pessimistic. Clearly there have been major setbacks for unions, with a loss of members, bargaining changes, and financial uncertainty. They faced a raft of legislative provisions weighted in favour of employers. Throughout the 1980s and 1990s, the state was at best indifferent, at worst hostile, about union representation. Unions, both individually and as part of the TUC, sought to address these problems. It was in these circumstances that union modernization became an issue. In some cases union leaderships, particularly in the public sector, sought to reform their internal organization by promoting local forms of representation. So as to address the declining membership, union leaderships began to promote strategies concerned with enhancing the service provision to members. These initiatives received support and encouragement from the TUC (TUC, 1997).

These initiatives were, by and large, predicated on a view that work and employment relations had become more individualized and individualistic, and that this should be reflected in the ways unions organize and operate. However, as Williams (1996) points out, this ignores the way in which union forms of organization have long been based on a subtle and changing interplay between individualism and collective forms of organization. More than this, these assessments of unionism ignore and overlook the way in which the form of unionism that has long prevailed in this country is at a crossroads. No longer is the shop-steward form of engineering and manufacturing unionism a model of effective and participative unionism.

It is now much more likely that such union groups will restrict their concerns to their workplaces and immediate employers, pursuing their economistic concerns via negotiation, consultation and occasional militancy.

In contrast, unions elsewhere, particularly in the public services and the privatized utilities, have begun to reorganize in distinctive ways, placing on the agenda, yet again, the position of unions in the polity. These previously centralized and often acquiescent unions have faced a dramatic restructuring of the social relations of production and service, of equal if not greater magnitude than in manufacturing. In such circumstances, these union groups have begun to reorganize. It is amongst these unions that more participative forms of organization have become evident. It is here that questions have been raised about public policy and steps taken to address questions relating to gender, race, youth and disability, in ways that have not been evident in unions elsewhere. However, it is also here that some union groups, faced with near continuous change, have all but disappeared. It is in these sections that the debate about the way unions are changing, and the form of unionism that is emerging in the British polity, is being played out.

The Future

These developments have provoked considerable debate about the place and position of unions in Britain. One strand of argument has focused on the further sophistication in the development of centralized and responsible forms of unionism. Advocates of this form of unionism emphasize the importance of developing more active and participative structures, albeit within a centralized framework that will ensure common purpose and unity between the sections that make up the union (McIlroy, 1995 and 1997; Terry, 1996). This advocacy implicitly recognizes the inadequacies of the 'responsible' unionism of the past, but the proponents of this case do not question the assumption that the future of unions lies with an accommodation with sympathetic governments, in this case a Labour Government. On the contrary, they make the case for a renewed and revised partnership with New Labour as a critical feature of this form of unionism. In making this case, they overlook the changes that have taken place in the political economy of employment and work relations. This is an argument for a return to the virtues and benefits of social partnership between the two wings of the labour movement in achieving a just and equitable society, at least in relation to work and employment (Flanders, 1970). The problem with this type of analysis is that it ignores the changing base of unionism in the current political economy and the implications this has for the way they organize and operate, as well as their relationship with the state and employers (Fairbrother and Waddington, 1990; Fairbrother, 2000a).

As part of this debate, Kelly (1996) reviewed the moves by the TUC and major affiliated unions to develop union policies based on the principles of 'social partnership'. In developing his analysis, Kelly argued that militancy was likely to be a better guarantee of the survival and recovery of unions in the 1990s rather than the embrace of the principles and practice of social partnership. He developed a multi-dimensional definition of union militancy and moderation, covering goals, methods, institutional resources, membership resources and ideology (pp. 79–81). For Kelly, militant unionism, an active and involved form of unionism, rests on a 'recognition of the antagonism of interests between workers and employers' (p. 102). In effect, this is an argument for active collective organization by workers, defending the right to strike and related collective acts, as well as expressing the ability to act in collective ways. It is a defence of collective organization and action at a workplace level.

However, in an earlier statement, Heery and Kelly (1994) argued that the 'servicing' relationship between trade unions and their members has passed through three distinct phases in the post-war period: 'professional unionism', characterized by membership dependence on a cadre of expert representatives; 'participative unionism' in which union officers facilitated self-reliance among union members; and 'managerial unionism' in which members are viewed as reactive consumers who must be attracted by well-researched and promoted servicing packages. The emergence of forms of managerial unionism implies that 'change in internal union relations can partially be explained by unions absorbing conceptions of desirable and effective organisation which are present in the wider society' (p. 19). These beliefs are in turn influenced by long-term cultural changes. Their argument is made with some recognition of the complexity and unevenness of actual developments. Nevertheless, their attempt to uphold the phases and the concepts has been contested by Smith (1995), who maintains, with some justification, that insufficient weight is given to the role of the state and employers, the economic context of union change and the possibilities of different relations through the conscious intervention of union members.

This last theme has been addressed elsewhere (Fairbrother, 1994a, 1996, 2000a and 2000b). The central proposition is that it is possible for unions to turn the new and weakened position they find themselves in to their own advantage. In a series of articles, linked to arguments about the possibility of union renewal (see, in particular, Fairbrother 1994a; 1996), it is argued that, particularly in the public services, the reorganization of employing units through privatization, marketization and compulsory competitive tendering, and the decentralization of collective bargaining which has attended it, provides the unions with an opportunity to begin to construct a different kind of unionism based on the workplace and overcoming the passivity that normally accompanied remote and bureaucratic forms embedded in national structures (cf. Colling, 1995). In this view, the restructuring of collective bargaining has not only weakened unions but also gives the possibility of transcending limitations inherent in old forms.

However, there is nothing inevitable about union renewal. The process necessitates a devolution of power and resources within the unions to workplace representatives and it is by no means automatic that workplace representatives will develop the vision, skills and confidence to demand this redistribution, nor that other layers of the union will simply watch with equanimity while power drains away from them. Moreover, it is not just a question of evacuating power from the centre: the centre has to nurture, encourage and sustain local activity through information, education and the mobilization of support through the construction of common interests from disparate disputes. Central union organizations continue to have a role, if a different one:

> It is a reversing of the traditional relationships characteristic of most unions, particularly in the state sector, so that the national level resources and facilitates rather than represents and thus controls. (Fairbrother 1996, p. 143)

The TUC's attempt to reinforce the dynamics of trade unionism and, in particular, its endorsement of membership activity, leaves unexamined the crucial dimension of the structural organization of trade unions. Any particular constituent union attempting to make concrete policies and decisions of necessity will have to confront this issue if renewal is to be sustainable.

It is possible that a form of unionism based on independent workplace-based unionism, as union members assert their immediate interests in a changing world, could provide the springboard for a union renewal (Fairbrother, 1994a, 1996, 2000a and 2000b). The strength of the union form of organization is that it is the institutional expression of the collective worker in a capitalist society, although it also carries with it the dangers of an assertive sectionalism. Nonetheless, the basis of such unionism is rooted in the notion that as employees, workers combine together for the purposes of production and the provision of services. In this respect, the union form of organization represents the possibility of these workers expressing their common concerns and interests. They represent a moment of collective organization and interests that is unusual in such societies. It is for this reason that unions give attention to the basis of organization, in the workplace and at a local level. The difficulty is to achieve the necessary balance between localized and workplace-based activity and the collective interests of the membership as a whole; in this form of unionism, the focus is from the workplace out and not vice versa. It is in this respect that there is thus a case for unions to seek to establish their organizational independence and autonomy from all liberal democratic governments.

It is likely that unions, such as those organizing workforces in utilities, will be caught up in a range of developments that will take them away from the Labour Party agenda. They will increasingly operate on an international scale and will be looking to governments to facilitate and support this type of involvement and concern. Further, it is likely to be the case that unions in the public sector, or its modern equivalent, will continue to build in the workplace, redefine their concerns in ways that distance themselves from all governments, and pursue their concerns accordingly. Of course, New Labour for these workers is more congenial than the Conservative Government, but there is no reason to expect favour or particular consideration from New Labour. These unions are on their own in their relationship with the state and there is likely to be a reconstruction of these unions accordingly.

The reconfiguration of unions in Britain is likely to remain tentative, uneven and ad hoc. On the one hand, the TUC and the traditional leading affiliated unions remain attached to the past, advocating continuity in approach and practice. On the other hand, the changes within the public services (and privatized utilities) have been such that there are signs of attempts to renew the basis of organization and operation, although often in hesitant and partially thought-out ways. In the context of an increasing internationalization of the economy, further state restructuring and an emergent unified European Union, the future looks bleak, at least in the short term.

References

Aris, R. (1997) *Trade Unions and the Management of Industrial Conflict*, Basingstoke: Macmillan.

Bain, G. and Price, R. (1980) *Profiles of Union Growth*, Oxford: Blackwell.

Bassett, P. and Cave, A. (1993) *All for One: The Future of the Unions*, Fabian Pamphlet No. 559, London: The Fabian Society.

Bird, D., Kirosingh, M. and Stevens, M. (1992) 'Membership of trade unions in 1990', *Employment Gazette, April*, 185–9.

Blyton, P. (1993) 'Steel', in A. Pendleton and J. Winterton (eds) (1993) *Public Enterprise in Transition: Industrial Relations in State and Privatized Corporations*, London: Routledge.

Carter, B. (1997) 'Adversity and opportunity: towards union renewal in MSF', *Capital & Class*, **61**, Spring, 8–18.

Carter, B. and Poynter, G. (1999) 'Unions in a changing climate: MSF and UNISON experiences in the new public sector', *Industrial Relations Journal*, **30** (5), 499–513.

Certification Office (1976) *Annual Report of the Certification Officer 1975*, London: Her Majesty's Stationery Office.

Certification Office (1980) *Annual Report of the Certification Officer 1979*, London: Certification Office for Trade Unions and Employers' Associations.

Certification Office (1991) *Annual Report of the Certification Officer 1991*, London: Certification Office for Trade Unions and Employers' Associations.

Certification Office (2000) *Annual Report of the Certification Officer 1999–2000*, London: Certification Office for Trade Unions and Employers' Associations.

Clegg, H. (1976) *Trade Unionism Under Collective Bargaining*, Oxford: Blackwell.

Clegg, H. (1979) *The Changing System of Industrial Relations in Great Britain*, Oxford: Blackwell.

Colling, T. (1991) 'Privatization and the management of industrial relations in electricity distribution', *Industrial Relations Journal*, **22** (2), 117–30.

Colling, T. (1995) 'Renewal or rigor mortis? Union responses to contracting in local government', *Industrial Relations Journal*, **26** (2), 134–45.

Colling, T. and Ferner, A. (1995) 'Privatization and marketization', in P. Edwards (ed.) *Industrial Relations: Theory and Practice in Britain*, Oxford: Blackwell, pp. 491–514.

Cully, M. and Woodland, S. (1997) 'Trade union membership and recognition', *Labour Market Trends*, May, 215–25.

Davies, P. and Freedland, M. (1993) *Labour Legislation and Public Policy*, Oxford: Clarendon Press.

Dickens, L. and Hall, M. (1995) 'The state, labour law and industrial relations', in P. Edwards (ed.) *Industrial Relations: Theory and Practice in Britain*, Oxford: Blackwell, pp. 255–303.

Edwards, P., Hall, M., Hyman, R., Marginson, P., Sisson, K., Waddington, J. and Winchester, D. (1998) 'Great Britain: From partial collectivism to neo-liberalism to where?', in A. Ferner and R. Hyman (eds) *Changing Industrial Relations in Europe*, Oxford: Blackwell Publishers, pp. 1–54.

Employment Gazette (1982) 'Membership of trade unions in 1980', *Employment Gazette*, February, 54–6.

Fairbrother, P. (1989) 'State workers: class position and collective action', in G. Duncan (ed.) *Democracy and the Capitalist State*, Cambridge: Cambridge University Press, pp. 187–213.

Fairbrother, P. (1994a) *Politics and the State as Employer*, London: Mansell.

Fairbrother, P. (1994b) 'Privatisation and local trade unionism', *Work, Employment and Society*, **8** (3), 339–56.

Fairbrother, P. (1996) 'Workplace trade unionism in the state sector', in P. Ackers, P. Smith and C. Smith (eds) *The New Workplace and Trade Unionism*, London: Routledge, pp. 110–49.

Fairbrother, P. (2000a) 'British trade unions facing the future', *Capital and Class*, **71**, 47–78.

Fairbrother, P. (2000b) *Trade Unions at the Crossroads*, London: Mansell.

Fairbrother, P. and Waddington, J. (1990) 'The politics of trade unionism: evidence, policy and theory', *Capital and Class*, **41**, 15–56.

Ferner, A. and Colling, T. (1991) 'Privatization, regulation and industrial relations', *British Journal of Industrial Relations*, **29** (3), 391–409.

Flanders, A. (1970) *Management and Unions: The Theory and Reform of Industrial Relations*, (2nd edn), London: Faber and Faber.

Fox, A. (1985) *History and Heritage*, London: Allen & Unwin.

Gallie, D., Penn, R. and Rose, M. (eds) (1996) *Trade Unions in Recession*, New York: Oxford University Press.

Hall, M. (1994) 'Industrial relations and the social dimension of European integration', in R. Hyman and A. Ferner (eds) *New Frontiers in European Industrial Relations*, Oxford: Blackwell Publishers, pp. 281–311.

Heery, E. and Kelly, J. (1994) 'Professional, participative and managerial unionism: an interpretation of change in trade unions', *Work, Employment and Society*, **8** (1), 1–22.

Hicks, S. (2000) 'Trade union membership and recognition: an analysis of data from the 1995 Labour Force Survey', *Labour Market Trends*, May, pp. 215–25.

Howard, B. and Williams, S. (1995) 'The relaunch of the TUC', in M. Erikson and S. Williams (eds) *Social Change in Tyne and Wear*, School of Social and International Studies Working Papers, No. 1, University of Sunderland.

Kahn-Freund, O. (1983) *Labour and the Law*, (3rd edn), London: Stevens.

Kelly, J. (1996) 'Union militancy and social partnership', in P. Ackers, C. Smith and P. Smith (eds) *The New Workplace and Trade Unionism*, London: Routledge, pp. 77–109.

MacInnes, J. (1987) *Thatcherism at Work: Industrial Relations and Economic Change*, Milton Keynes: Open University Press.

Martinez-Lucio, M. and Weston, S. (1992) 'Human resource management and trade union responses: bringing the politics of the workplace back into the debate', in P. Blyton and P. Turnbull (eds) *Reassessing Human Resource Management*, London: Sage, pp. 215–32.

McIlroy, J. (1995) *Trade Unions in Britain Today*, (2nd edn), Manchester: Manchester University Press.

McIlroy, J. (1997) 'Still under siege: British trade unions at the turn of the century', *Historical Studies in Industrial Relations*, **3** (March), 93–122.

McIlroy, J. (2000) 'New labour, new unions, new left', *Capital and Class*, **71**, 11–45.

Minkin, L. (1991) *The Contentious Alliance, Trade Unions and the Labour Party*, Edinburgh: Edinburgh University Press.

Nichols, T. (1986) *The British Worker Question: A New Look at Workers and Productivity in Manufacturing*, London: Routledge & Kegan Paul.

Ogden, S. (1992) 'Decline and fall: national bargaining in British water', *Industrial Relations Journal*, **23** (1), 44–58.

Pendleton, A. and Winterton, J. (eds) (1993) *Public Enterprise in Transition: Industrial Relations in State and Privatized Corporations*, London: Routledge.

Service Employees International Union (1997) *Bold Action: How SEIU Local Unions are Changing to Organize*, New York: Service Employees International Union.

Smith, P. (1995) 'Change in British trade unions since 1945', *Work, Employment and Society*, **9** (1), 137–46.

Taylor, R. (2000) *The TUC: From the General Strike to New Unionism*, Basingstoke: Palgrave.

Terry, M. (1995) 'Trade unions, shop stewards and the workplace', in P. Edwards (ed.) *Industrial Relations*, Oxford: Blackwell, pp. 203–28.

Terry, M. (1996) 'Negotiating the government of unison: union democracy in theory and practice', *British Journal of Industrial Relations*, **34** (1), 87–110.

Trades Union Congress (1984) *TUC Strategy*, London: Trades Union Congress.

Trades Union Congress (1988a) *Meeting the Challenge: First Report of the Special Review Body*, London: Trades Union Congress.

Trades Union Congress (1988b) *Services For Union Members: Special Review Body Report on Services*, London: Trades Union Congress.

Trades Union Congress (1989) *Organising For The 1990s: The Special Review Body's Second Report*, London: Trades Union Congress.

Trades Union Congress (1991) *Towards 2000*, London: Trades Union Congress.

Trades Union Congress (1994a) *Human Resource Management: A Trade Union Response*, London: Trades Union Congress.

Trades Union Congress (1994b) *Employee Representation*, London: Trades Union Congress.

Trades Union Congress (1995) *Representation at Work: A TUC Consultative Document*, London: Trades Union Congress.

Trades Union Congress (1996) *New Unionism: Organising for Growth. New Unionism: A Message from John Monks*, London: Trades Union Congress.

Trades Union Congress (1998) *Congress 1998 – General Council Report*, London: Trades Union Congress.

Undy, R., Fosh, P., Morris, H., Smith, P. and Martin, R. (1996) *Managing the Unions: The Impact of Legislation on Trade Unions' Behaviour*, Oxford: Clarendon Press.

Waddington, J. (1992) 'Trade union membership in Britain, 1980–1987: unemployment and restructuring', *British Journal of Industrial Relations*, **30** (2), 287–328.

Waddington, J. (1993) 'Trade union membership concentration, 1892–1987: development and concentration', *British Journal of Industrial Relations*, **31** (3), 433–58.

Waddington, J. (1995) *The Politics of Bargaining: The Merger Process and British Trade Union Structural Development, 1892–1987*, London: Mansell.

Waddington, J. (2000) 'United Kingdom: recovering from the neo-liberal assault', in

J. Waddington and R. Hoffmann (eds) *Trade Unions in Europe: Facing Challenges and Searching for Solutions*, Brussels: European Trade Union Institute, pp. 575–626.

Williams, S. (1996) *Meeting the Needs of the Individual: The Nature and Differences of Recent Trade Union Modernisation Policies in the UK*, PhD, University of Sunderland.

Willman, P., Morris, T. and Aston, B. (1993) *Union Business: Trade Union Organisation and Financial Reform in the Thatcher Years*, Cambridge: Cambridge University Press.

4 Unions in Canada: Strategic Renewal, Strategic Conundrums[1]

Gregor Murray

Three strands underlie the recent evolution of trade unionism in Canada. First, in an international economic and political environment, which has been extremely adverse for trade unions in general and for selected national trade union movements in particular, unions in Canada have fared relatively well over the last two decades. In contrast with many other labour movements, the 1980s were in fact a decade of relative expansion. Although the 1990s proved more difficult, Canadian unions have just about held their own, maintaining their membership but suffering a slight decline in union density. Second, it can be argued that this relatively good performance is the result of considerable innovation and a sustained effort to develop and pursue strategies likely to reinforce union presence. Third, in the current context, such strategic renewal is probably insufficient to ensure enhanced union strength. The union movement in Canada faces a number of strategic conundrums and it is not yet apparent which strategies are most likely to bear fruit.

Union movements are, of course, the result of particular institutional trajectories; themselves embedded in the political economy of national settings. The first part of this chapter gives a brief overview of the political economy of union representation in Canada in order to locate the union movement as a social actor *vis-à-vis* the state, both in terms of the evolution of the legal regulation of collective representation and the broader role of unions in the society. The following parts of the chapter then focus on the 'nuts and bolts' of Canadian unionism, first in terms of the evolution and distribution of membership, then with regard to union structure and to union objectives and ideology. The final parts of the chapter present and assess the underlying dynamics of union renewal in Canada, specifically with regard to union strategies, the degree of success achieving them and the prospects for the future.

GREGOR MURRAY

The Political Economy of Collective Representation in Canada

Historical Development of Unions

The development of unions in Canada closely parallels that of unions in the United States. It is important, however, to distinguish the distinct phases of union growth, since they strongly imprint its current character.

As in many of the most developed economies, the emergence of local craft unionism dates from the early nineteenth century. With the development of inter-city rail travel and the greater labour mobility that characterized it, 'national' and 'international' craft unions began to take shape in North America. Industrialization was also associated with the emergence of an urban working class and the attendant social problems that characterized it. Concern with working standards, child labour, and the representation of workers were issues at the core of the 'labour problem' that sparked the emergence of national unions, workers' political parties and even the study of industrial relations throughout the developed world (see Giles and Murray, 1988). It was thus that city-wide and, eventually, national labour organizations emerged. Indeed, the Knights of Labor represented a spectacular but ultimately failed attempt to bring a form of mass or general unionism to the North American working class. Despite the real weakness of organized labour centres until well into the twentieth century, the current labour central, the Canadian Labour Congress, can legitimately trace its lineage from the mid-1870s.

A distinct feature of Canadian labour, also shared with Ireland, is the presence of international unions (based in the USA in the Canadian case) that organized workers in both the USA and Canada. From 1902 onwards, the Canadian labour movement was largely dominated by these international organizations. It is important to stress that this was more the result of an effort to assure effective organization of cross-border labour markets than any imperialist imperative. The increasing importance of secular, international unions also prompted a reaction in the largely French-speaking province of Québec where the Catholic Church encouraged rival Catholic unions more closely aligned with the value structures of the Church. The roots of contemporary union pluralism in Québec, the only province where there are competing labour confederations, can be traced back to this rivalry.

With collective representation largely confined to skilled industrial workers, the emergence of the large-scale firm in the USA, but also in Canada, with its huge numbers of semi-skilled and unskilled production workers, meant that there was an increasing representation gap as existing structures did not respond to the needs of this growing workforce. Closely mirroring the emergence of industrial unions in the United States under the auspices of the Congress of Industrial Organizations (CIO), mass industrial unionism arrived in Canada in the mid-1930s. It was not until the Second World War and its immediate aftermath, however, that there was substantial growth in the number of union members and the rate of unionization. Whereas absolute union membership and relative union density were stable from 1920 to 1940, membership tripled and density grew from 16.3 per cent to 28.4 per cent of the labour force during the 1940s (see Table 4.1 on p. 102). It was also at the end of the war that the federal government promulgated a legal framework largely inspired from the US Wagner Act of the 1930s, which defined the major features of the modern regime of collective labour representation. We shall examine this framework more closely in the next section of this chapter.

Although there continued to be a rivalry between a labour central dominated by the older craft unions and a labour central composed mainly of the new industrial unions and some Canadian unions, as in the USA, these rival centres merged in the mid-1950s to form a single labour centre, the Canadian Labour Congress (CLC). It was shortly thereafter that many of the industrial labour organizations played a significant role in the creation of the New Democratic Party (NDP), Canada's equivalent of a Labour Party.

Another impetus to the growth of the labour movement came with public sector unionization from the late 1960s onwards. In particular, this sparked a major growth in the number of union members, as total union membership grew from 2.17 million in 1970 to 3.39 million in 1980 and relative union density from 33.6 per cent to 35.7 per cent (see Table 4.1).

The Legal Framework of Collective Representation

The basic legal regime for collective representation is similar in Canada and the United States. It is especially important to give an overview of this regime since it so strongly influences basic union activities such as recruitment, servicing, bargaining and political action.[2]

The right to belong to a union for the purposes of collective bargaining is a positive right which can only be exercised when a union is recognized as the exclusive bargaining agent for a group of workers. A union gains exclusive bargaining rights when it demonstrates that it has majority support from the workers in the particular unit that it seeks to organize. There is inevitably some form of administrative determination as to what the 'appropriate bargaining unit' might be in a particular case and, therefore, whether the union has secured majority support in that particular unit. In contrast to the United States where the most common method of determining majority support is a certification election, the predominant method in Canada is the verification of membership cards. In other words, a union conducting an organizing campaign is obliged to have potential union members sign cards, which constitute proof that they have joined the union. This process is generally overseen by an administrative tribunal, which is also charged with the determination of the certification or bargaining unit. These latter are typically highly decentralized – a single establishment being the norm – unless it can be demonstrated that many separate units of a larger firm are effectively managed as a single unit or that there is a sufficient overlapping community of interest in cause. The parties may ultimately agree to conduct bargaining at some higher level, meaning that the effective bargaining unit could be made up of many certification units. As a rule, however, bargaining is very decentralized and the patchwork system of representation further contributes to this decentralization.

Where the union is not recognized as a majority agent, workers are effectively disenfranchised from collective representation rights; they must first form a majority. Although employers nominally cannot play any role in the exercise of these rights, employer opposition to the formation of unions is widespread and, where it can be demonstrated that employers have interfered with the formation of a union, administrative tribunals are empowered to impose union representation on the employer.[3] Access to collective representation is restricted in other important ways. Workers generally must be deemed to be salaried or waged employees: independent workers do not therefore qualify for union representation rights. These rights are further restricted to employees who do not exercise a managerial or supervisory function.

Once the union is designated as the monopoly bargaining agent, it is the exclusive agent for all workers covered by that particular unit. All workers generally pay union dues, whether they are a member of the union or not. Employers are obliged to deduct the union dues at source. Unlike in the United States, this union shop provision is a legal requirement in most jurisdictions in Canada. The union must conduct membership votes in order to undertake strike action and to ratify collective agreements. Workers also have the right to alter the bargaining agent or to renounce their collective representation rights during a specified period before the end of the collective agreement.

Employers are further obliged to deal with the union 'in good faith', although that does not mean that they are obliged to sign agreements with their unions. Given the inherent anti-unionism of many employers, administrative tribunals in most jurisdictions are also permitted to impose first collective agreements in order to 'regularize' the relationship. Collective agreements are legally binding, usually for a fixed term, and the union is a joint custodian in the observance of that agreement. In other words, strikes during the term of an agreement are generally illegal. Instead, the parties have recourse to a several-stage process of grievance resolution within the workplace before any such 'rights' disputes are put to binding third-party arbitration.

Even at the term of the agreement, strikes or lockouts may be delayed until a process of conciliation has been completed. This particular aspect of the legal requirements of collective bargaining in fact precedes the modern legal framework of the immediate post-war period. It dates from the first decade of the twentieth century when the government feared that industrial conflict in vital transportation infrastructure and commodity production industries would damage the Canadian economy. Not unlike in Australia and New Zealand, an elaborate process of compulsory conciliation was therefore put in place. Although this has gradually become less constraining over recent decades, the state maintains the power to limit the right to strike or lockout during periods of conciliation. In exceptional circumstances, the state can also impose an agreement and has increasingly had recourse to special legislative intervention to do so in a number of federally regulated industries over the past decades (see Panitch and Swartz, 1993).

The strike is, however, made more effective in several jurisdictions where the use of strikebreakers is illegal. This legislative movement began in Québec in the late 1970s with the election of a 'sovereignist' government basically sympathetic to labour, and was subsequently extended to Ontario and British Columbia and, most recently, albeit in a very limited way, to the federal jurisdiction. When a Conservative Government replaced a Social Democratic Government in Ontario in the mid-1990s, however, this provision was repealed and the movement to prohibit the recourse to strikebreakers in different Canadian jurisdictions has since slowed.

This legal framework has a number of strengths but also many weaknesses. In its favour, and in contrast to more centralized regimes of labour representation, the accountability of unions to their membership is very direct. Not only must trade unions directly recruit their members but they are also directly accountable to them at significant moments during the collective bargaining calendar; notably for strike action and the ratification of collective agreements. Workers, moreover, may choose to withdraw their support or decertify their union. The framework also provides a degree of institutional stability to the labour movement in as much as it guarantees revenue from all persons covered by the union within the bargaining unit. Finally, the tendency to decentralization offers the possibility to vary the terms and conditions of employment in accordance with local conditions. This relative flexibility is particularly conducive to a variety of forms of experimentation at local level.

The legal regime also suffers from a significant number of drawbacks. First, access to collective representation rights can be onerous for those who choose to attempt to unionize. Indeed, those who are in situations where a majority of colleagues do not opt for collective representation are completely excluded from the regime. The extremely high degree of decentralization also makes access to these rights increasingly problematical in a context, particularly in private services, where employment is located in a multitude of small units, with employees who are often in positions of contingent employment. Second, the entire process suffers from what has been labelled 'judiciarization'. The collective agreement has tended to evolve into a complex legal document. Recourse for a variety of problems is invariably tied up in procedural wrangles and can end up in lengthy procedures before administrative tribunals. Third, the regime provides few tools for the democratization of workplaces. While there are considerable procedural obligations related to the bargaining process, there are few obligations as to what should be bargained about. Moreover, unions are entirely reliant on their power to secure access to information and a role within the processes of change affecting so many workplaces. Finally, the administrative decentralization of the regime in the federal system and its permeability to provincial political pressures means that its basic coherence is vulnerable over the long term. It is currently safe to say that there have rarely been such contrasting trends within the broader framework of the legal regime. Several provincial jurisdictions have been experimenting with reinforcing different aspects of the regime, be it in terms of facilitating access, alleviating the onerous aspects of different procedures or introducing greater obligations about the content of bargaining. In contrast, several other regimes have tended to render access more difficult, most notably by introducing elections on a more frequent basis, reducing collective representation rights for certain groups and limiting the right to strike. This contradictory trend reflects the broader pressures on labour and social policy in Canada.

Unions, Political Action and the State

Unions generally engage in both industrial and political actions. Political action concerns both the defence of the worker as wage earner in the political realm as well as the defence of the worker as citizen (see Murray and Verge, 1999). The relative importance of political as opposed to industrial action varies greatly from one national labour relations regime to another. Moreover, the relative equilibrium between a narrower conception of the defence of the worker as wage earner and as citizen varies considerably from one union to the next.

The overall legitimacy of political activities as a dimension of union action was recently confirmed by an important Supreme Court of Canada decision. When a member of the Ontario Public Service Employees Union challenged the right of his union to use his compulsory union dues for purposes other than collective bargaining, the court ruled that political activity was a legitimate extension of collective bargaining.

Unions exhibit varying attitudes to the role of the market and the need for social change. On the one hand, many union leaders are content to continue in the tradition of 'bread and butter' unionism. This *business unionism* broadly accepts the operative assumptions of the market place and seeks to get the best deal possible for its members within these limits. Many unions also use political means to improve the terms and conditions of their members. These union leaders generally express a more critical view of the workings of the market and argue the need to promote social and political change as an integral part of union activity. Such *social unionism* plays an increasingly important role in the analysis of economic restructuring advanced by unions in Canada (Pupo and White, 1994; Kumar, 1995). There are also some unions that seek to effect political change, not through alliances with political parties but through alliances with the new social movements. This might be labelled *social movement unionism* (see, in particular, Robinson, 1994).

Union political involvement therefore varies from no political involvement whatsoever, to pressure-group activity that seeks to influence the parliamentary or governmental process, to direct partisan political action in favour of a particular political party, to coalition activity designed to work with other social groups towards common objectives. There are a variety of examples of each in Canada.

Many of the affiliates of the major labour confederation in Canada, however, have long maintained an important relationship with the New Democratic Party of Canada. This special relationship has translated into active organizational and financial support. Many, but not all, CLC affiliates are organically linked to the NDP. While the NDP has formed the government in several provinces (Saskatchewan, British Columbia, Manitoba and Ontario) at various points over the last three decades, it has never enjoyed more than minor electoral success at federal level.

Unions in Canada have been increasingly involved in a variety of other kinds of political activity, most notably in coalition with other groups, as they have sought to influence the outcome of public debates on a range of issues. Faced with the question of how to reflect the new labour market developments and the preoccupations of their new membership into the larger sets of political and social action, there is considerable evidence of union attempts to effect broader coalitions with other social groups.

Most important have been the successive debates on the free trade agreement with the United States and the North American Free Trade Agreement (NAFTA) in which Canadian unions worked with many other social groups against these free trade treaties (see Robinson, 1994). Similarly, some unions have increasingly shared platforms with other groups on questions such as the environment, equal rights and international solidarity. A number of unions have also created special funds to assist their work in this domain. The Steelworkers Union, in particular, created its Humanity Fund to assist international development projects. Similarly, the Autoworkers' social justice fund is designed to promote worthy projects both in Canada and abroad. Many unions have, of course, long maintained an active civic and community role in philanthropic work such as the United Way or other special charitable causes.

Membership

Membership Trends

Faced with a variety of significant structural adjustments, unions represent a diminishing proportion of the labour force in many of the industrialized Western economies. The recent history of Canadian trade unionism, then, is somewhat of an anomaly, particularly when compared with the fortunes of the neighbouring US labour movement. While the number of union members in the United States has diminished in both absolute and relative terms over the past two decades, the Canadian union movement experienced a steady but gradual growth in aggregate union membership: from 2.2 million in 1970 to 3.4 million in 1980 to 4.0 million in 1990 (Table 4.1). Since then, from 1990 to 1999, aggregate union membership has remained stable at just over 4.0 million members. The absolute growth during the 1980s was remarkable given that so many other labour movements experienced membership declines over the same period (see ILO, 1997). The relative stability of the last decade, in the 1990s, belies significant changes in the composition of union membership to which we shall return; it also is indicative of the scale of the challenge facing unions in Canada if they are to make significant progress in relative union density over coming years.

Given the extent of detailed legal regulation of union representation in Canada, detailed above, the notion of a union member in Canada closely approximates that of a dues payer. It is, of course, possible to be a member of a union without enjoying access to collective representation rights but this is a very marginal phenomenon. Some unions also make provision for unemployed members to retain their membership at reduced rates. It is highly unusual in Canada for retired members to retain their membership although there have been some recent efforts to activate associations for retirees.

Measures of union membership are subject to some confusion because the figures vary according to the source of the data. Two main sources are used in this chapter. Human Resources Development Canada (HRDC), formerly known as Labour Canada, conducts an annual survey of union membership. All union organizations report their membership and their affiliation to a labour centre. This provides an historical statistical series for assessing the evolution of union membership and density over time (see Table 4.1). Statistics Canada also conducts a detailed monthly survey of individuals' labour market activity, which has recently begun to ask respondents whether they are union members and, if not, whether their wages and conditions of employment are determined by a collective agreement. This enables extrapolation of union membership and collective bargaining coverage for particular industries and for the economy as a whole. It also provides detailed information about the demographic and socioeconomic composition of the union movement (see Tables 4.2 and 4.3 on pp. 104 and 106). While these sources of information are, by and large, convergent and complementary, the overall estimations of the number of union members and the rate of union density vary by several percentage points according to the source used.[4]

At the beginning of 1999, the HRDC survey estimated that 32.3 per cent of paid non-agricultural workers were members of a union (Table 4.1). The rate of collective bargaining coverage, including those workers whose terms and conditions of employment were negotiated by a union but who were not themselves union members, tends to be several percentage points higher. In

Table 4.1 *Evolution of union membership in Canada, 1911–99*

Year	Membership (thousands)	Membership as percentage of non-agricultural paid workers	Year	Membership (thousands)	Membership as percentage of non-agricultural paid workers
1910	133	–	1990	4,031	34.5
1920	374	16.0**	1991	4,068	34.7
1930	322	13.1	1992	4,089	35.7
1940	362	16.3	1993	4,071	35.8
1950***	1,029	28.4	1994	4,078	35.6
1960	1,459	32.3	1995	4,003	34.3
1970	2,173	33.6	1996	4,033	33.9
1975	2,884	36.9	1997	4,074	34.1
1980	3,397	35.7	1998	3,938	32.5
1985	3,666	36.4	1999	4,010	32.3

Percentage change for selected periods

Period	Membership (%)	Union density (%)	Period	Membership (%)	Union density (%)
1910–20	181.2	–	1970–75	32.7	9.8
1920–30	−13.9	−18.1	1975–80	17.8	−3.3
1930–40	12.4	24.4	1980–85	7.9	2.0
1940–50	184.3	74.2	1985–90	10.0	−5.2
1950–60	41.8	13.7	1990–95	−0.7	−0.6
1960–70	48.9	4.0	1995–9	0.2	−5.8

* 1911 ** 1921 *** 1951

Note: Data from Annual Union Survey conducted by Human Resources Development Canada (HRDC).

Source: Calculated from Murray (2000).

1999, for example, it can be estimated that collective bargaining coverage was 2.5 percentage points higher than union density (calculated from Akyeampong 1999, see Tables 4.2 and 4.3 on pp. 104 and 106).

Absolute membership figures reflect the relative health of unions, especially in terms of dues income and levels of organizing. Measures of relative union membership are especially useful for understanding the importance of unions in different industries and occupations. Absolute union membership in Canada grew during the 1980s and remained stable through the 1990s, declining slightly between 1990 and 1995 but increasing between 1995 and 1999 (Table 4.1). Relative density as a percentage of non-agricultural paid workers declined significantly through the later half of the 1980s and, again, in the latter half of the 1990s, moving from 34.3 per cent in 1995 to 32.3 per cent in 1999.[5]

Nonetheless, the growth of Canadian union membership in the 1980s and its relative stability through the 1990s compare relatively favourably with membership trends in other industrialized economies. When we compare Canadian union growth with that of other industrialized economies in the 1985 to 1995 period, only the union movements in Denmark, Malta, Norway and Spain demonstrated a comparable stability. The aggregate membership performance of Canadian trade unions contrasts markedly with the more significant declines in union membership in countries such as Australia, France, Japan, the United Kingdom and the United States (ILO, 1997).

Trade union membership by province reflects these national trends. In absolute terms, union membership in all provinces increased significantly over the last two decades. There are, however, significant differences in the levels of union density from one province to another (see Akyeampong, 1999). At one end of the scale, Newfoundland consistently exhibits the highest union density (38.0 per cent), followed by Québec (35.9 per cent), Manitoba (35.5 per cent) and British Columbia (33.9 per cent). Alberta has the lowest level of union density (23.0 per cent) followed by Ontario (26.5 per cent). These differences reflect various factors: differing industrial structures, particularly the concentration of highly unionized industries in certain provinces; more rapid expansion of labour markets in some provinces (particularly Alberta and Ontario); differences in community attitudes to unionism which, despite initial differences in industrial structure, tend to spill over into other sectors as regards the acceptability of unionism as a way of regulating employment relations; and, by extension, given the high degree of decentralization in the legal regulation of unions in Canada, changing public policy on access to unionism, particularly in terms of a more adverse climate in certain provinces such as Alberta and Ontario.

Distribution of Union Membership

Union membership is not evenly distributed throughout the economy. There are significant variations by sociodemographic characteristics, industry, occupation, firm size and employment status.

A first source of variation is by gender. Historically, the rate of unionization of women has tended to be less than that of men, but the proportion of male and female union members is now roughly equivalent (30.9 per cent of men as opposed to 29.3 per cent of women were union members in 1999, see Table 4.2). This represents a significant change over the last three decades because women accounted for only 23.5 per cent of union members in the early 1970s. Moreover, while male union membership has either grown very slowly or, in some cases, declined slightly over the last two decades, female union membership has increased substantially. Thus, underlying a relative stability in union membership over the last several years is an increasing feminization of the union movement, which has significant implications for the changing character of unions in Canada (see White, 1993; Briskin and McDermott, 1993).

There are also considerable variations in the degree of unionization by industry, particularly on terms of the disparity between the rates of public and private sector unionization (see Table 4.3). According to Statistics

Table 4.2 *Union membership and collective bargaining coverage by gender, age, employment status, and establishment size, Canada, 1999*

	Percentage union membership (%)	Percentage collective bargaining coverage (%)
Sex		
Male	30.9	33.5
Female	29.3	31.6
Age		
15–24 years	12.0	13.8
25–44 years	30.4	33.0
45–54 years	41.8	44.6
55 years or more	34.8	37.1
Employment status		
Full time	32.0	34.7
Part time	21.8	23.2
Establishment size		
Less than 20 employees	12.2	13.8
20–99 employees	30.5	33.3
100–499 employees	44.1	47.3
500 or more employees	56.6	59.4
Total	30.1	32.6

Note. Estimates calculated from Statistics Canada labour market survey for the first six months of 1999.
Source. Akyeampong (1999).

Canada figures for 1999, workers in the education sector are by far the most unionized group (69.1 per cent), followed by workers in utilities (68.3 per cent), civil servants in public administration (64.3 per cent) and workers in healthcare and social assistance (53.2 per cent). Manufacturing, which has traditionally been highly unionized, has experienced both an absolute decline in union membership and a relative decline in union density over the last two decades, falling from approximately 44.3 per cent in 1982 to 31.2 per cent in 1999.

Private services remain little unionized, particularly the huge concentrations of workers in the trade sector (12.6 per cent), finance, insurance and real estate (8.3 per cent) and accommodation and food services (6.4 per cent). In common with many other industrialized economies, the least unionized industries in Canada include those that have been growing most quickly, such as trade and finance. It should be emphasized that the degree of unionization in these two industries has increased steadily over the past two decades, but the overall degree of unionization remains extremely weak.

The composition of the union movement continues to change, as new members come from areas of weaker unionization while membership is lost in traditional industries. The most significant change over the past decades has been the declining proportion of union members in manufacturing and the increased proportion of public sector workers in the union movement. For example, 38.9 per cent of union members came from manufacturing in 1966 as opposed to only 18.2 per cent in 1999. The public sector accounted for more than half (53.4 per cent) of union members in Canada in 1999. As the employment structure continues to shift towards the private services, the future of the Canadian union movement, in many ways, hinges on its ability to negotiate this change.

The distribution of union members by firm size is also highly variable. Drawing on the estimates of collective bargaining coverage provided by Statistics Canada (Table 4.2), the overall level of collective bargaining coverage was 32.6 per cent of paid workers in 1999. This figure was only 13.8 per cent for firms with less than twenty employers, 33.3 per cent for establishments with twenty to one hundred employees, 47.3 per cent for establishments with between 100 and 500 employees, and 59.4 per cent for establishments with more than 500 employees. Clearly a much higher proportion of union members work in larger firms than is the case with the active labour force as a whole. This reflects the more difficult time unions have in securing their presence in small firms.

Employment status also exerts an effect on the degree of unionization, as full-time workers (those working more than 30 hours per week) tend to be

Table 4.3 *Membership and union density by industry, Canada, 1999*

Industry	Membership	Union density (%)
Public	1,912,000	70.9
Private	1,676,000	18.2
Goods	939,000	31.1
Agriculture	3,000	2.5
Other primary sector	56,000	26.4
Utilities	83,000	68.3
Manufacturing	651,000	31.2
Construction	146,000	30.2
Services	2,654,000	29.8
Transportation and warehousing	253,000	42.3
Trade	238,000	12.6
Finance, insurance, real estate	62,000	8.3
Professional, scientific and technical	23,000	4.0
Management, administrative and support	36,000	9.9
Education	645,000	69.1
Healthcare and social assistance	667,000	53.2
Information, culture and recreation	148,000	28.0
Accommodation and food	52,000	6.4
Other	37,000	8.1
Public administration	493,000	64.3
Total	3,593,000	30.1

Note: Estimates calculated from Statistics Canada labour market survey for the first six months of 1999.
Source: Akyeampong (1999).

more unionized than part-time workers. According to Statistics Canada estimates (Table 4.2), collective bargaining coverage for full-time workers was 34.7 per cent in 1999 as opposed to 23.2 per cent for part-time workers. This differential constitutes a challenge for Canadian trade unions because there continues to be a more rapid expansion of part-time employment than full-time employment and of contingent or atypical jobs, such as short-term contracts, as opposed to full-time, permanent jobs.

The age of a person also exercises a very powerful influence on union membership. Younger persons are much less likely to be union members than other age categories. For example, in 1999 it was estimated that only

12.0 per cent of persons between 15 and 24 years of age were union members as opposed to 30.18 per cent of those between 25 and 44 and 41.8 per cent of those between 45 and 54. This marked differential reflects younger people's more tenuous hold on regular, full-time employment in the labour market; a trend that has accelerated over the last two decades of the twentieth century.

It has thus become increasingly apparent that the membership pressures operating on unions in Canada are very intense. The employment areas in which unions have traditionally been most representative, particularly manufacturing and public administration, are shrinking, while the areas in which unions are less representative, particularly private services, are the most important sources of employment growth. While union growth has largely kept pace with the growth in public service employment, this is not the case with the private services, which is of particular importance as public service employment growth stagnates while private services continue to expand. Yet there is considerable evidence that the Canadian union movement has proved highly adaptable and fairly innovative over the last two decades. Several indicators point in this direction: the overall growth in aggregate union membership, continuing high levels of recruitment activity, the entry of women into the labour market and a certain success in obtaining changes in provincial labour laws that facilitate new recruitment. However, these changes in employment structure continue to exert a significant impact on union structures, which we shall explore further in the next section.

Union Structure[6]

Union structure in Canada might be envisaged as being made up of several basic building blocks: the certification unit, the local union, the national or international union, the central labour body or congress, and affiliations to international labour organizations by one of these other levels of union structure.

The cornerstone of all union structures is the *certification unit* or *appropriate bargaining unit*. This is the definition of the group of workers for which a labour board or other similar administrative body grants exclusive bargaining rights to a designated agent, after a majority of those workers has indicated support for union representation.

Bargaining units in Canada are generally quite small and bargaining is highly decentralized. With the notable exception of the public sector, the norm is the negotiation of a single agreement between an employer and a union for a single site. The focus of union activity is generally at the level of the certification unit and, unlike many countries characterized by national-level bargaining, Canadian union structure is highly decentralized with weak vertical integration between different hierarchical levels of union organization. The division of powers over labour matters within the Canadian federation further exacerbates this decentralization. Roughly 10 per cent of Canadian workers fall under federal jurisdiction; the other 90 per cent are subject to the different provincial jurisdictions, whose labour codes vary considerably.

Despite this decentralization, the certification unit is most frequently also part of a larger union structure. At the local level, a *union local* may be made up of one or more such certification units. Union locals in industries such as construction are typically made up of multiple certification units. In large manufacturing establishments, on the other hand, the local union generally consists of a single certification unit. There were approximately 17,365 such local unions in Canada at the beginning of 1998 (see Table 4.4).

Whatever their degree of autonomy, most local unions are part of a larger structure.[7] A union local is typically chartered by a *national* or *international union organization* from which it receives its name and its statutes. National and international unions organize and charter locals in the industries or professions defined by their statutes or policies. This is known as a union's jurisdiction. Such jurisdictions are increasingly being altered by changes in industrial structure and the consequent strategies pursued by unions to diversify their membership base. There were roughly 279 such national and international unions operating in Canada at the beginning of 1998. Among these, the ten largest accounted for 47.3 per cent of all union members in Canada (see Table 4.5 on p. 111). This represents an increasing trend towards greater concentration since the similar figure was 40.0 per cent in 1980 and 41.8 per cent in 1990.

Most, but not all, of these unions are, in turn, affiliated to *central labour bodies* or *congresses*. These central labour bodies or peak organizations have both a national presence and, in the case of the Canadian Labour Congress, a significant provincial and territorial presence in the form of twelve *provincial and territorial federations of labour*. In Québec there are also several autonomous central labour bodies or confederations, notably the Confédération des syndicats nationaux (CSN) and the Centrale de l'enseignement du Québec (CEQ). Labour congresses or confederations are also present at district or regional levels. These central labour bodies, as well as many of the national and international unions affiliated to them, also generally maintain *international affiliations*.

Labour Centres

The Canadian Labour Congress is the principal central labour congress in Canada. It represented 2.67 million members in 1998, approximately 66.7 per cent of union members in Canada. There were 93 national and international unions affiliated to the CLC. They pay affiliation fees to the CLC on a per member basis. It is such organizations and not the CLC or its provincial federations of labour that provide the bulk of direct services to members. In general, with the exception of the CSN in Québec, labour congresses do not negotiate for their members, nor do they recruit new members.

Table 4.4 *Union membership by congress affiliation, Canada, 1998*

	Locals	Membership	Percentage of membership
Canadian Labour Congress (CLC)*	9,827	2,626,740	66.71
Confédération des syndicats nationaux (CSN)	2,399	242,830	6.17
Centrale de l'enseignement du Québec (CEQ)	305	113,510	2.88
AFL–CIO only	153	82,510	2.10
Centrale des syndicats démocratiques (CSD)	490	73,070	1.86
Confederation of Canadian Unions (CCU)	38	17,020	0.43
Unaffiliated national unions	3,793	637,270	16.18
Unaffiliated international unions	8	230	0.00
Independent local organizations	352	144,610	3.67
TOTAL	17,365	3,937,790	100.00

Note: *CLC includes 2571 locals with both CLC and AFL–CIO affiliations.
Source: Human Resources Development Canada (1998).

Labour congresses are thus confined to representational and policy-making activities in the social, economic and political spheres. For example, CLC representatives participate in a number of national and international bodies on issues such as training, unemployment insurance and social policy on behalf of its members. Representatives of provincial federations of labour do likewise at the provincial level.

Affiliated unions zealously maintain their autonomy and the CLC has very weak formal authority over the activities of its affiliates. Given this weak vertical integration and its relative lack of financial resources, coordination depends more on consensus-building on policy issues among its principal affiliates and persuading them to commit resources to particular campaigns.

However, because of increasing conflicts between affiliates over jurisdictional issues, the CLC has in recent years bolstered its disciplinary powers over individual affiliates. This was, in particular, the result of a bitter dispute in the Maritimes between the United Food and Commercial Workers Union (UFCW) and the Canadian Auto Workers (CAW) over the decision of many certification units in the fishing industry to transfer their allegiance from the former to the latter. However, there have been many other examples of inter-union conflicts over jurisdictional issues, not least of which is a recent dispute over charges that the CAW has raided the membership of an international union in Canada (the Service Employees International Union), leading to the temporary suspension of the CAW from the CLC in 2000–.

The Confédération des syndicats nationaux (CSN) is the second labour congress in size. Formerly a confessional or Catholic union movement but fully secular since the early 1960s, its membership is located almost exclusively in Québec. The CSN represents approximately nine union organizations covering 2,399 local unions and 242,830 members. Unlike the CLC, but like some of the labour congresses in continental Europe, the degree of vertical and horizontal integration of locals within the CSN is highly developed.

Other labour congresses in Canada include the CEQ, a confederation of Québec public sector unions located primarily but not exclusively in the field of education; the Centrale des syndicats démocratiques (CSD), a small grouping of Québec unions that broke away from the CSN in the early 1970s; and the Confederation of Canadian Unions (CCU), a loose grouping of independent local Canadian unions with a specific nationalist perspective.

The Canadian union movement became increasingly fragmented from 1975 to 1985 as the proportion of union membership represented by the CLC fell from 71.1 per cent to 57.8 per cent. The trend has been partially reversed in the 1990s as the CLC represented 66.7 per cent of union members in Canada in 1998 (see Table 4.5). The initial decline was not the result of a decline in overall affiliated membership of the CLC but rather of three factors: (1) continued increases in membership of non-affiliated unions, particularly those representing professionals in the health and education sector; (2) a modification in the reporting requirements of Statistics Canada, which further 'increased' the number of unaffiliated union members; and (3) the breakaway of a number of US-based affiliated unions, especially in the construction trades, from the Canadian Labour Congress in 1982 to form the Canadian Federation of Labour (CFL). The more recent move towards a greater concentration of union membership in the CLC is the result of the reaffiliation of a number of unions that had previously quit or been excluded from CLC membership (notably the Teamsters), the disappearance of the CFL as a labour centre and, increasingly in the context of public sector cutbacks, the interest in previously unaffiliated public sector unions (notably teachers' unions) in joining broader labour coalitions.

Table 4.5 *Percentage share of membership in the ten largest unions and in the CLC, Canada, 1975–98*

	CLC (%)	Ten largest unions (%)	Unaffiliated or independent unions (%)
1975	71.1	37.2	20.8
1980	68.5	40.0	23.8
1985	57.8	40.9	24.6
1990	58.6	41.8	21.7
1995	60.8	44.4	22.8
1998	66.7	47.3	19.9

Source: Human Resources Development Canada (1999).

National and International Unions

In terms of the organization of resources and the development of strategies, national and international unions are undoubtedly the most significant organizational level. It is generally at this level that major decisions about approaches to bargaining, recruitment and political activity are made. As befits the decentralization of the Canadian labour movement, national and international unions in Canada are highly diverse in their structures and policies.

By international standards, one of the more peculiar features of Canadian unionism has been the interpenetration of Canadian and American union structures. Indeed, among the industrialized economies, only in Ireland and Britain are union structures linked in this way. Because of the high degree of integration of the two economies, the two major phases of union development in the United States, craft and industrial unionism, spilled over the northern US border and a large proportion of Canadian union members have belonged to such 'international' unions. An important trend has been the relative decline in the importance of international or American unionism. At the beginning of 1998, 29.9 per cent of union members in Canada belonged to unions whose headquarters were based in the United

States (HRDC, 1997). This represents a complete reversal in the importance of international unionism in Canada, as three decades earlier, in 1969, 65 per cent of union members in Canada belonged to international unions.

National unions have been growing much faster than international unions, particularly because of the spread of unionization in the public sector where almost all union members belong to national unions. There have also been some significant splits from parent US unions. One of the most visible separations was that of the Canadian Auto Workers union in 1985, which split from the United Auto Workers.

The move to greater Canadian autonomy has not necessarily resulted in secession by Canadian members within US-based unions. There has been a growing movement towards more self-governance by the Canadian members of international unions (Thompson and Blum, 1983). International unions remain a significant feature of Canadian union structure. Of the ten largest unions, only three are now international unions. As workers strive to construct cross-border alliances to deal with common problems in the context of the internationalization of production, not only are many forms of international unionism likely to endure, but new forms of international unionism will also probably emerge.

Unions have a wide variety of internal structures, which tend to reflect the evolution of particular visions of territorial, occupational and industrial solidarities as well as administrative arrangements for providing service to members. The great historical conflict was, of course, between craft unionism, which favoured occupational solidarities, and industrial unionism, which sought to organize workers on the basis of industries. Most unions continue to be based on either an occupational or an industrial principle. These organizing jurisdictions have become blurred over time. In particular, changes in the sectoral distribution of employment have led to significant modifications in union structure.

First, many previously single industry unions are involved in mergers. In 1992, for example, three major industrial unions in the paper, energy, and chemical and communications industries merged to create a single new union, the Communications, Energy and Paperworkers Union of Canada. The Canadian Auto Workers has also been extremely active, merging successively in the 1990s with a number of other unions, notably in the transport, electrical, mining and aluminium industries (see Yates, 1998). Other mergers have resulted from a consolidation of unions in the AFL–CIO in the United States. Thus, Union of Needletrades Industrial and Textile Employees (UNITE) is the result of a 1995 merger between the Amalgamated Textile and Clothing Workers and the International Ladies Garment Workers.

Second, many of the industrial unions in the manufacturing sector have been faced with declining membership and diminished opportunities for new recruitment activity in their traditional jurisdictions. This has prompted some unions to diversify their areas of recruitment. One of the more striking examples of this phenomenon is that of the Steelworkers Union, which is increasingly involved in recruitment in the service sector (see Murray, 1998). This trend accelerated throughout the 1980s as the Steelworkers, seeking to compensate for significant membership loss in traditional areas of strength such as mining and manufacturing, began organizing among security guards, department store, hotel and restaurant workers. There are many other examples of this larger trend, as private and public sector unions both compensate for membership loss and respond to changes in the organization of production that affect the employment conditions of existing membership.

Thus, industrial unionism is slowly giving way to new varieties of general unionism. In the past, there were a few unions that organized in a wide variety of sectors. Such *general unions* were based on neither craft nor industrial jurisdictions. The search for appropriate union structures to take root in the new service sector is likely to exacerbate this transformation of industrial and craft unions into modified forms of general unionism over the coming decade.

At the same time, there is a reaction to this trend in terms of the importance of different occupational groupings, both within and between unions. In particular, unaffiliated national unions are typically representative of professional groups in the public sector such as nurses and other healthcare professionals. Wary of political activity, they have traditionally opted not to affiliate to a central labour body such as the Canadian Labour Congress. In an era where the jurisdictional lines have become increasingly muddled, the clearer professional focus of some of these unions has proved to be an impetus for growth at the same time as public sector cutbacks have sparked greater political activity.

Union Locals

The decentralization of Canadian union structure means that many local unions have a high degree of autonomy. Local unions tend to reflect either their craft or industrial union servicing traditions, though pressures on existing union structures are contributing to the emergence of other hybrid local models.

The craft tradition tends towards a very autonomous local union, which organizes a large number of certification units on a regional basis. All dues are paid to that local union. With the growing demands for specialized union services centrally, unions organized along this model have added more centralized services but their ability to do so is limited by both the autonomy of local unions and their weak financial capacity at central level.

The industrial tradition is more centralized. The local union traditionally, but not exclusively, consisted of one certification unit. Local unions had part-time presidents, who did not draw their salary from the union, and were serviced by a cadre of full-time officials employed by the national or international union. Dues were paid by members to the national or international union. The central union body or the head office generally developed specialized services, which were delivered through fieldstaff. Many of the new public sector unions tended to adopt some variation of this industrial union model.

There is considerable pressure on all of these models because of changes in industrial structure. Some models appear to be better suited to the new exigencies of the service economy than do others. The changing organization of the firm and larger trends in the labour market have also had a marked, if highly differential, impact on the structures and strategies of local unions. Most notably, the declining size of existing bargaining units and the small size of many new certifications have prompted some unions to amalgamate different certifications into larger, composite locals. This is particularly evident in many of the older unions, which are characterized by a craft structure and have traditionally organized a multiplicity of units within a single local union and built their servicing structures around this type of arrangement. The local structures of 'industrial model' unions, such as the United Steelworkers of America, are also undergoing significant change. With the infusion of smaller certification units, particularly in the private services, the Steelworkers Union has gradually altered its local structures, with the average number of certifications per local union increasing. This represents a conscious organizing and servicing strategy designed to better meet the needs of new membership groups in both the service sector and in small manufacturing units. Indeed, it aimed to create union locals, which are better able to adjust to the small size of new units typically being organized during this period. It also sought to achieve a viable servicing strategy in terms of the relative cost of reaching a multiplicity of small units and providing access to basic services, sometimes assured by newly trained full-time lay representatives rather than professional business agents or servicing staff.

Objectives and Ideology

Unions are, of course, collective organizations of workers premised on the defence and the advancement of the interests of their members. How they define those interests, which interests they choose to put forward and how they choose to defend and advance those interests is a more open question – hence the variations in union objectives, character and ideologies.

Six simple distinctions should help to clarify this terrain of interest and the way in which those interests should be defined and advanced.[8] The first two concern the definition of interest while the latter four address the way in which those interests are to be advanced. First, in terms of job territory or the extent of the collectivity, the union might seek to represent particular interests, and only those interests, be it a particular craft or locality, or it might seek to cover a broader range of interests; for example, waged workers in general. Second, in terms of the range of interest, as has previously been suggested, a union might seek to defend the worker, primarily, indeed exclusively, as a wage earner. It might also seek to defend the worker as citizen: his or her conditions of life over and beyond the wage relationship. Third, in terms of its posture towards social relations in general, a union might seek to regulate the wage relationship within existing economic and social parameters, broadly defined, or it might seek to transform those parameters. In terms of market relations, is it possible to work within the market or must it be transformed? Fourth, in terms of the level of representation, does the union focus primarily on the place of work and the role of the worker within it, or does the union focus more broadly on an industry or on the labour market as a whole or, indeed, on the society in general? Fifth, in terms of methods, are those objectives to be achieved primarily by economic means, directly *vis-à-vis* the employer, or by political means in terms of lobbying, founding a political party, or working with other social groups to effect changes in state policy or even in the society as a whole? Finally, union objectives may be achieved cooperatively or through conflict. While there will invariably be some combination of both, a union's action might be more oriented in one direction or another. Each of these distinctions suggests a continuum of possibilities. They are not either/or propositions. Indeed, it is even possible to find permutations of the two ends of the continuum.

Union objectives, character and ideology represent some combination of these six axes of differentiation. Three prototypical configurations spring readily to mind but it should quickly become apparent that the definition of union character defies these simple distinctions, not least because the definition of union objectives and character, as befits collective, democratic organizations, is the subject of continuous internal debate and process. For heuristic purposes, we shall first attempt to set out a number of simple configurations of union character and/or ideology and to locate their relative importance in the Canadian union movement.

A first configuration might be labelled 'business unionism'. In terms of the definition of interests, it tends to privilege a narrower conception of the extent of solidarity; particular interests are usually more important than the general interest. It follows that the defence of the worker as wage earner is more important than that of the worker as citizen – hence the focus on a narrower, economic instrumentality, a kind of '*bread and butterism*'. As regards the advancement of these interests, business unionism is most likely to work within the confines of existing market relations. It is also more likely to focus on the workplace than on the market in general unless, by its various nature, the occupation or job territory in question is characterized by such a high degree of mobility that the union will naturally address some level other than the establishment. Typically, this would be an occupation or a sector. Moreover, it is usually a form of unionism that tends to utilize economic rather than political means, although that certainly does not preclude political action as a method of action. Finally, there is no fixed ideological space for business unionism as regards conflict and cooperation: it is possible to pursue membership interests in a cooperative manner or with a high degree of militancy. However, in a highly decentralized bargaining regime, it is more likely to be conflictual than cooperative in the pursuit of its primarily economic objectives.

Such a union configuration has certainly been an important model in North America. Certain craft unions probably approximate it in a more prototypical form. The prevailing model has been one predicated on job control in the workplace, often defended with a high degree of militancy, in which political action is less important except when the political impinges on the organizational possibility of defending members' interests at the place of work. It is then that the lobby, irrespective of political affiliation, becomes an important method of action. The creation of the Canadian Federation of Labour in the 1980s represented a certain triumph for this approach. Disillusioned with the increasingly political orientation that they felt drove the industrial and public sector unions in the Canadian Labour Congress, these unions sought to found a labour central that did not engage in partisan politics nor seek to transform the social order. The underlying ideological orientations of many of the new professional public sector unions, notably the nurses and other professionalized union groupings, also approximates a form of business unionism.

A second configuration might be broadly defined as 'social unionism'. Without excluding the defence of particular interests, for what union can do so, it starts from a wider definition of solidarity. In other words, its vision of the job territory to be defended is broader and subject to extension. Moreover, this form of unionism is likely to embrace the interests of the worker as citizen as well as the interests of the worker as wage earner. It is an open question to what degree this type of unionism can work within the confines of existing market relations. Social unions clearly vary in this orientation but tend to seek some transformation of market relations, even if, in that memorable expression of Commons, it is only to 'save capitalism from itself' (see DeBrizzi, 1983). It follows that such unionism must focus on both the workplace and the market in general. This unionism is also most likely to engage in political as well as economic action. In that respect, relations with political parties are important. Social unionism might be conflictual or cooperative at the level of the workplace but its at least partially transformative character tends to leave a more conflictual imprint.

In terms of union practice in Canada, social unionism covers a fairly large territory as many unions could safely be included in such a definition. Indeed, such an ideological configuration is undoubtedly the dominant union mode in Canada. In particular, industrial unionism as practised in Canada corresponds very closely to this definition. In the case of the major industrial unions in industries such as auto, meatpacking, paper and steel, the predominant notion of fighting for the improvement of working conditions and wages has historically entailed a twofold agenda of collective bargaining and political action. The former typically involved some combination of contractually based job control and pattern bargaining for semi-skilled and unskilled workers, while the latter involved the pursuit of a social and political agenda that addressed the conditions of workers in general, as both wage earners and citizens. These were also the unions most involved in the creation of the New Democratic Party and they continually bankrolled its electoral efforts. Many of the new public sector unions organizing among less-skilled workers also fit this political space except that their members demonstrated much greater ambivalence about the political role that they should play and they often avoided an implication in partisan politics. There are clearly considerable differences both between and within the various industrial and public sector unions as regards their orientation on one or the other of the axes identified. As the dominant ideological construct, social unionism has been a 'very broad church'.

A third configuration might be described as 'social movement unionism'.

It closely resembles social unionism but the differences of degree are sufficiently important to suggest a different ideological configuration altogether. First, in terms of its posture on market relations, it tends to pursue a more important social transformation as the way of truly advancing worker interests, both as wage earner and as citizen. Second, given the objective of social transformation, politics is a vital dimension of union action. Finally, such a vision is more likely to embrace the transformative potential of conflict as a method of action. Such an approach to union practice is again present in many unions but has rarely been entirely dominant, even in unions where political activists, notably from the Communist Party, were in positions of leadership.

This approach has often played an important role within Canadian unions but as an ideological counterpoint to the prevailing social union philosophy. The automobile workers provide an interesting case study in as much as this approach was much more in evidence in the Auto Union in Canada than it was in the Steelworkers' Union (see Yates, 1993). The United Electrical Workers was a rare example of where such an approach was actually the dominant union philosophy.

Union character is, of course, forged over time. It changes gradually unless some larger societal forces are at work to prompt more rapid changes. Moreover, it reflects the broader political economy from which it emerges. For example, given the importance of the state for both the Canadian economy and the legal regulation of unions, it has been difficult for Canadian unions to adopt a purely 'business unionism' approach. It was an ideological space for which there was simply less scope. At the same time, however, the distance of the social unions' political preference, the NDP, from parliamentary political power in most jurisdictions has meant that the economic dimensions of social unionism have generally been more prevalent. Social unionism in Canada has rarely had to contend with the paradoxes of proximity to power that is the case with so many other labour movements that have organic links to social democratic parties in power. Among examples of this is the oftentimes tempestuous relationship between unions in Québec province and the Parti Québécois governments of the last two decades. Similar tensions have been observed, particularly in British Columbia, Saskatchewan and Ontario, when the NDP has been in power.

Strategic Responses

The strategic response of unions in Canada to their new environment has been both defensive and proactive. It is certainly defensive in as much as many unions have been reeling as a result of their inability to protect basic wages and working conditions. The environment is a very hostile one and repeated surveys point to a deterioration of working conditions on the part of unionized workers: decreased job security, increased workload and greater stress on the job. In this respect, the priority has typically been to mitigate the worst effects of this trend. Yet, Canadian unions have also been engaged in substantial innovation in their attempts to renew their membership and their organizations and to engage in new avenues of strategic endeavour. The decentralized nature of the regime of collective representation in Canada and the strategic focus on national and international unions as the most salient levels of strategy-making mean that union strategies vary considerably from one union to the next. The role of the labour centres is quite limited in the development of these strategic orientations, most often confined to political representation. We briefly explore four areas of union action: union membership and recruitment; structural reform, membership participation and servicing; bargaining and workplace change; and political action.

Union Membership and Recruitment

There are essentially two generations of innovation in union organizing. The first, during the 1980s, marked an initial response to drastic membership decline during the recession of the early 1980s and the first wave of public sector cutbacks. From the early 1980s onwards, several of the largest Canadian unions began to make substantial new investments in organizing. This prompted new thinking about organizing, efforts to dedicate a certain proportion of resources to recruitment, a number of local structural adjustments to accommodate new membership groups and so on. A second generation of innovation, in the 1990s, has seen a generalization of the effort to organize to a much larger proportion of unions, particularly in the private sector. There are also considerable new resources expended on organizing and a number of unions have increased dues on this basis. This second generation of strategic renewal in organizing is further reinforced by the new emphasis of several of the international unions operating in Canada on organizing. Greater resources are available and, indeed, as was previously mentioned, organizing in Canada is often seen by international union leaderships to be more effective because of the more accommodating legal framework than that in the United States.

In these organizing efforts, we can distinguish three generic strategies:

consolidation, selective diversification and unfettered diversification.

Consolidation represents the classic jurisdictional union strategy for a particular industry. There are numerous examples of this type of strategy in recent years. In the retail food industry, the only way to 'take wages out of competition' is to ensure that all major competitors are unionized and the main union in this industry (the United Food and Commercial Workers Union) has usually spent a significant proportion of its resources on organizing. The restructuring of the retail food industry through the 1980s and 1990s, with the dismemberment of certain corporate entities into distinct franchises and the entry of new non-union superstores, has meant that this strategy has become even more important. Similarly, when the Canadian Autoworkers Union was created in 1985, after its separation from the United Auto Workers, it put substantial new resources into the organization of non-unionized auto parts plants and Asian assembly transplants. It should be emphasized that in the face of considerable employer opposition these jurisdictional strategies have often met with mixed results. Unions have continued, however, to maintain the pressure on wages and working conditions by a continuing organizing effort.

Selective diversification typically involves following membership into related sectors. As public sector unions have had to contend with the privatization of certain services and recourse to sub-contractors in other cases, they began to put more effort into the reorganization of their own former members as well as the organization of other workers in these new sectors. Not all public sector unions have pursued these initiatives but a number have done so very successfully and, in the process, have changed in nature. In the early 1980s, most of the members of what was then the British Columbia Government Employees Union were covered by a single master agreement in the public sector. The union today, now known as the British Columbia Government and General Workers Union, is larger in size, covers a multitude of collective agreements and has less than half of its membership in the public sector. A number of private sector unions have also attempted to stem membership decline through selective diversification into related sectors. Not all unions have pursued diversification with such vigour. Indeed, it can be a divisive internal issue as existing membership asks instead for increased delivery of services in what is often a difficult context, resulting in membership backlash.

There has also been a marked trend towards *unfettered diversification* as unions seek new membership in any sector where they are able to organize. The Steelworkers in Canada began to identify their union as a general union from the late 1980s. In particular, the union in Québec organized security guards, taxi drivers, hotel and restaurant employees, to name but a few.

Similarly, although the Autoworkers Union did not initially engage in unfettered diversification, successive mergers with a variety of organizations in different sectors have meant that it now organizes workers in almost all areas of the private sector and, increasingly, even in the public sector.

Structural Reform, Membership Participation and Servicing

A significant dimension of union strategies has been the attempt to adapt internal structures and practices to the exigencies of the new environment. There are a number of common internal adjustments in order to reflect the changes in membership composition, the movements in corporate structure, the rise of new identities at work and the real problems of organizing new groups of workers into unions.

Structural reform

There is an increasing trend towards amalgamations and mergers. The actual benefits of such mergers have often yet to be realized but external union structure increasingly gravitates towards a smaller number of large unions. Unions have also sought to adopt their internal structures to accommodate new groups of workers. The shift in employment to the service sector, notably in small firms, has meant that traditional forms of local union organization were unlikely to be viable. Instead, they have increasingly promoted the composite local union, which is both more sensitive to the challenges of organizing workers in the service sector and better able to accommodate the worker mobility that so characterizes this sector. At other levels, there is the question of how to achieve effective coordinating mechanisms in an effort to organize the new groups into viable structures and make links between core and peripheral workers. There has also been considerable movement by different groups of public sector 'professionals' attempting to enhance the representation of their specific identities.

The challenge of fostering participation and giving a sense of ownership in their organizations is, of course, a major preoccupation behind attempts to achieve structural adjustments at different levels of union organizations. This is especially so for the newer groups of workers in the labour market, such as women and immigrants, who have traditionally been excluded from such a sense of belonging.

New identities and membership participation

As women have participated in the labour force in growing numbers, a major focus has been the opportunities for women to participate in the life of their unions. The unionization of the public sector brought large numbers of women members into the ranks of unions and the growth of private service sector employment suggests even greater potential for union membership growth among women. However, for many women members, unions have not necessarily reflected their concerns, nor have they accommodated their needs in terms of the opportunities to participate. Thus, through the 1970s and 1980s, there has been a continuing debate as women have sought to introduce issues such as sexual harassment, child care, maternity leave, affirmative action and pay equity on to union agendas; to ensure that women were adequately represented in elected positions and the different structures of their unions; and to address the barriers to active participation in the life of the union (see Briskin and McDermott, 1993, p. 5). Indeed, women's groups and the feminist movement more generally have been a major source of renewal in many unions and some union leaderships are now beginning to reflect their formative experience in union women's committees or in coalition activity with other feminist groups. The relative success of women in this endeavour has served as an example to other groups, such as visible minorities, to claim equivalent recognition within the political channels of their unions.

Thus, many Canadian unions have adopted a variety of affirmative action measures to ensure greater participation of different membership groups. Special internal structures based on specific identities, such as gender, ethnicity or sexual orientation, have also provided a focus for new types of activism. Most unions have sought to express these new work-mediated identities through new committees and electoral practices for designated groups, in their services and bargaining policies through the expression of a wider range of concerns on issues such as employment equity, and in their political action through coalition activity with a wider range of community groups. Indeed, it can be argued that the relative success of Canadian unionism over the past decade might be attributed at least in part to the relative success in giving expression to such concerns within its internal structures and bargaining policies. The strategy has been one of enhancing their sense of ownership about the future role of unions.

Many unions have not, however, fully come to terms with this much greater diversity within their membership and its implications for internal democracy. Union leaderships are thus increasingly confronted with the cultural implications of the changing composition of their union's membership, not least in order to avoid potential backlash from traditional sectors of the union where there may be some nostalgia for an older industrial structure. Certainly one of the more daunting challenges is ensuring membership participation. Indeed, in a recent survey of the organizational priorities of national and international union federations in Canada, promoting membership participation was identified as the second highest priority, after the protection of wages and working conditions of their members (see Kumar, Murray and Schetagne, 1998a). There has also been substantial new investment in union educational services with a number of unions founding their own residential education centres.

Servicing

Canadian unions face increasing demands from their members to provide a wide range of sophisticated services. Basic services start, of course, with the negotiation and application of a collective agreement in a particular workplace. While such a service might be provided by a lay official such as a local union president or a shop steward or by a full-time official working either for the national or the local union, larger certification units generally require increasingly complex back-up services, such as research and legal services. The wider the range of issues dealt with in the collective agreement, the more complex are the range of services required. In recent years, most unions have employed health and safety, pension and pay equity specialists. There is also an increasing demand for information and advice on company finances, work reorganization, new technologies, quality initiatives and environmental regulation. Many unions also seek to provide some supplementary services. Unions began, of course, as mutual insurance societies to provide benefits to craft workers in times of hardship. Strike pay and supplementary health and insurance schemes are examples of such benefits. Some unions have expanded into other types of individual services such as legal, financial and employment advice to members. Other unions have sought to develop collective instruments, such as investment funds, in order to safeguard and promote employment in particular workplaces.

There is a decreased capacity, however, to pay for these services. In particular, structural changes in the labour market have resulted in reduced real dues income per member as overall income has remained stable with new members often either working part time or earning less in the general service occupations. This has increased the pressure on union services and led to a certain rethinking of the role of full-time staff in some unions, particularly as regards the relative division of labour between staff and activists, and the role of education and self-empowerment in the provision of services by activists. This has potentially important cultural ramifications for the way that members think about their organizations, though it is altogether less clear that widespread changes have actually taken place.

GREGOR MURRAY

Bargaining and Workplace Change

One of the most fundamental problems for Canadian unions has been the development of appropriate strategies to deal with industrial restructuring and workplace change. There are two major areas of concern: maintaining and improving conditions of work and ensuring a union and/or worker role in the process of workplace change.

There are clearly considerable pressures on employment security, wages and working conditions in a large number of unionized establishments in Canada. By the very nature of the representation regime, worker protection involves the negotiation of detailed enterprise or establishment agreements. In the past, the prevailing pattern has been characterized by highly detailed legal agreements, which ensured a degree of contractual protection to unionized workers through job control and procedural protections. Given the high degree of decentralization, some form of pattern bargaining – the integrity of which was ensured by internal union-coordinating mechanisms – permitted unions to pursue common targets and to generalize them across a range of employers. In the context of enhanced employer-bargaining power and reduced union-bargaining power, this trend has been reversed with employers engaged in coercive comparisons in order to secure greater organizational flexibility and increased competitiveness. Canadian unions, by and large, resisted the trend towards wage and benefit concessions in the early and mid-1980s and demonstrated considerable militancy in doing so. Helped by a favourable exchange rate, they were more likely to engage in greater organizational flexibility in a context where there was less pressure on employment than in the United States. The introduction of free trade with the United States in the late 1980s made unions in a number of vulnerable sectors more amenable to concessions in an effort to protect jobs. The experience of such concessions, however, has typically been that such savings do not ultimately alter corporate location strategies. Despite some successes in introducing increased contractual controls over practices such as outsourcing (notably in the automobile industry), the inability of unions to protect jobs through collective bargaining has prompted exploration of new avenues of strategic engagement.

A number of Canadian unions, starting in 1984 in Québec, have introduced worker investment funds. Afforded a highly favourable fiscal treatment by the state, these mutual investment funds are designed to channel worker savings for their retirement into investments that protect and promote employment. Unions have also been involved in a wide range of initiatives, which seek to promote industrial adjustment through training.

Sponsored notably by the federal government and the Québec Government (many similar initiatives in Ontario have been abolished by a Conservative Government), sectoral training committees are bipartite or tripartite initiatives designed to involve employers and unions in particular sectors in long-term discussions about the evolution of skills in relation to the competitive profile of these sectors and the design of programs to enhance employee skills (see Gunderson and Sharpe, 1998; Charest, 1999). Such strategic initiatives have been more in evidence in the private sector. Indeed, in the 1990s, as restructuring continues apace in the public sector, there is a much greater sentiment of fatalism about the lack of union power to resist these changes.

The current wave of work reorganization and the increased participation of workers in the management of their work alter many of the forms of regulation that typified the workplace compromises of the post-war period. Reworking the relationship between employers and union members has raised a number of strategic issues for unions. There has been a continual tension between acceptance of these new forms of worker participation and a more critical posture. Indeed, this issue has been the cause of significant tensions between a number of unions (see Kumar, 1995). The status quo is generally not an option since workers themselves are not necessarily enamoured with their traditional role in the workplace. Yet many of these new participative initiatives do not fulfil their initial promise. Most unions have therefore sought to make the argument for greater workplace modernization and increased employee involvement as part of a larger thrust for democratization at work (see Kumar *et al.*, 1998b; Wells, 1996). Such an approach has, however, often been at odds with an employer agenda focused more narrowly on downsizing. There have, therefore, been a large number of experiments with work organization. An increasing problem has appeared, however, in that employee efforts to modernize work practices do not appear to carry much weight in the light of larger trends towards corporate restructuring.

Political Action

Political action is undoubtedly one of the most divisive issues in the Canadian labour movement in which the differentiation between business unionism, social unionism and social movement unionism increasingly comes to the fore. The primary conflict would appear to be between a social union orientation that favours traditional links with unions' political ally, the NDP, and a social movement orientation that has been sharply critical of the performance of NDP governments when in office. Also criticized by this last group has been the increasing penchant of many members of the parliamentary caucus to espouse 'modernist' views along the lines of the 'third way' repositioning of the British Labour Party under Tony Blair. It should also be noted that the poor showing of the NDP in successive federal elections has led some business union leaders to query whether a strong identification with the NDP is really an asset for the representation of their members' interests.

The recent experience of the NDP Government in Ontario in the mid-1990s, in particular the implementation of its so-called Social Contract legislation, provides a good illustration of some of the tensions over political strategy. The scars caused by this particular episode, in which the government suspended free collective bargaining and enacted wage-restraint legislation in the Ontario public sector, caused many public sector unions and some private sector unions to refuse to support this particular government. This episode has left a legacy of bitter divisions between unions in Ontario; divisions that have spilled over into the larger labour movement in Canada. In one camp is a coalition of public sector and left-leaning unions, which blame the NDP for not pursuing with sufficient vigour appropriate labour policies. In the other camp are a group of unions loyal to the NDP, which tend to blame the public sector and left-leaning unions for sabotaging the fortunes of the NDP's first experience of power in Canada's largest province. This particular division has spilled over into current divisions in strategy between Ontario unions, which now face a hostile, neo-liberal government that has reversed most of the policies that the previous social-democratic government had implemented over the preceding four years. Although the Ontario Federation of Labour has organized a series of one-day strikes in various communities throughout the province in protest at the neo-liberal agenda of a new conservative government, a rift between competing orientations became increasingly apparent. On the one side are a number of international unions, particularly loyal to the NDP, that perceive diminishing marginal returns in extra-parliamentary protest and a need to reinforce traditional forms of support for the parliamentary wing of the NDP. On the other side is a coalition of public sector unions and the Canadian Auto Workers that makes the argument that the NDP, when in government, had actually initiated many of the policies against which it was now protesting. This coalition maintains that the future of unionism lies in public protest and the forging of strategic alliances with different community groups on the role of public services in fighting inequality.

Nor are such strains unique to the unions' relationship with the NDP. Similar tensions were observed between Québec labour unions and the Parti Québécois (PQ) government of the 1970s and the early 1980s and again in the 1990s. They are currently very much in evidence as the PQ government pursues a variety of policy initiatives that are opposed by the Québec union movement. At the same time, however, this government has a much greater proclivity to consult with labour and has organized a number of multipartite summits to engage actors in the civil society on overall economic policy orientations.

Overall, there exists significant consensus between social unionism and social movement unionism adherents on a number of key issues such as the provision of public services and the importance of a high profile for the labour movement on social justice issues like pay equity, sexual harassment and the rights of visible minorities. However, the competition between the two union orientations continues to be a source of bitter dispute between different union leaderships.

The State of Canadian Unions

How, then, might we assess the relative success of these strategic endeavours outlined above? In fact, it is possible to tell two quite different tales. Arguably, few labour movements have engaged in such a sustained period of strategic renewal. Yet, the basic dilemma for Canadian unions – their strategic conundrum – is that despite this substantial organizational innovation and strategic engagement at a number of levels, the basic pressures on unions are acute and are likely to remain so.

Union Membership and Recruitment

Larger labour market trends continue to exert tremendous pressures on levels of union membership. Despite substantial investment in new forms of organization, unions appear to have to run faster and faster to stand still. Organizing efforts in Canada were initially facilitated by successive legislative changes in provincial jurisdictions, notably the widespread introduction of first contract arbitration, which meant that unions could effectively cross the hurdle of initial employer opposition after the organizing campaign. However, the election of more conservative and/or populist governments in at least two jurisdictions in the 1990s – Alberta and Ontario – has resulted in a certain narrowing of the legislative framework. In Ontario, in particular, there is now a much greater likelihood of a certification election which, as seen in American experience, provides considerable scope for the expression of employer opposition and the development of employee uncertainty. They must contend with the basic limits of a highly decentralized regime of collective representation where access to such rights is severely limited in the absence of some form of sectoral representation (see Murray and Verge, 1999).

Efforts to innovate in recruitment encounter two types of obstacles. In terms of the external environment, there are judicial obstacles, employer opposition and employee uncertainty. In terms of the internal political processes of unions, union leaderships must arbitrate between the exigencies of organizational renewal through new membership drives and the claims of existing members to maintain and enhance services. This is a complex process, subject to internal political vagaries. A significant organizing victory can consolidate political resolve to invest yet greater resources in organizing, just as a defeat can undermine this resolve. In this respect, there is considerably more effort expended on organizing but it would be an exaggeration to suggest that the majority of unions have a deeply ensconced and unwavering organizing culture.

Bargaining and Workplace Change

A recent Human Resources Development Survey on union federation bargaining priorities permits us to make an overall assessment of union achievements through the 1990s (see Kumar, Murray and Schetagne, 1998b). First, it appears quite clear that the unions surveyed are able to achieve a relatively high degree of success on traditional distributive issues when they figure among a union's most important bargaining objectives. Second, there is much less success on work control issues. Indeed, these might be divided into two groupings since there appears to be a higher degree of success on the procedural aspects, such as protocols and protections around the control of work, and a very low rate of success on issues that limit organizational flexibility such as subcontracting, restricting overtime and minimum employment guarantees. Third, union attempts to enhance their members' participation in the change process, particularly through the union, meet a very low degree of success, be it in terms of an enhanced union role in workplace decision-making, access to financial information or increased worker control and responsibility. This result is of particular significance because it suggests that it is probably more difficult to achieve an enhanced union and worker role in the workplace change than much of the discourse would suggest.

Union Objectives and Ideology

Unions in Canada now face a vastly different environment than they did two decades ago: increased competition, economic restructuring, challenges to traditional forms of job control, pressures on membership, modifications in state policy, to name but a few. How have these recent transformations in the political economy affected union objectives and ideology? We briefly discuss each of three configurations identified earlier in the chapter.

Business unionism as an ideological construct is greatly affected by current transformations. In essence, there would appear to be even less political and economic space for this construct. First, economic restructuring and pressures on membership make it much more difficult to maintain a narrow definition of collectivity. In particular, organizational pressures to survive mean that such unions are likely to seek new sources of membership, to broaden their definition of collectivity, either through mergers or new recruitment. As a construct, business unionism is arguably ill-suited to new recruitment because it involves going beyond the traditional definition of collectivity to embrace new groups whose interests might not necessarily be defended by its predominant focus on the economic interests of workers.

Second, the combination of changes in state social policy associated with neo-liberalism and an apparently declining economic bargaining power on the part of unions tends to translate into an increased emphasis on the citizenship aspects of union representation. This trend is far from unequivocal but business unions are, again, drawn on to a terrain on which they are less well equipped.

Third, the tremendous pressures to restructure workplaces and industries in many ways reinforces that intuitive understanding, so characteristic of business unionism, that firms need to be competitive. The exigencies of economic restructuring also mean, however, that unions are engaged in a search to alleviate the worst aspects of market restructuring. In Canada, this has tended to take the form of investment vehicles for worker pension funds in order to assist the economic survival of firms in trouble. While this is highly consistent with a social vision that accepts the parameters of capitalist markets, it takes business unionism on to new and often very tricky ideological terrain. It is difficult for unions to be purely instrumental in these circumstances as unions become deeply enmeshed in the complexities of ensuring the survival for firms and the jobs in which they have invested.

Fourth, economic restructuring tends to demonstrate that an exclusive focus on the workplace is insufficient. There is an increasing embrace with different kinds of sectoral mechanisms concerned with skill development, workplace change, and so on. This focus is certainly not incompatible with business unionism but it does entail a significant shift in focus.

Fifth, changes in the labour and social policy agenda mean that there are greater pressures to engage in various kinds of political action. Indeed, these pressures are so great that it can be argued that certain business unions, such as the Teamsters in Canada, have evolved towards a form of social unionism as they began to emulate many of the political practices of the old industrial unions in the private sector.

Finally, the emphasis on workplace restructuring and competitiveness means that there is a much greater premium attached to workplace cooperation. In particular, the search for greater organizational flexibility means that traditions of tight union job control are directly challenged. This poses a basic dilemma about the blend of conflict and cooperation. A broad philosophy of 'jointness' is increasingly in evidence but, once again, this is a new and often complex terrain for business unionism, not least because it can bring it into conflict with its own members about the extent of possible cooperation.

There would appear to be more space for social unionism as a philosophy in the new environment but it also faces considerable challenges to its prevailing configuration. As with business unionism, the threat or reality of declining membership means that unions are likely to extend their job territories and notions of collectivity. Social unions are, in fact, well equipped to do so. As was outlined in the discussion on union structure above, what is most characteristic of industrial unions in Canada is their gradual evolution into general unions (see also Murray, 1998). There is also a greater likelihood of defending the worker as citizen in this new environment. The key dilemma concerns how such unions are to do so. In the context of diminishing bargaining power and an ability to influence state policy in the context of globalization, the question of the extent to which the union should seek to transform or to regulate the market is at the core of strategic thinking. Some unions seek to develop new forms of institutional regulation, be they worker investment funds such as the Solidarity Fund initiated by unions in Québec or new parity mechanisms that promote dialogue between business and labour such as the Canadian Centre for Labour Market Productivity and Cooperation. Other unions, such as the automobile workers, are more drawn by the need to engage in the transformation of the market, which pushes then in the direction of social movement unionism. The new context certainly reinforces the basic position of social unionism to engage in representational activities at both the level of the workplace and the society in general. It too has become engaged in a variety of sectoral mechanisms that seek to address the limits of actions based exclusively at micro- and macro-levels, typically in the area of training but sometimes in the area of industrial adjustment and workplace change.

Environmental change similarly reinforces the need for both economic and political action. In particular, public sector cutbacks have greatly reduced the ambivalence of social unions in the public sector about engaging in political action. One important dilemma here concerns the limits of traditional social democratic politics. This is a question which divides social unions in Canada, particularly between public and private sectors, as many of the older private sector social unions tend to emphasize the importance of traditional links with the NDP, while a number of the public sector unions are embittered by their experience of cutbacks at the behest of NDP governments in power at the provincial level. This has sparked a sharp, ideological cleavage in Ontario between a group of unions predominantly in the private sector and a coalition of public sector unions and the automobile workers.

Finally, we can observe considerable differences between unions as regards their orientations towards conflict and cooperation. A significant number of social unions, usually concentrated in the private sector, have sought to promote a cooperative workplace change policy. Given the importance of the diffusion of new models of work organization, they have largely bought into the discourse of 'jointness' at workplace level. These unions have tended to innovate in terms of new approaches to bargaining as well as in the promotion of a positive union agenda on workplace change. This does not mean that they did not also continue to pursue their traditional social objectives in other forums of union activity. Other social unions have demonstrated greater scepticism about the cooperative potential of workplace change. They have tended to focus on the negative trends in the workplace and, often through industrial action, have sought to develop a new generation of contractual controls to limit the worst effects of workplace change. This is notably the approach adopted by the Autoworkers union.

The new environment, in many respects, invigorates social movement unionism. Its orientation towards a broader definition of collectivity, its emphasis on the worker as citizen as well as wage earner, its dedication to the transformation rather than the regulation of the market, its focus on both the workplace and society, the importance of political action and its emphasis on the transformative character of conflict are all reinforced. Perhaps the greatest change for this unionism is the greater political space afforded to it by the emergence of coalition politics. Political action has been largely transformed by the development of larger coalitions of community or civil society groups around issues such as free trade and the quality of public services. In this context, the philosophy of social movement unionism is much less isolated and indeed more likely to work with many of the traditional social unions.

To summarize, all three ideological constructs remain in place. Overall, there is probably some movement towards social unions and social movement unionism but the greatest changes are occurring within each of these ideological configurations. In particular, economic and political contingencies are prompting a certain repositioning along the axes that define each of these configurations.

Conclusion: Future Prospects

Canadian unions face a real strategic conundrum. If judged by international standards, they have engaged in substantial strategic innovation, which is arguably a factor in their relatively good standing as a national union movement. Yet, they face most of the same intractable problems that characterize the current international environment for other national union movements. This conundrum runs through most of their major areas of activity.

First, as regards membership trends and recruitment of new members, Canadian unions have generally maintained membership levels, not least through continuous organizing initiatives, yet overall union density has decreased slightly. Indeed, there are significant downward pressures on the current level of union density that are unlikely to be reversed without a substantial increase in the resources dedicated to organizing, coupled with important changes in the public policy framework for union representation. There can be little doubt that organizing is likely to be a major priority for unions in Canada over the coming decade.

Second, despite many bargaining innovations and considerable militancy, unions in Canada were not able to prevent a deterioration of wages and working conditions in a number of industries through the 1990s. Nor does it appear that they have made major gains in the consolidation of a worker and union role in workplace change. Although they have also pioneered sectoral initiatives to promote training and industrial restructuring, many of these initiatives appear vulnerable to the withdrawal of state support. When this latter has occurred, notably in the context of political hostility to the labour movement, such bipartite institutional initiatives have not frequently survived. These trends are likely to translate into an increasingly volatile patchwork of local cooperation and militancy as more favourable labour market conditions reinforce traditional economic demands, while the pressures associated with globalization reinforce the need to underwrite new local compromises on job security through greater flexibility and concession bargaining. This will likely lead to even greater dissension both between and within the different union types and orientations outlined earlier in the chapter.

Third, Canadian unions have been very active in their opposition to neo-liberal policy reforms. Moreover, they have developed a wide variety of initiatives involving coalitions with other groups in the civil society on issues such as trade, healthcare and pay equity. This agenda increasingly reflects the transformations in the internal composition of the labour movement. Yet, Canadian unions have, by and large, been unable to prevent the implementation of these same neo-liberal political reforms. This has led to an increasingly virulent internal political debate between the social and social movement union traditions, in particular as regards the relevance of so-called 'third way' politics for the social democratic party.

Fourth, despite the many pressures operating on internal union solidarity, there is considerable empirical evidence that unions in Canada have not lost the support of their members. On the contrary, membership confidence in the institution, despite unions' relative loss of power, may have actually increased. Indeed, the context is one in which workers increasingly look to their collective institution to promote and protect their lives at work. However, Canadian unions are also subject to the many cross-cutting contingencies that fragment internal solidarity and draw their members in different political directions. The virtual strategic dilemma then is how to develop internal coalitions likely to engender new collective values and projects.

A pessimistic view running through this strategic conundrum, and certainly one that is present in the labour movement itself, would suggest that Canadian unions might have hitherto been sheltered from some of the most acute pressures of the neo-liberal era. Consequently, they are likely to experience a decline in influence over the coming years. A more optimistic view, and one that the extent of past innovation certainly supports, points to the many avenues of renewal currently evident in the Canadian union movement. Unions in Canada thus appear condemned to this Sisyphean task of further continuous strategic renewal. While the exact path to enhanced gains and influence is not entirely apparent, the very process of working towards such renewal, particularly through membership participation and the emergence of new union projects, may well lead to a qualitative breakthrough. It is from this process of strategic engagement, membership participation and continuous renewal that new union forms and practices, adopted to the exigencies of the new political economy, may well emerge.

Notes

1. This chapter draws on the author's work funded by the Social Sciences and Humanities Research Council of Canada, as well as his contribution to an International Institute for Labour Studies ILO project on trade union responses to globalization. Thanks are due to the many trade unionists and colleagues who have contributed to the information compiled in this chapter and to Gerry Griffin for comments on an earlier version.

2. For more detailed overviews of the collective regime for union representation, see Murray and Verge (1999).

3. A typical recent case is that of a Walmart store in Windsor, Ontario, where the Ontario Labour Relations Board determined that the employer had interfered in its employees' attempt to secure representation rights. The particular significance of this case is that representation rights were imposed on an employer, which hitherto had avoided unionization in any of its huge chain of retail outlets across North America. In keeping with the absence of unions elsewhere in this retail chain, the employees in this particular store have since 'decertified' their union, which no longer is recognized as the majority agent.

4. For example, the HRDC data in Table 4.1 provides an overall estimate of union density in Canada of 32.3 per cent at the beginning of 1999 while the Statistics Canada data in Tables 4.2 and 4.3 estimates that union density was 30.1 per cent during the first six months of 1999.

5. It should be noted that a slight improvement in reporting requirements in the HRDC survey in 1998 probably yields a more accurate reading of overall union membership but tends to overstate the change in union membership between 1997 and 1998.

6. This section draws on Murray (2000).

7. In 1998, only 3.7 per cent of union members in Canada belonged to independent local unions; that is, those with no form of affiliation whatsoever (see Table 4.4).

8. Thanks to Ian Robinson for various discussions, which helped me to clarify these issues.

References

Akyeampong, E. (1999) 'Unionization – an update', *Perspectives on Labour and Income*, **11** (3), 45–65.

Briskin, L. and McDermott, P. (ed.) (1993) *Women Challenging Unions*, Toronto: University of Toronto Press.

Charest, J. (1999) 'Articulation institutionnelle et orientations du système de formation professionnelle', *Relations Industrielles/Industrial Relations*, **54** (3), 439–71.

DeBrizzi, J. (1983) *Ideology and the Rise of Labor Theory in America*, Westport: Greenwood Press.

Giles, A. and Murray, G. (1988) 'Towards an historical understanding of Canadian industrial relations theory', *Relations industrielles/Industrial Relations*, **43** (4), 780–811.

Gunderson, M. and Sharpe, A. (eds) (1998) *Forging Business–Labour Partnerships*, Toronto: University of Toronto Press.

HRDC (Workplace Information Directorate), (various years; annual until 1999, then website from 1999) *Directory of Labour Organizations in Canada*, Ottawa: Canadian Government Publishing, http://labour-travail.hrdc-drhc.gc.ca.

HRDC (1999) 'Union membership in Canada 1999', *Workplace Gazette*, **2** (3), 62–3.

ILO (International Labour Organization) (1997) *World Labour Report: Industrial Relations Democracy and Stability*, Geneva, Switzerland: International Labour Office.

Kumar, P. (1995) *Unions and Workplace Change in Canada*, Kingston, Ontario: IRC Press, Queen's University.

Kumar, P., Murray, G. and Schetagne, S. (1998a) 'Adapting to change: union priorities in the 1990s', *Workplace Gazette*, **1** (3), 84–98.

Kumar, P., Murray, G. and Schetagne, S. (1998b) 'Workplace change in Canada: union perceptions of impacts, responses and support systems', *Workplace Gazette*, **1** (4), 75–87.

Murray, G. (1998) 'Steeling for change: organization and organizing in two USWA districts in Canada', in K. Bronfenbrenner, S. Friedman, R. Hurd, R. Oswald and R. Seeber (eds) *Organizing to Win: New Research on Union Strategies*, Ithaca: ILR Press, pp. 320–38.

Murray, G. (2000) 'Unions: membership, structures, actions, and challenges', in M. Gunderson, A. Ponak and D. Tarras (eds) *Union–Management Relations in Canada*, (4th edn), Toronto: Pearson, pp. 79–116.

Murray, G. and Verge, P. (1999) *La représentation syndicale*, Québec: Les Presses de l'Université Laval.

Panitch, L. and Swartz, D. (1993) *The Assault on Trade Union Freedoms*, Toronto: Garamond Press.

Pupo, N. and White, J. (1994) 'Union leaders and the economic crisis: responses to restructuring', *Relations industrielles/Industrial Relations*, **49** (4), 821–45.

Robinson, I. (1994) 'NAFTA, social unionism, and labour movement power in Canada and the United States', *Relations industrielles/Industrial Relations*, **49** (4), 657–95.

Thompson, M. and Blum, A. (1983) 'International unionism in Canada: the move to local control', *Industrial Relations*, **22**, 71–86.

Wells, D. (1996) 'New dimensions for labor in a post-Fordist world', in W. Green and E. Yanarella (eds) *North American Auto Unions in Crisis*, Albany: State University of New York Press, pp. 191–208.

White, J. (1993) *Sisters and Solidarity: Women and Unions in Canada*, Toronto: Thompson Educational Publishing, Inc.

Yates, C. (1993) *From Plant to Politics: The Autoworkers Union in Postwar Canada*, Philadelphia: Temple University Press.

Yates, C. (1998) 'Unity and diversity: challenges to an expanding Canadian autoworkers union', *Canadian Review of Sociology and Anthropology*, **35** (1), 93–118.

5 IRISH UNIONS: TESTING THE LIMITS OF SOCIAL PARTNERSHIP

William K. Roche and Jacqueline Ashmore

Introduction and Context

Entering the new millennium, Irish unions occupy a pivotal role in Irish economic and political governance, having engaged in thirteen years of centralized tripartite bargaining with employers and the state. The Irish economy is the envy of the European Union, registering annual levels of economic growth and job creation which outstrip the major European economies. Progressive though modest wage rises have been negotiated during the 1990s, combined with a gradual easing of the tax burden on employees. Foreign direct investment is flowing briskly into Ireland, creating sizeable numbers of new jobs in high technology electronics and pharmaceutical companies and in a range of service industries. Under the current tripartite national agreement, unions are seeking to extend macro-level social partnership to enterprises and workplaces, through instituting voluntary mutual gains arrangements in dialogue with employers. The 'Irish model' of economic management and governance is attracting growing international attention. These developments in many ways reflect the high-water mark of trade union influence in Irish society. Unions had engaged in national-level and tripartite bargaining at various times in the past. The 1970s and early 1980s, in particular, had witnessed nine successive national pay agreements. What is different about tripartism since 1987 is a general conviction that the model had worked well, supporting first recovery from the acute economic crisis of the late 1980s and subsequently a rapid acceleration of economic growth and transition to European economic and monetary union.

At another level, Irish unions have faced major problems. Density has declined progressively since the early 1980s. Union engagement in neo-corporatist arrangements has done little to halt or slow the trend. Employer strategies of 'union substitution' and 'suppression' have become more pronounced in the 1990s, and large dynamic industrial sectors have little union presence. Union attempts to resolve problems with recognition and bargaining rights in tripartite forums have severely tested the partnership process. The progress of workplace partnership is modest. This chapter will explore these themes in some detail and end with a commentary on the possible future scenarios facing unions in Ireland.

Unions, the State and Political Parties

As in the UK, the first stable unions in Ireland organized skilled craftsmen. In the second half of the nineteenth century, Irish craftsmen were organized mainly by local branches of UK-based craft unions. Unskilled workers, particularly located in the main trading towns of the 'maritime' economy on the East and South coasts, were organized, often fleetingly, by nascent British general unions from the late 1880s and early 1890s. The first two decades of the twentieth century witnessed dramatic growth in union membership among unskilled workers. The unionization of the unskilled was spearheaded by James Larkin's Irish Transport (and General) Workers' Union. The rapid expansion of the militant union sparked a series of bitter and protracted lockouts, culminating in the Great Dublin Lock-out of 1913–14. The virtual collapse of the Irish Transport (and General) Workers' Union in the wake of the Dublin lockout halted union expansion for a time. The imperatives of food production during the First World War and consequent rising demand for farm labourers led to a sharp recovery of union membership in the increasingly syndicalist Transport Union. A wave of rank-and-file militancy and radicalism was further spurred by the political dislocation attending the Anglo-Irish War (1916–21) and resulted in a spate of seizures of large farms and factories, often operated as short-lived 'Soviets'. The economic slump following the end of the Great War and the restoration of political order in the newly independent Irish Free State resulted in a sharp decline of union membership and the disappearance of radical militancy (cf. O'Connor, 1992; Roche, 1992b).

The Law, Unions and Collective Representation

In legal terms the Irish system of industrial relations remains a 'voluntary system'. Legislation has progressively extended individual employment rights but, in comparison, collective bargaining and collective representation have remained largely outside the sphere of legal regulation. In the 1990s, a number of changes have nonetheless occurred and others have been mooted.

Spurred by European Union (EU) regulatory initiatives, legislation began to play a more central role from the 1970s in enshrining individual employment rights in areas like equal pay and opportunities and unfair dismissals. This trend continued in the 1990s with EU-initiated proposals for the regulation of maximum working hours. Irish legislation has also historically regulated working-time arrangements in general. Pay and conditions in low-paid, labour-intensive industries have also been regulated through joint labour committees that establish minimum rates of pay. Irish unions have also supported the institution of a minimum wage in Ireland and pressed for the establishment of a National Minimum Wage Commission to examine the issue. The Commission reported in 1998 and recommended the introduction of a statutory minimum wage in the year 2000.

The UK 1906 Trade Disputes Act was enshrined in Irish law at the foundation of the independent Irish State in 1922. This famously provides immunity from civil and criminal actions for persons lawfully acting in contemplation or furtherance of a trade dispute, and protects the funds of trade unions from lawsuits arising from industrial disputes. The law was altered with the passage of the 1990 Industrial Relations Act. The Act removed immunity from inter-union disputes (disputes between employees) and from secondary industrial action, unless undertaken against employers whose actions seek to undermine employees engaged in an industrial dispute. The Act also introduced mandatory secret balloting in advance of industrial action. Collective agreements remain legally non-binding unless the parties register agreements with the Labour Court – a little-used facility available since 1946. The third-party facilities for dispute resolution available to employers and unions, the Labour Relations Commission (LRC) (conciliation service) and the Labour Court (dispute adjudication service) remain voluntary and issue non-binding proposals or recommendations, unless the parties have agreed under company disputes procedures to be bound by Labour Court recommendations. This is not a common practice. In the public sector, the position is similar. Commercial public enterprises (owned by the state but governed by state-appointed independent Boards) generally resort to the LRC and the Labour Court, with the exception of the state electricity utility, ESB, which operates an internal tribunal for resolving disputes. In the public services, health, education and the local authorities, disputes are referred either to a public service conciliation and arbitration system or to the LRC and Labour Court.

Under the 1937 constitution of the Irish Republic, citizens enjoy the right to be trade union members. The courts have established a parallel right of persons not to join a trade union and this has rendered unlawful industrial action undertaken to enforce closed-shop arrangements. The constitutional right to union membership does not impose an obligation on employers to recognize a trade union or to negotiate with trade unions representing employees. In this critical respect, trade union recognition comes within the voluntary process of industrial relations between employers and trade unions. In practice, the Labour Court has generally recommended in favour of unions in recognition disputes and does not appear to have applied any fixed rule with respect to making a recommendation for recognition conditional on some proportion of the workforce in the bargaining unit already having unionized. In the public services, health, education and local government recognition is granted to unions under ministerial authority. In commercial public companies, recognition is based on the voluntary principles that hold in the private sector, and the tradition has been for management to grant recognition while seeking to promote more 'rational' representative structures by fostering inter-union cooperation with respect to membership domains and industrial relations activity more generally.

No changes in the legal position regarding union recognition have occurred to date during the 1990s. As will be discussed later in the chapter, a major High Court judgment in 1994 found against Ireland's largest union, Services, Industrial, Professional and Technical Union, in a case concerning the union's resort to industrial action to win recognition and to defend existing members. The judgment was overturned on appeal to the Supreme Court in 1998. The recognition issue had become a key strategic concern for trade unions in response to falling density and a rise in the incidence and intensity of employer resistance to unionization during the 1990s. A High Level Group, with representation from trade unions, employers and the state, was set up to consider how the recognition issue might be handled. The question of recognition became part of the contested terrain of social partnership in Irish industrial relations. The proposals of the High Level Group will be examined later in the chapter.

Since 1977, Irish legislation had provided for the election of worker directors to the boards of commercial public enterprises. The range of companies covered by the worker director arrangements was progressively widened over the next decade. One-third of the seats on company boards are reserved for worker directors elected by all full-time employees but nominated by recognized trade unions. A further statute enacted in 1988 provided for sub-board structures in companies with worker directors. No similar legislative provisions exist for the private sector, where worker participation arrangements have been subject to voluntary collective agreements or other voluntary arrangements entered into between employers and employees. In practice, those initiatives which evolved in the private sector were focused on joint consultative committees or works councils at sub-board level. One survey estimated the incidence of such arrangements in private sector enterprises at 21 per cent in 1995 (Gunnigle *et al.*, 1997, Chapter 7). The first legislative initiative on worker participation in the private sector in Ireland emerged in 1996 in response to an EU directive of 1994. The Transnational Information and Consultation of Employees Act of 1996 makes provision for the establishment of European Works Councils (EWCs) in 'community-scale' undertakings with at least 1,000 employees within EU member states and at least 150 employees in each of at least two different member states. EWCs are consultative forums in which employee or union representatives meet management to exchange information and consult on a range of stipulated transnational business issues and concerns. These include the development of the business, production and sales; the probable trend of employment and investments; and plans with respect to new working methods and production processes. It has been estimated that some 300 multinationals with operations in Ireland are affected by the EWC legislation. Unions support the principle of extending EU-level legislation into works council arrangements for domestic companies. During the 1990s, however, the union policy agenda has focused primarily on extending voluntary joint arrangements for 'partnership' at enterprise and workplace levels, as will be considered in detail below.

The Politics of Industrial Relations and Neo-corporatism

A number of unions in Ireland, including some of the largest unions, have long been affiliated to the Labour Party. Affiliation involves contributing political subscriptions, providing support for union-backed election candidates and offering general support and facilities, especially during elections. In the late 1980s, it was estimated that affiliated unions totalled 262,000 members, or about 57 per cent of all trade union members. However, these unions choose to affiliate only in respect of 187,000 members – 41 per cent of total union membership (see Katz and Mair, 1992, p. 402). However, the main political parties have never differed sharply as to the conduct of industrial relations in general, or the status and rights of unions. Unlike the historical situation in the UK, where elections have been fought on the issue of union power and where class politics have found expression in sharply differing party-political postures on union rights, unions have seldom figured to any significant degree in ideological divisions between the main Irish parties. This reflects a party system in which the two main parties formed out of the Irish Civil War, Fianna Fail and Fine Gael, have sought historically to mobilize cross-class support around political programmes differing primarily in regard to their postures on the 'national question', especially the status of Northern Ireland. Fianna Fail has been particularly successful at mobilizing cross-cutting political support and enjoys the votes of the majority of trade union members. While Fianna Fail and Fine Gael have also differed significantly with respect to their stances on economic issues and priorities, and in respect of the social composition of their core electoral support, both parties have adopted a broadly 'centrist' position on unions, fusing elements of the European Social Democratic and Christian Democratic traditions. In recent decades, the parties have moved even closer together in the areas of industrial relations, pay determination and the role of trade unions in a modern economy. While Fianna Fail historically pursued a more active industrial relations policy and adopted a more favourable stance towards engaging unions in tripartite, neo-corporatist arrangements, Fine Gael in the 1990s appears to have tempered its traditional liberal scepticism of the economic and constitutional implications of tripartism and now explicitly embraces centralized neo-corporatist bargaining over pay and economic and fiscal policy as an essential element of the 'Irish model' of economic management. Of the smaller parties, Labour and Democratic Left have advocated the case for industrial democracy and income redistribution more vigorously than other parties on the left, and in earlier periods of their histories have proposed radical programmes of nationalization. The parties of the left have entered government only as coalition partners to one or other of the main political parties. The impact of their policies on unions and industrial relations has thus been affected by the need to find accommodation with the policies of their major coalition partners. Reflecting wider developments in European socialism, the two parties of the left now support a social market economy and are committed to tripartism as a core element of Irish economic management. Moreover, Labour's major – and, as it proved, fleeting – electoral breakthrough in the 1992 general election, when it attained an unprecedented 19 per cent of the vote, was based on the party gaining a high level of support from among salaried middle-class voters (Sinnott, 1995, Chapter 7).

Of the other political parties, the small Progressive Democrats (PDs) Party is characterized by a strongly liberal posture on economic, business and labour market issues. The PDs are currently in a coalition government with Fianna Fail but under threat as a viable political party following a sharp drop in their level of electoral support in the 1997 general election. In the run up to the 1997 election, a prominent member of the PDs appeared to question the constitutionality of an incoming government being expected to endorse a tripartite national agreement negotiated by the previous administration. In power, the PDs have nevertheless accommodated to the present regime of neo-corporatism, the party leader (who is deputy prime minister) even giving her backing to proposals on the minimum wage in the face of hostile reaction from sections of Irish business.

Given the nature of Irish party politics it is hardly surprising that the level of trade union organization – as indexed by the trend of trade union membership – has been unaffected by the political complexion of governments, controlling for business cycle and institutional influences on union growth and decline (Roche and Larragy, 1990). Nor is it surprising that single-party (Fianna Fail) and coalition governments of different hues have at various times entered tripartite national bargaining arrangements with trade unions. Since 1987, five successive national agreements covering pay, economic industrial and social policy and taxation have dominated Irish industrial relations. Each of the agreements, or 'programmes' as they were to become known, has run for a three-year period. The advent of a regime of national tripartite bargaining in 1987 reflected a severe economic crisis marked by high inflation, spiralling public debt, high and persistent unemployment and rising emigration. Unions had operated under a regime of enterprise and sectoral-level bargaining since the early 1980s, and had suffered large declines in membership and density. Inflation and penal levels of taxation on even modestly paid workers whittled away the gains from pay bargaining in an increasingly slack and difficult labour market. Events in the United Kingdom raised the spectre of progressive union exclusion and marginalization – a scenario given sharp focus by the electoral success of the newly formed Progressive Democrats and the possibility at the time of a realignment in Irish politics towards the liberal right, centred on a PDs–Fine Gael alliance. The first of the recent national tripartite agreements, the Programme for National Recovery (PNR), gave priority to stabilizing and reducing public debt, imposing severe deflationary pressures on the economy and in particular on public spending. As the economy began to recover, unions entered a second programme with employers and government: the Programme for Economic and Social Progress (PESP). The PESP continued the pattern of the PNR, unions trading pay restraint for concessions on taxation and a voice in determining the main parameters of economic, industrial and social policy. The PESP and subsequent agreements – the Programme for Competitiveness and Work, Partnership 2000 and the recently negotiated Programme for Prosperity and Fairness – retained the formula of trading wage moderation for tax reform and increasingly addressed the policy implications of European economic integration and monetary union. At the behest of the unions, both Partnership 2000 and the Programme for Prosperity and Fairness also sought to promote voluntary partnership arrangements at enterprise and workplace levels, effectively breaking new ground in tripartite bargaining.

In the more competitive and stable economic regime associated with tripartism, Ireland has enjoyed high levels of foreign direct investment, particularly in sectors like electronics and pharmaceuticals, and increasingly in teleservices. Rapid job creation in multinationals and increasing competitiveness fuelled economic growth and fostered a recovery in indigenous and small business. By the early 1990s, commentators were referring to the Irish economy as the 'Celtic Tiger'. Annual GDP growth was outpacing EU and OECD countries, reaching close on 10 per cent by the mid-1990s. Employment expanded sharply and the level of unemployment fell towards the EU average. By 1998 tripartism was encountering labour market, economic and industrial relations problems associated with a boom economy, radically different in performance terms from the economic and social crisis which led to the emergence of the present phase of neo-corporatism in the late 1980s. The dominance of the neo-corporatist model remains largely unshaken. Liberal economic commentators who question the viability of the current national programme in the light of growing inflation and labour market pressures remain in the minority. The weight of opinion among academic and professional economists strongly favours tripartism.

Membership

Trends in Membership and Density

Notwithstanding the constitutional right to union membership, unions are regulated in representing their members in a number of ways. Associations representing the police ('gardai') and defence forces are prohibited from engaging in collective bargaining in the normal way and from undertaking industrial action. Both groups, however, are well organized and have engaged *de facto* in collective bargaining over pay and conditions. The army has protested over terms and conditions through the expedient of army spouses standing as protest candidates in a general election. During 1998, the gardai undertook mass work stoppages – the so-called 'blue flu' epidemic – in support of a pay relativity and productivity claim, and a demand that they be permitted to enter national pay negotiations.

Otherwise, unions are entitled to negotiate terms and conditions of employment and to engage in industrial action covered by the protection of the 1990 Industrial Relations Act only if they have been 'licensed' for this purpose. A negotiating licence is granted to unions meeting a minimum membership threshold of 1,000 members resident in the state and depositing between £20,000 and £60,000 (depending on the size of membership) with the Registrar of Friendly Societies. Recognized public service unions and associations may be 'excepted' from this provision.

Irish unions appear to organize significant numbers of self-employed workers. No time-series indicators of the share of membership among the self-employed are available. Retired members are likewise included in trade union membership returns as are unemployed members and again there is no way of identifying the numbers of members in these categories returned as union members. In studies of trends in Irish trade union membership and density, it has thus been standard practice to confine both membership and employees/workforce series to civilian employees and civilian employees, plus numbers unemployed.

The most authoritative time-series indicators of trade union membership and density for Ireland are those reported in Table 5.1. These data were collected as part of the 'DUES Project'; a thirteen-nation study of post-war trade union membership and organization in Western Europe and Scandinavia, centred at the University of Mannheim, Germany. The Irish DUES series[1] was constructed by freshly recording membership data from the annual returns of all unions registered in Ireland or the UK (membership of Irish branches only) and from comparable sources or union files in the case of non-registered unions. The time-series, thus constructed, overcame many of the problems associated with pre-existing estimates of annual union membership. These often drew on annual aggregate Registry estimates which omitted unions failing to make returns in any given year, or drew excessively on the membership levels for which unions had chosen to affiliate to trade union confederations. The DUES series covers civilian trade union membership and union density, measured as percentages of civilian employees at work and the employee workforce. The series is inflated by the inclusion in Registry returns and union records of undetermined numbers of self-employed and retired members. Table 5.1 indicates clearly that the 1980s were difficult years for Irish unions. In 1980, trade union membership and density reached their historic peaks. Between then and 1988, Irish unions suffered their most serious and sustained declines in membership and density since the 1920s. In net terms, 87,000 members were lost. Employment density measured by this series dropped by nearly 10 percentage points from 62 per cent to 53 per cent and workforce density by 14 percentage points from 55 per cent to 41 per cent.

Table 5.1 *Levels of unionization in Ireland, 1930–95[a]*

	Membership	Annual rate of change %	Employment density %	Workforce density %
1925[b]	123,000		21.20	18.70
1930[c]	99,450		19.98	19.98
1935	130,230		22.58	18.61
1940	151,630		26.21	22.88
1945	172,340		27.72	25.26
1955	305,620		45.69	41.61
1965	358,050		52.39	48.84
1975	449,520		60.02	53.19
1980	527,960		61.93	55.34
1985	485,050	−3.36	61.31	47.47
1986	471,740	−2.74	58.56	45.27
1987	458,050	−2.90	56.95	45.56
1988	440,890	−3.75	55.14	42.35
1989	459,920	4.32	57.37	44.51
1990	474,590	3.19	57.10	44.95
1991	484,730	2.14	57.12	43.96
1992	487,320	0.53	57.31	43.00
1993	485,700	−0.33	56.38	42.02
1994	492,820	1.47	54.96	41.80
1995	504,450	2.36	53.07	41.07

Notes:
[a] Series presented here differ from previously published DUES estimates due to data revisions.
[b] Value for 1926.
[c] Value for 1931.
Sources: DUES Data Series on Trade Unions in Ireland (Business Research Programme, Department of Industrial Relations, University College, Dublin, and University of Mannheim Centre for European Social Research, Germany).

Membership recovered from the late 1980s and has grown progressively during the 1990s. By the mid-1990s, trade union membership had revived to levels comparable to the early 1980s. The growth in membership had not, however, kept pace with the growth in employment or the workforce, with the result that trade union density has continued to decline significantly. Continuing decline in trade union density, especially employment density, in the 1990s is particularly significant given that the decade has been the most successful ever in Irish economic history. Unions have also participated in tripartite national agreements and gained considerable influence over economic, industrial and social policy. Employment has grown sharply, especially around mid-decade, but Irish unions have nevertheless been unable to sustain or increase their levels of organization.

The determinants of annual trade union growth and decline in Ireland have been identified in a series of quantitative studies (Roche and Larragy, 1990; Roche, 1992a). Of possible business-cycle influences, the annual rate of change in nominal earnings and the annual rate of change in employees at work are positively associated with trade union growth. Price inflation exerts no consistent influence on the annual trend; a reflection of the historical concurrence of inflationary peaks and labour market stagnation in the Irish economy and possibly of the importance of the cost-of-living criterion in determining the levels of recurring pay-round adjustments over most of the period. The rate of change in employment proves to be a better indicator of trends in labour market slackness than the rate of unemployment – the latter affected by migration flows in Ireland. Two institutional influences significantly affected the trend at different points of time. Legislation on trade union rationalization in 1941 combined with the imposition of statutory pay control contributed to a sharp drop in membership. The transition to free collective bargaining in the second half of the 1940s, which witnessed the advent of recurring pay rounds and the establishment of the modern system of conflict resolution in Irish industrial relations, account for a major part of the unprecedented growth of those years.

Structural change in the composition of the workforce is poorly captured in econometric modelling as it is characterized by long-time trends or little annual variability. The density term is conventionally treated as capturing part of such an effect by picking up the so-called 'saturation effect' (Bain and Elsheikh, 1976).

In terms of this framework, the factors influencing the trend of membership and density during the 1980s and 1990s can be identified. Successive national tripartite programmes made provision for modest pay rises of no more than a few per cent per year. The level of employment fell over most of the 1980s, recovering during the 1990s. Over both decades, however, employment growth was concentrated in sectors characterized by relatively low trade union density and considerable barriers to union organization: in particular, high-technology manufacturing, especially electronics and pharmaceuticals, and financial services (no longer a consistently highly organized sector). Levels of part-time working and contract employment also rose significantly. Employment stagnated and then fell in the high-density public sector. The trend in Irish trade union membership and density during the 1980s and 1990s can then be attributed mainly to modest wage growth (accompanied by low inflation) combined with significant structural change in the composition of the workforce.

It is clear from the statistical results that the regime of tripartite bargaining had little positive effect on the membership fortunes of trade unions over and above that which can be attributed to the modest wage increases of the past decade. This is consistent with the historical pattern. Trade union growth and decline in Ireland since 1930 appears to have been unaffected in any direct sense by whether centralized or decentralized pay-bargaining regimes prevailed (Roche and Larragy, 1990). Unions in the 1990s showed signs of being concerned, however, that centralized agreements since 1987 may have *depressed* union growth and organization by imposing tight constraints on local bargaining activity and by removing unions from the workplace to a pronounced degree. The econometric evidence fails to accord with this view. Tripartite agreements in Ireland since 1987 appear to have had no direct generalized effect in depressing the level of trade union membership. Union critics of tripartism could, of course, still argue that higher pay rises under a free-for-all bargaining regime might have led to higher levels of trade union growth than those recorded during the 1990s.

A more detailed breakdown of the recent pattern and trend of trade union density can be obtained from the data in Table 5.2. The data were collected in the annual Labour Force Survey which contained a question on trade union and staff association membership between 1992 and 1997; unfortunately, no official data is available for later than 1997. The table is restricted to employees at work and thus excludes self-employed trade union members and unemployed and retired members. It is evident that the estimates of employment density are substantially lower than those based on annual trade union membership returns. The figures nevertheless confirm that trade union density has declined continuously during the 1990s.

The data also reveal sharp differences in levels of union density across sectors and some differences between male and female density levels. Density

Table 5.2 *Labour force survey estimates of trade union density by sector and gender, Ireland, 1992–7*

Industrial sectors	1992			1993			1994		
	Male %	Female %	All employees %	Male %	Female %	All employees %	Male %	Female %	All employees %
Agriculture, forestry and fishing	12.3	13.6	12.4	10.7	16.7	10.9	10.0	19.2	11.1
Building and construction	45.0	17.9	43.7	44.5	25.8	43.3	40.1	21.6	38.9
Other production industries	55.0	52.6	54.3	55.2	52.5	54.4	53.9	51.4	53.1
Commerce, insurance, finance and business services	31.6	31.7	31.6	28.9	31.8	30.3	29.0	30.7	29.8
Transport, communication and storage	70.7	59.0	68.0	75.3	54.2	70.6	69.2	52.8	65.7
Professional services	58.7	58.7	58.7	55.9	58.4	57.6	55.7	59.2	58.1
Public administration and defence	72.2	76.5	73.4	74.7	77.7	75.6	75.9	80.2	77.5
Other	28.2	21.5	24.2	27.0	22.1	24.0	25.9	19.8	22.4
Total	49.5	46.7	48.3	49.2	46.4	48.0	47.6	46.1	47.0

Industrial sectors	1995			1996			1997		
	Male %	Female %	All employees %	Male %	Female %	All employees %	Male %	Female %	All employees %
Agriculture, forestry and fishing	8.2	6.9	8.4	10.2	5.9	9.5	8.1	3.7	7.5
Building and construction	42.1	24.3	40.9	39.4	26.3	38.4	37.2	17.1	36.0
Other production industries	52.9	49.1	51.7	51.3	47.4	50.1	48.5	43.4	46.9
Commerce, insurance, finance and business services	28.1	31.6	29.7	27.4	33.1	30.2	27.2	30.8	29.0
Transport, communication and storage	68.4	55.9	65.3	65.6	56.0	63.4	64.5	50.0	60.9
Professional services	57.3	56.6	56.8	57.6	56.3	56.7	55.6	56.1	56.0
Public administration and defence	76.2	76.8	76.4	77.1	73.9	75.9	74.3	73.8	74.1
Other	23.3	19.0	20.8	25.6	20.0	22.4	25.6	19.9	22.3
Total	46.8	44.3	45.8	46.3	44.5	45.5	44.3	42.6	43.5

Notes: Data are based on numbers of employees at work responding in the affirmative to a question on membership of a trade union or staff association. Data on membership of unions or staff associations are not available in the case of relatively small numbers of non-respondents to this question. The numbers vary from between 6,000 to 8,000 in total. These respondents appear in the employment totals for each sector from which the density levels are estimated.

Source: Labour Force Survey data (unpublished), made available by the Central Statistics Office.

levels are predictably low in agriculture, forestry and fishing. The highest levels of unionization are found in public administration and in transport, communication and storage, an industry sector that includes major public utilities. Three out of ten employees in financial services are unionized in the 1990s. Four out of ten employees in building and construction are unionized. More than half of those employed in manufacturing ('other production industries') were unionized in 1992. This had fallen to just under half by 1997. In fact this sector represents a miscellaneous group of industries characterized by sharply diverging levels of density. Density levels are known to be lowest in high-technology sectors, such as computer hardware and software manufacturing, dominated by foreign-owned multinationals, and to be highest among established indigenous Irish companies in traditional industries. Employment growth has been concentrated mainly in the high-technology sectors, imposing a drag on the overall density level in manufacturing. Levels of density in professional services have held up at under 60 per cent of employees.

The gender gap in union density in Ireland is not particularly pronounced and appears to be closing. 50 per cent of male employees were unionized in 1992 compared with 47 per cent of women. The levels in 1997 were 44 per cent of men compared with 43 per cent of women. Table 5.2 shows that gender differences are more pronounced within specific sectors, but also appear to be changing in some sectors. Men are significantly more likely to be unionized in building and construction (which has a very small female workforce), in manufacturing and in transport, communications and storage. In commerce, insurance and finance, and business services a gender gap is opening up in favour of women. This may reflect the operation of the twin forces of women being disproportionately concentrated in junior grades and of senior-grade employees being encouraged to leave unions, or not to join on appointment to new and existing financial institutions (Roche and Turner, 1998). In public administration and defence a gender gap in the early 1990s in favour of women had been reversed by 1997, when men had become slightly more likely than women to be union members. Annual density levels by gender, as indexed by the Labour Force Survey, appear to fluctuate in this sector, but the underlying pattern is one of declining female density and rising male density.

The Labour Force Survey does not permit a breakdown of density by public and private sectors. Manifestly, however, given the spread of employment in the sectors identified in Table 5.2 across the public and private domains, union density is very significantly higher in the public than in the private sector. Apart from public administration and defence, which shows the highest level of trade union density, the public sector share of employment in the relatively high-density transport and communications sector is substantial. Also, public sector professional services, like education and health, are highly unionized. Table 5.3 provides a public and private sector profile of the membership of unions affiliated to the Irish Congress of Trade Unions (ICTU) (accounting for 95 per cent or more of total trade union membership). The table shows that the Irish trade union movement is now a predominantly public sector movement with a changing gender composition in favour of women, who still remain a minority of the membership. Given the pattern of the data reported in Table 5.2, however, it is likely that the estimates of the share of public sector membership in Table 5.3 are conservative. Table 5.3 also contains data on ICTU affiliated membership for 1998 and 1999. In the absence of official Labour Force Survey data, the increase in combined affiliated membership for these years points to some growth in overall membership. However, given both a growing workforce and declining rates of unemployment, significant changes to density were unlikely to have occurred.

Table 5.3 *The sectoral and gender composition of the membership of unions affiliated to the Irish Congress of Trade Unions, 1990–6*

	Total affiliated membership in the Irish Republic	Public sector membership %	Private sector membership %	Female membership %
1990	459,336	n.a.	n.a.	36.0
1991	454,777	49.0	51.0	36.0
1992	463,647	52.0	48.0	38.0
1993	467,199	52.0	48.0	37.0
1994	473,611	52.0	48.0	38.0
1995	482,835	55.0	45.0	38.0
1996	491,164	n.a.	n.a.	40.0
1997	499,560	n.a.	n.a.	41.0
1998	521,036	n.a.	n.a.	43.0
1999	523,624	n.a.	n.a.	44.0

Source: ICTU Annual Reports on Affiliated Membership (unpublished) and data made available by ICTU (1997–9).

To summarize the pattern of change in membership and density during the 1990s, the following trends can be highlighted. Trade union membership levels recovered during the 1990s, but employment and workforce density levels have fallen significantly. Union membership growth has been assisted by rising employment and an increasingly tight labour market. The modest rate of growth in nominal earnings, combined with a concentration of employment growth in relatively low-density sectors help account for the modest rise in membership given the level of employment growth. Other than through instituting a regime of modest pay rises, there is no compelling evidence that neo-corporatist bargaining since 1987 depressed union growth or density by taking unions out of the workplace or transforming union officials into policemen and women of tight national pay norms. The trend in union density during the 1990s has been of particular concern to unions, particularly the part played in declining unionization by the increasing incidence of foreign-owned multinationals opting to establish non-union establishments in Ireland, and by the growing resistance to union recognition among indigenous firms. Union policy responses to these forces will be examined below.

Structure and Governance

Composition of Union Membership

Table 5.4 outlines the changing composition of trade union membership by union type or character. After having grown progressively in their member-ship share up to the 1960s, general unions' share of total trade union membership declined, the trend apparently bottoming out in the 1990s. The decline and stagnation of the share of the most inclusive type of unions obscures the counter-trend for general unions to have become in reality more 'general' in their membership composition, as they have succeeded in recruiting significant numbers of white-collar, craft and technical workers. The share of (ex-)craft unions has continued to decline, a reflection of the blurring or disappearance of many of the traditional craft domains around which they had organized and the growing absorption of craft unions by general unions. The growing share of white-collar unions reflects changes in the industrial and occupational composition of the workforce in favour of clerical, technical, administrative and managerial jobs. Like general unions, white-collar unions have become more encompassing or 'inclusive' over time: unions of single or allied white-collar occupations giving way to more general, multi-occupational unions (Roche, 1992b).

The share of unions with headquarters in the United Kingdom of overall trade union membership has continued to decline in the 1990s. This trend

Table 5.4 *Membership shares by union type, congress affiliation and location of union headquarters[a], Ireland (percentage)*

Year	General unions	White-collar unions	(Ex-)Craft unions	Other manual[b]	ICTU/ITUC[d]	CIU	British unions[c]
1940	45.5	24.1	16.9	13.5	90.0		22.4
1945	44.3	28.6	15.8	11.3	44.0	45.5[d]	21.4
1950	55.3	21.5	14.1	9.2	38.8	53.4	18.0
1955	57.1	20.7	13.4	8.8	39.0	54.5	14.2
1960	57.2	20.9	13.2	8.7	93.6		13.0
1965	55.8	22.0	13.6	8.7	91.4		14.0
1970	52.9	24.9	13.7	8.5	91.3		14.3
1975	48.6	31.3	11.5	8.6	91.1		15.3
1980	49.4	33.7	11.8	5.1	91.0		14.1
1985	45.0	38.4	11.6	5.0	91.4		14.3
1990	46.9	38.9	12.0	2.2	93.7		13.7
1995	46.3	42.1	10.2	1.4	97.4		11.5

Notes:

[a] Membership of unions with headquarters in the Irish Republic includes a small percentage of Northern Ireland members (varying around 3%). Hence Congress affiliation will be slightly overestimated and a small margin of error is unavoidable in the case of shares of different union types.

[b] Includes one union, the National League of the Blind, the membership of which comprises both manual and non-manual employees.

[c] Net membership excludes Northern Ireland members of unions based in the Republic.

[d] Membership shares for 1945, 1950 and 1955 reflect a split within the Irish Trade Union Congress and the existence for a time of two rival peak federations following the emergence of the Irish and nationalist-union-dominated, Congress of Irish Unions (CIU). The two federations subsequently merged to form the current Irish Congress of Trade Unions.

Source: DUES Series.

cannot be accounted for in simple structural terms by being attributable to a concentration of British union membership in domains characterized by lower organic or 'natural' growth potential. British unions were and are more heavily concentrated in craft domains than Irish unions, but their growth record in those domains is substantially less impressive than that attained by Irish unions. British unions' relative membership decline can better be explained in terms of the retarding effects during certain periods of resurgent nationalism and the policy decisions of UK head offices as to the viability and value of Irish branches (Roche, 1994).

It will be clear from Table 5.4 that the monopoly of representation of the Irish Congress of Trade Unions is now almost total – ICTU affiliated unions accounting for 97 per cent of total trade union membership by the mid-1990s.

Merger Activity

Table 5.5 presents data on levels of merger activity and highlights the intensive merger wave that occurred during the 1980s and 1990s. In examining merger levels in Ireland the coexistence of unions with headquarters in Ireland and British-based unions needs to be borne in mind. Table 5.5 distinguishes between 'Irish mergers' and total mergers. Irish mergers comprise in the main mergers between Irish-based trade unions, whether achieved through amalgamations or through transfers of engagements. The latter path to merger is usually followed where small organizations are absorbed by substantially larger unions. The 'Irish mergers' category also includes some instances where the Irish branches of British unions have merged with Irish-based unions. 'Irish mergers' are likely to reflect prevailing *domestic* economic and industrial relations conditions. Mergers between the Irish branches of British unions will reflect the conditions in the UK influencing the mergers of parent unions. Both types of mergers are combined to provide an overall indication of the intensity of merger activity affecting Irish trade union members at various points of time since 1922.

It is clear from the data that the merger wave that occurred from the mid-1980s is without historical precedent. Larger numbers of unions merged during the second half of the 1980s and first half of the 1990s than in any previous period of Irish industrial relations history. Relative to the total population of unions, a substantially higher proportion of trade unions were affected by mergers than at any other time. The trends in Table 5.5 reflect

Table 5.5   *Merger intensity in Ireland, 1922–94*

Five-year periods	Number of unions in mergers		Average number of unions extant over period		Merger intensity	
	(a) 'Irish mergers'	(b) All mergers	(c) Irish unions	All unions	(d) 'Irish mergers'	All mergers
1920–4(e)		6		96		6.3
1925–9		0		101		0.0
1930–4		1		105		1.0
1935–9		1		106		0.9
1940–4	0	0	67	109	0.0	0.0
1945–9	1	2	70	111	1.4	1.8
1950–4	4	3	69	109	5.8	2.8
1955–9	1	2	70	109	1.4	1.8
1960–4	0	4	77	118	0.0	3.4
1965–9	7	12	78	113	9.0	10.6
1970–4	2	6	80	107	2.5	5.6
1975–9	7	9	75	100	9.3	9.0
1980–4	6	8	69	91	8.7	8.8
1985–9	12	15	62	82	19.4	18.3
1990–4	9	17	50	68	18.0	25.0

Notes:
(a) Mergers between Irish-based unions and between Irish branches of UK-based unions and Irish unions.
(b) All mergers: 'Irish mergers' and mergers between UK-based unions.
(c) Average number of unions extant over corresponding five-year periods.
(d) Merger intensity = $\dfrac{\text{number of mergers} \times 100}{\text{average number of unions extant}}$
(e) Value is for period 1922–4.

Source: DUES Data Series.

both the merger wave in the United Kingdom during the 1980s and 1990s and a merger wave among Irish trade unions. Confining the analysis to Irish mergers, which reflected prevailing domestic conditions and pressures on unions, about 18 per cent of Irish unions were affected by merger activity in the ten-year period from the mid-1980s. Irish mergers during this period also occurred among some of the country's largest trade unions, with the result that the numbers of trade union members affected by merger activity were also quite without historical precedent.

Mergers fell into three broad categories. Large general unions were involved in mergers, particularly Ireland's largest trade union, the Irish Transport and General Workers' Union, which was involved in 1990 in a merger with the Federated Workers' Union of Ireland, resulting in the birth of the 'super union', Services, Industrial, Professional and Technical Union. A wave of merger activity also occurred among public service white-collar unions, leading to a significant shift away from the single-grade unions that had dominated public service representation and to the emergence of multi-occupational or conglomerate unions. Groups of craft unions also engaged in merger activity, either with other craft unions in contiguous or similar membership domains – the dominant pattern – or with general unions.

Merger activity represented one line of response by unions to the economic and industrial relations conditions prevailing during the 1980s and 1990s. The large general unions, which had built up extensive branch networks and sometimes head-office support divisions during the phase of rapid membership expansion in the 1960s and 1970s, now faced problems sustaining levels of organization and services as membership fell and income was squeezed. Similar pressures bore down on craft unions, with additional pressures arising from the blurring of membership territories as technologies changed, core craft skills were eroded and employers more frequently pressed for multi-skilling and craft integration arrangements.

In the public services, merger activity was spurred by the general merger wave affecting the trade union movement and by factors specific to that sector. While density did not decline on a par with the private sector, unions nevertheless faced the prospect of stagnation and decline in public sector employment. Merger activity sparked off further mergers. Once merger activity was initiated by unions absorbing organizations in contiguous membership domains, other unions were forced to follow suit for defensive reasons. Not to absorb smaller organizations in job territories close to their existing core membership categories was to run the risk that other unions might do so, 'invading' and threatening the existing domains of unions disinclined to become involved in mergers. Irish unions had sought to promote rationalization since the 1930s and various programmes and models of reorganization were canvassed at different points (McPartlin, 1994). Legislation and public policy also addressed the issue of more rational trade union structures in various ways. It is ironic indeed that the parlous circumstances of the 1980s were a more potent force for trade union rationalization than more than fifty years of union endeavours on the issue and a succession of initiatives by the state.

Governance

Compared with the United Kingdom, where workplace organization and quasi-autonomous workplace bargaining led by shop stewards was extensive during the 1960s and 1970s in the private sector, unions in Ireland have tended to be highly centralized. Union headquarters, working through geographical branches, have dominated decision-making and governance in many unions, particularly in the large general unions and public service unions. Some white-collar unions, like the UK-based Manufacturing, Science and Finance Union, have adopted more decentralized strategies, delegating bargaining activity to workplace-based representatives within an overall policy framework laid down by professional union officials. In the case of craft unions, the workplace-based shop has traditionally played an important role in representation and defending the job territory of the craft.

In general, Irish unions have never been characterized by militant workplace bargaining. Shop stewards have mainly acted as recruiters and grievance handlers rather than as primary pay bargainers. The reasons for the centralization of decision-making and governance in Irish unions can be traced to the size structure of Irish companies and the dynamics of pay bargaining. Workplace activism has been pronounced in large Irish establishments such as the electricity utility, ESB, or large manufacturing companies like Waterford Crystal. In these enterprises, union activity during specific periods or generally has been dominated by workplace shop-steward organization. The more common pattern among the great majority of small to medium-sized companies, was for the professional local trade union official to be the dominant force, acting within national-level policies.

The centralization of decision-making was further bolstered by a wage-bargaining system dominated by sectoral-level bargaining in all but the largest enterprises. With the advent of recurrent 'rounds' of pay bargaining in Irish industrial relations during the second half of the 1940s, wage adjustment in free-for-all or decentralized rounds was pitched mainly at a sectoral level, where national or branch-level professional union officials were the key actors. Nationally determined pay rounds during the period further underscored centralized decision-making. In the case of public service unions, the pay-bargaining system for different grades and categories of public servants was highly centralized, in line with the pattern internationally until the 1980s and 1990s.

The advent of a decade of national pay bargaining during the period from 1970 to 1980, when there was an unbroken sequence of nine national pay agreements, further bolstered union centralization. Though extensive second-tier wage bargaining occurred under the 1970s national pay regime, the advent of second-tier bargaining failed to disrupt prevailing patterns of decision-making in unions in the manner that had become familiar in the UK. In the British case, workplace bargaining effectively undermined industry level bargaining, forcing unions to respond by decentralizing union government and bargaining activity (Undy *et al.*, 1981). With the return to free-for-all bargaining in Ireland over the period 1982–7, sectoral bargaining gradually gave way to enterprise bargaining in the private sector, but without any manifest change in the locus of decision-making in trade unions. This may have reflected both the short period of time over which pay bargaining became more focused on the enterprise and the centralizing effects of the highly recessionary conditions of the early to mid-1980s.

The resurgence of national pay bargaining from 1987 to date has thus underscored a tradition in which union governance and decision-making has always been vested in mainly national organizations and in union branches acting for the most part as agents of national policy. Paradoxically perhaps, given the centralized system of union governance, the authority of the Irish Congress of Trade Unions has always been clearly delimited. Nor has ICTU authority grown in any formal sense as a result of a long-running regime of tripartite bargaining. Despite enjoying a now near total monopoly of union representation, ICTU has limited formal powers over the activities of affiliated unions. The peak federation has no powers to sanction or withhold sanction in the area of industrial action and possesses no strike funds. The last formal powers accorded to ICTU – the power to intervene in inter-union disputes and to regulate picketing among affiliated unions – were gained in the 1970s. Commentators on the fragility of tripartite bargaining during the 1970s, which was manifest in extensive pay drift and soaring strike levels, have pointed by way of explanation to the weak 'concertative capacity' of the ICTU. This has been traced to the vertical, fragmented and sectional pattern of organization of the Irish trade union movement (Hardiman, 1987, Chapter 5). While the merger wave of the 1980s and 1990s has led to a degree of 'rationalization' in the structure of Irish unions, commentators on the functioning of pay bargaining since 1987 emphasize that little has changed with respect to the formal capacity of the ICTU to control affiliated organizations or police national pay norms (Sheehan, 1996).

Irrespective of the formalities of power and authority as provided for in constitutions and resources commanded, the ICTU has enjoyed considerable 'moral authority' and 'strategic authority' as a centre for formulating union policy on major common issues and challenges facing all unions. The stature of ICTU in both these areas has probably grown significantly during the 1990s; in particular its 'strategic authority' to articulate trade union priorities with respect to economic, fiscal, social and industrial policy. Since 1987, as will be discussed below, ICTU has emerged as the major strategic actor on the trade union side in pay determination and tripartite governance.

If wage drift and sectional militancy were significant factors in the eventual collapse of the 1970s regime of national pay bargaining, pay drift and sectional bargaining were more muted during the first three national programmes since 1987. Reviews of pay determination have concluded that drift was limited, due less to greater pay discipline or greater central control by unions or employer federations than to the operation of competitive forces and, for much of the period, recession and slack labour markets (Sheehan, 1996). Where drift occurred, it appears to have been more closely related to changes in work organization and more general restructuring and reorganization at workplace level.

Indications of growing membership restiveness with national pay agreements have emerged in recent years. The vote in favour of Partnership 2000 was much closer than anticipated in the largest union, Services, Industrial, Professional and Technical Union. Several public service unions that had traditionally supported national agreements voted against Partnership 2000, due to their failure to make headway with special category claims, and other unions supported the deal only when sectional claims were conceded. Nevertheless, at a special ICTU conference held in late 1999, an overwhelming majority of delegates voted in favour of entering new tripartite talks (EIRR, 1999). As noted above, a new agreement was reached, and subsequently ratified by the union movement in February and March 2000.

Given the sharp growth in the economy from the mid-1990s and associated rises in employment and emerging skill shortages, indications of sectional bargaining pressures and pay drift are beginning to emerge more prominently. In the public sector, in particular, pay claims backed by industrial action have been pursued by gardai, local government and health-service craft workers. In the private sector, skills shortages in high-growth sectors have led to the bidding up of rates, and probably to various forms of disguised pay drift focused on bonuses and grade drift.

To summarize the pattern of governance in Irish unions during the 1990s, it can be concluded that national pay bargaining has underpinned a largely centralized model of governance, with the major decisions on pay determination being taken in the ICTU and at national level in the main affiliated unions. The pivotal role of ICTU since the late 1980s has further centralized decision-making into a multi-union coalition with near total representative monopoly and dominated by national-level trade union leaders. This does not, however, represent any radical departure from the dominant model of governance in Irish unions since 1922. Even in periods of free-for-all pay bargaining, union governance was generally concentrated in the hands of national union officers and full-time branch officials – a mode of governance buttressed by the dominance of sectoral pay determination. More recently a tightening labour market and rapid economic growth have imposed perhaps the most serious pressures on the national pay regime since the return to centralized bargaining in 1987.

Orientation and Strategies

With the exception of a phase of militancy and syndicalist radicalism during the first two decades of the century, spurred by the economic conditions of the First World War and the political and social dislocations of the Anglo-Irish War, Irish unions have, by and large, adopted a reformist and pragmatic philosophy. A philosophy of class struggle has never guided the policies of Irish trade unions as organizations, though it has of course found support from individual union leaders and among union activists. The reformist, gradualist and social democratic outlook of Irish unions has facilitated dealings with employer bodies at national and local level and allowed unions to come to an accommodation with governments comprising different political parties and groupings. In general, British trade unions in Ireland have tended to be more left-leaning than their Irish counterparts and they have opposed, or less consistently supported, national pay bargaining – a reflection of the ideologies and policies of their UK parent organizations. At various points, particularly during the 1930s and 1940s, a number of Irish unions have adopted staunchly nationalist postures, lobbying for state proposals on union rationalization which worked to the disadvantage of British unions. Clashes of ideology, combined with organizational vested interests and deep enmity between a number of major trade union leaders led to a split in Congress in the 1940s and the emergence for a time of two rival trade union federations.

British unions, whether general, craft or white-collar, mostly oppose and vote against national tripartite agreements, while working within the parameters of those agreements once ratified by Congress. Irish craft unions also commonly oppose national agreements on the grounds that decentralized pay bargaining results in higher levels of pay increases for craft categories.

Tripartite agreements commonly seek to favour lower-paid employees through the manner in which wage norms are specified. At various points in the history of national pay bargaining, minimum cash increases, cash ceilings and tapering percentage rises have been agreed in pursuit of a broad policy of 'wage solidarism'. During the 1970s' generation of national agreements, these devices were usually overridden by wage drift (O'Brien, 1981). By the mid-1990s, national agreements appear to have halted the growing dispersion of pay in the the private sector associated with the return to decentralized bargaining in the early 1980s; pay dispersion with the public sector appeared however to be widening (Teague, 1995).

While a significant section of the trade union movement favours decentralized bargaining and declares itself opposed to tripartism, the majority of unions favour centralized bargaining. They do so more on the balance of advantage accruing from tripartism than on any explicitly ideological or philosophical terms. The approach adopted to tripartism over the past decade by the ICTU and its affiliated unions has been highly iterative. Succeeding agreements reflected changing union priorities rooted in changing labour market, economic and political conditions. The early agreements reflected union priorities shaped by economic and labour market crisis and by fears of progressive union marginalization. Subsequent agreements more vigorously sought to trade income tax reform and increases in the social wage for pay moderation. In Partnership 2000, unions sought to promote workplace and enterprise partnership – the new frontier of tripartism. European economic integration, impending monetary union and the modernization of the Irish economy were an important backdrop to the parameters agreed in the more recent deals. While ICTU negotiating strategy was thus in major respects pragmatic, it is possible to detect a growing philosophical current among sections of the union leadership which views tripartism as the path ahead for unions in an advanced industrial or post-industrial economy and society. Some union leaders have interpreted the 'Irish model' of social partnership of the last decade as a historic break with the British industrial relations tradition and a shift towards a continental European industrial relations tradition – problematic though such a portrayal may be.

During the 1980s and 1990s, the ICTU and its major affiliated unions have actively supported European Monetary Union and moves to a single currency, endorsing public policy proposals aimed at a gradual reduction of the debt/GNP ratio and limits on public spending consistent with meeting the Maastricht Treaty criteria on European Monetary Union (EMU). Support for a consistent state policy of maintaining the value of the Irish currency within a narrow band of the main EU currencies caused considerable controversy in periods when sterling has devalued sharply, threatening jobs in sectors heavily dependent on trade with the UK. ICTU's vision of the future competitive advantage of the Irish economy is that Irish business must compete in upstream international markets on the basis of economic stability, high skills and high levels of education and training. A low-cost, low-wage route to competitiveness is emphatically rejected.

The ICTU – a body organized on an all-Ireland basis – has vigorously supported moves to find a political settlement in Northern Ireland acceptable to both the Protestant/unionist and nationalist communities. Congress has consistently campaigned against sectarianism, employment discrimination and political violence. The internal political schisms of earlier periods, focused around the 'national question', have largely given way to consensus on the imperative of finding a democratic settlement. At a more general level, ICTU has espoused support for a range of progressive policies in areas such as harassment at work, gay rights, the environment and more flexible working-time options, including parental leave.

With the exception of local area employment initiatives in high unemployment areas, no significant new patterns of alliance or partnership – for example, with community groups or social movements – have been apparent. The primary channels of union engagement with members' interests remain the industrial and political arenas – the two increasingly fused under the current regime of neo-corporatism. Congress has supported the more explicit incorporation of social policy pressure groups and the Irish National Union of the Unemployed – the so-called 'social pillar' – into tripartite institutions and negotiations.

Union strategies regarding pay determination, the minimum wage, macroeconomic management, European integration, industrial policy and competitiveness have already been considered above, as has the pivotal role of the ICTU in articulating and negotiating such policies in tripartite agreements and institutions. These areas mark out the 'agreed terrain, of social partnership in Ireland around which it has been possible to find accommodation with employers and the state.

While working within these parameters, unions have also sought to respond to organizational pressures through internal measures focused on service enhancement and mergers. In response to falling membership and declining density from the second half of the 1980s, unions in Ireland undertook some of the recruitment and organizational initiatives apparent in other countries. Attempts were commonly made to extend the range of services available to members with a view to enhancing the 'selective incentives' for unionization. Alliances were entered into with financial institutions to provide preferential services in areas like health insurance, general insurance and holiday travel. In some ways, this was an interesting reversion to what the Webbs (1920) had famously referred to as the 'method of social insurance' in their classic treatise on the early history of British unions. Now, however, union benefits were being offered as a top-up to state welfare or private insurance provisions and as additional financial products in a growing consumer market for services of various kinds. In addition to attempts at enhanced service provision, growing numbers of unions were forced to countenance the prospect of mergers. The dramatic effects on union structure of this more traumatic line of response to the membership setbacks of the 1980s have been examined above.

Organizational pressures and attempts to respond to industrial challenges have also led unions to revise their established modes of representing members. Following a series of strategic reviews, unions have tried to implement new policies in major respects through social partnership channels. The ICTU and its major affiliated unions, in particular the Services, Industrial, Professional and Technical Union, have again been pivotal in coordinating trade union responses. In seeking to extend the boundaries of social partnership, unions have entered 'contested terrain', exposing areas where the scope for accommodation with employers and the state presently appears limited. Union policy changes have tested and continue to test the boundaries of social partnership in two major areas: strategies to promote partnership at workplace and enterprise levels, and strategies to promote recognition and bargaining rights.

Workplace Partnership

In the early 1990s, ICTU undertook an important review of commercial trends and new production strategies in manufacturing industries (ICTU, 1993). Based on detailed case studies of twelve companies, the review confirmed that a series of competitive pressures were impacting on employer manufacturing strategies, leading to growing experimentation with new forms of work organization involving team working, a continuous improvement programme, world-class manufacturing and other post-Taylorist innovations. In the case-study companies, new approaches to work organization were found to be commonly complemented by supporting human resource policies. The ICTU review noted that union and worker involvement in formal structures to implement new initiatives was minimal (ICTU, 1993, p. 8). The review advocated that unions should choose one of three strategies in responding to the growing incidence of new forms of work organization:

- A *minimalist approach*, where unions would cooperate with employer initiatives given explicit assurances. Specific guidelines would be given to officials as to the initiatives with which they should cooperate and under what terms. These guidelines would provide a 'floor' below which unions would not be prepared to go in their dealings with employers.

- A *proactive approach*, where unions form the view that on balance new forms of work organization will operate to the benefit of their members. Here unions would seek as much input as possible into decisions on the introduction and monitoring of new initiatives. This approach was held to have much in common with the approach being adopted to new forms of work organization by German unions.

- A *maximalist approach* based on unions actively promoting their own agenda. In this approach, unions would seize opportunities (for example where commercial crises required radically new approaches to running firms) to promote the introduction of new forms of work organization, believing these to be in the best long-term interest of their members. This was portrayed as similar to the approach of Swedish unions.

The review advocated that strategies should be adopted on a company-by-company basis, depending on current and past relations between management and unions, business circumstances and the quality and depth of management commitment to new work-organization initiatives (ICTU, 1993, Chapter 7). These approaches appear to overlap, and the injunctions given as to the conditions that should guide strategic choice appear difficult to reconcile with the 'universalistic' postures that define the second and third strategies. Nevertheless, under the aegis of this review, the ICTU had begun to develop a policy on union and employee involvement which shifted ground from the classical posture of subjecting work organization to unilateral regulation, wherever possible, to joint regulation through collective agreement or custom and practice.

A subsequent ICTU review published in 1995 returned to this theme on the wider canvas of union involvement in change and company restructuring. This review noted that companies most commonly approached the management of change through 'hard HRM' or through 'cherry picking', involving the use of the language and tools of culture change without any serious intent to engage in serious change (ICTU, 1995, pp. 20–1). The review endorsed the imperative for 'strategic reorganization' in companies and identified a series of principles that should focus union policy in the area. These included union involvement in business or competitive strategy, partnership and participative structures, greater team and worker autonomy and a system for sharing benefits to be delivered. It was envisaged that unions would develop goals to be achieved in these and allied areas in the context of national agreements.

In the run-up to negotiations on a new national agreement in 1996, the ICTU leadership was proclaiming that a deepening of social partnership through provisions for workplace partnership would be a precondition of any new agreement. Reflecting the sharply diverging views of their membership on workplace partnership, the employers' confederation were cautious and opposed legislative measures or an interventionist public policy in the area (Roche, 1998). The agreement, concluded early in 1997, contains a set of provisions to promote 'partnership for competitive enterprise'. Partnership is defined broadly and encompasses forms of direct employee involvement, union-based structures and financial participation (Partnership 2000, Chapter 9).

Union efforts in this area subsequently took shape within the parameters of the national agreement. A new tripartite institution, the National Centre for Partnership, was established to encourage and monitor workplace partnership. The limited incidence of workplace partnership based on union involvement at the outset of Partnership 2000 is clear from national survey data on unionized workplaces conducted in mid-1997. Partnership with trade unions has been relatively little used by management as a means of handling workplace change. The survey showed that fewer than 20 per cent of workplaces had pursued partnership-based approaches involving unions in their handling of any single aspect of operational workplace change. Partnership with unions seldom extended to the handling of strategic aspects of change in areas like new product development, setting business targets or plans with respect to mergers, acquisitions and sell-offs. In fact 'strategic partnerships' which give unions a voice in business and competitive strategy are very uncommon outside commercial state-owned companies (Roche and Turner, 1998).

When respondents were asked in the survey to indicate how they intended to handle change *in the future* the prospects for partnership arrangements with trade unions covering operational areas appeared brighter: from 20 to 30 per cent of workplaces indicating that this would be their preferred strategy for different aspects of operational change. Direct employee involvement, however, also appears likely to grow in popularity and collective bargaining to attenuate. There is no indication from the data that the prospect of unions being accorded a role in strategic decision-making in the future is any greater.

Where partnership has emerged in both the private and public sectors, its occurrence to date has generally reflected unusual sets of forces, including actual or impending commercial trauma, major programmes of reorganization and rationalization, highly organized unions – capable of blocking attempts by management at bypass or marginalization – and visionary human resources and senior executives willing to pioneer new and untried approaches to industrial relations (Roche and Turner, 1998).

Unions manifestly faced very substantial challenges in pursuing their strategy of extending social partnership to the workplace under the Partnership 2000 agreement. While the pace of activity appears to have picked up during the late 1990s, with partnership agreements coming into force in companies in a number of areas of the private sector, overall progress has been modest. Where partnership arrangements exist in the private sector, they are more likely to take the form of consultative mechanisms, or 'exploratory arrangements', than 'joint governance' models (see Roche and Turner, 1998).

The ICTU issued guidelines to assist local union efforts under the enterprise partnership provisions contained in Partnership 2000. Congress guidelines clearly favoured the institution of partnership, including forms of direct employee involvement, under formal steering-group arrangements, involving trade union officials (ICTU, 1998, pp. 4–5). However, notwithstanding efforts on the part of ICTU and major affiliated unions like the Services, Industrial, Professional and Technical Union to forge ahead with workplace partnership, the priority accorded to the area varies from union to union and within unions across different levels and branches. The partnership agenda may well be competing for attention at workplace level with more traditional union agendas centred on pay and conditions and defending members' interests in circumstances of change. The union position is made more difficult by apparent divergences of view among employers on the advisability of entering partnership arrangements with unions and on the form any such arrangements should take. For example, the membership of the main employers' federation, the Irish Business and Employers' Confederation (IBEC), fearing that the workplace partnership agenda might be exploited by unions to pursue wage gains and to extend the scope of traditional collective bargaining, and faced with a diverse membership base with significant differences of approach to partnership, has adopted a very cautious posture (IBEC, 1998).

Union Recognition and the Right to Bargain

As discussed earlier, the issue of recognition became very significant for Irish unions from the 1980s. Historically, the incidence of disputes and strikes over trade union recognition waxed and waned in Ireland, rising in periods of labour market slackness and declining in periods of relative prosperity. A significant rise in recognition disputes occurred during the 1980s and the issue of recognition remained a flash-point in Irish industrial relations during the 1990s (Roche, 1992a).

Union concerns over recognition obviously reflect the decline in density, examined earlier. Resistance to recognition among employers is concentrated in two main areas: foreign-owned, and especially US-owned, multinational companies in high-technology sectors like computer hardware and software and pharmaceuticals, and usually small but sometimes large Irish companies in manufacturing and service industries. The character of employer resistance is quite different in each area.

In seeking to organize workers in a number of US multinationals in electronics and pharmaceuticals, established during the 1980s and 1990s, unions have faced classic 'union substitution strategies'. Employers adopt well-integrated sets of 'soft' human resource policies, characterized by good pay and conditions, profit sharing, extensive provision for the exercise of employee voice, high levels of investment in training and development, team working and employee involvement and sophisticated approaches to recruitment, selection, appraisal and other aspects of 'flow' management. These policies are adopted in support of union avoidance, as well as to avail of their direct contribution to fostering employee commitment. There is no compelling empirical evidence that the simple adoption by employers in Ireland of these types of human resource policies, even at high thresholds of intensity, of itself reduces the likelihood of union recognition (see Roche and Turner, 1994). What matters is that they have been adopted in certain cases to give force to an explicit policy of union avoidance. In these cases, their effectiveness may be further underpinned by the recruitment of young and well-educated workforces and by locating plants in areas with little tradition of industrial employment or trade union activity. These 'union substitution' companies now manifestly pose a significant obstacle to unions by reducing the incentive to unionize among their employees.

Among new and established Irish companies, unions are more likely to encounter traditional 'union suppression' tactics, focused on the isolation of union activists and on stratagems aimed at removing the possibility of viable union organization. In some instances, recognition is conceded either formally or *de facto*, but unions may not enjoy any meaningful right to bargain: when talks become deadlocked, employers refuse resort to established third-party channels for conflict resolution and dispute settlement.

Union concern over recognition was heightened in 1994 when the High Court found in favour of a small family-trucking company, Nolan Transport, in a dispute with Ireland's largest union, the Services, Industrial, Professional and Technical Union. In what was essentially a recognition dispute, the Services, Industrial, Professional and Technical Union was found to have instituted industrial action to bring all employees into membership. The union was also found to have 'rigged' the ballot for industrial action, contrary to the balloting provisions of the 1990 Industrial Relations Act. Damages and costs of £1.3 million were awarded against the union. The union appealed the decision to the Supreme Court.

Of the options available to unions to counter growing resistance to recognition, a militant campaign aimed at forcing concessions from employers on a company-by-company basis was not seriously countenanced. There were serious doubts as to the effectiveness of such an approach, particularly in the case of multinational companies, where the real danger of 'capital flight' could rebound seriously on investment and job creation. Serious and intense recognition disputes have nevertheless occurred and have been pursued vigorously by unions, though more often and arguably more vigorously in Irish-owned than in multinational companies. Moreover, union leaders have raised the spectre of militancy in the event of no other avenue being open to progress the issue. As in the case of workplace partnership, unions have opted to make progress on recognition mainly within the ambit of social partnership, by seeking to negotiate proposals on union recognition with employers and the state.

In the case of the growing incidence of non-union multinationals, ICTU has expressed concern about the posture of the main industrial development agencies (ICTU, 1995, p. 33). Up to the 1980s, it had been common practice to encourage incoming multinationals to concede recognition and adapt to local traditions of industrial relations. Given the more competitive market now existing for foreign direct investment, this is no longer the case. Currently incoming companies enjoy greater scope to develop models of employee relations reflecting their wider corporate strategies and priorities. The development agencies are no longer persuaders for any one model. ICTU leaders favour a more vigorous presentation to incoming companies of successful unionized models of employee relations.

An ICTU review in 1995 advocated that the general issue of recognition should be taken up nationally and at a European level through the European Trade Union Confederation. It further proposed that the issue should 'not be considered in the abstract', as what was really at issue was the 'right to bargain' through a trade union and to have terms and conditions of employment determined through a collective agreement (ICTU, 1995, p. 34). The prospect was raised of unions changing their stance on the voluntarist principle that third-party machinery for dispute resolution should not be mandatory. A shift to mandatory use of third-party machinery was seen as a potentially effective means of securing a right to bargain in the case of employers who resisted recognition, or in the case of unionized employers who refused to engage in collective bargaining. In the mid-1990s, a bitter and protracted strike over conditions had occurred in Ireland's largest retail chain, and one of its largest employers, Dunnes Stores. The Dunnes dispute pointed to the limits of a union's capacity to represent members when the employer refused to resort to standard third-party mechanisms. In a recognition dispute with the US pharmaceutical company, Elan, the Services, Industrial, Professional and Technical Union had signalled its willingness to countenance a binding third-party disputes mechanism in an attempt to counter the employer's concern that unionization might threaten continuity in the Irish plant's production. In spite of a positive Labour Court recommendation, the union's bid for recognition was unsuccessful. The union's strategy in Elan seemed to amount to an offer of a 'no-strike deal', though it was not presented in such terms.

Unions' willingness by the 1990s to question core aspects of voluntarism reflected the serious situation they faced over recognition and bargaining rights, but some initiatives had also grown up at company level where unions had agreed to forms of binding third-party dispute resolution. These initiatives originated less in problems over bargaining rights *per se* than in wider programmes of change in industrial relations. In both Waterford Crystal and the state-owned broadcasting service, unions had accepted a departure from the classic voluntarist principle of non-mandatory and non-binding third-party mechanisms.

Faced with increasing difficulty in gaining recognition from employers and a legal context made more uncertain by the Nolan Transport judgment, in 1996 the Irish Congress of Trade Unions (ICTU) sought to negotiate provisions on union recognition into Partnership 2000. No agreement on the handling of union recognition was forthcoming, but agreement was reached on the establishment of a tripartite High Level Group to make recommendations on the question. The Group reported in 1998 and advocated a voluntary procedure for resolving recognition disputes, culminating in a non-binding Labour Court recommendation. The unions had favoured the principle of binding recommendations in circumstances where voluntary agreement was unobtainable. The release of the report coincided with a bitter recognition dispute between the Services, Industrial, Professional and Technical Union and the independent Irish low-cost airline, Ryanair. The dispute over recognition for 30 baggage handlers closed down Dublin airport and resulted in a government-brokered investigation. For some sections of the trade union movement, already critical of the failure of the High Level Group to agree a mandatory recognition procedure, the Ryanair dispute only confirmed the impotence of a voluntarist approach in circumstances where employers doggedly refused to concede recognition. During the course of the Ryanair dispute, union leaders claimed that the posture of employers generally towards both the dispute and the issue of recognition showed that support for social partnership was hollow. Some claimed that the dispute and the recognition question endangered social partnership and made it considerably less likely that a further national agreement could be negotiated.

The Supreme Court delivered its judgment in the Nolan Transport case in May 1998. The Court overturned the original judgment and found that the union had validly undertaken strike action primarily to seek the reinstatement of dismissed members. The balloting procedure was heavily criticized but the union was not found to have forfeited its statutory immunities or to be open to damages (see *IRN*, 1998, **20**, pp. 15–17). The publication in mid-1998 of proposals for a mandatory system of trade union recognition in the United Kingdom, based on the balloting of employees in the bargaining unit affected, gave further impetus to trade union calls for a stiffening of the law on recognition in Ireland.

The pressures resulting from the Ryanair dispute, the Nolan Transport judgment and developments in the UK led the High Level Group to review its original proposals and to make new proposals in March 1999. The new proposals retain the emphasis on resolving recognition disputes through voluntary procedures. A significant change was made, however, to apply to 'exceptional' circumstances where disputes proved intractable to the voluntary approach, or the parties failed to follow the steps outlined in the voluntary procedure. In such circumstances the Labour Court will be empowered, under a proposed amendment to the Industrial Relations Act of 1946, to take a series of steps. The Court may summon witnesses and subpoena documents relevant to matters in dispute, hold an investigation and issue a recommendation. Should the parties fail to resolve the dispute within the framework of this recommendation, the Court may issue a determination binding for a period of one year. If at the end of this period the dispute remains unresolved, the Court can issue a recommendation that is binding on the parties in respect of pay, conditions of employment and procedures. These proposals have met with the agreement of the union and employer federations. Their aim is to institute a voluntary procedure for resolving recognition disputes, backed by a so-called 'special fallback position' intended to be invoked only in a small number of exceptionally intractable disputes.

The State of the Unions

In some respects unions in Ireland have gained significant power, influence and legitimacy in the 1990s. As a 'social partner', unions have a voice in formulating macroeconomic strategy, industrial policy, fiscal policy and a range of areas of social policy. The tripartite formula is now commonly adopted in managing public institutions and agencies. The national wage agreements since the late 1980s, combined with changes in taxation, have delivered progressive if modest rises in real disposable incomes. Employment creation in Ireland has outstripped other EU countries and unemployment has declined significantly. Labour-supply shortages have become a problem across both high- and low-pay industrial and service sectors. Economic growth has reached annual levels close to 10 per cent and average living standards in Ireland have converged on levels in hitherto much wealthier EU countries.

In repeatedly entering tripartite agreements, unions in Ireland avoided the marginalization and wholesale demoralization experienced by the British trade union movement in the 1980s and early to mid-1990s. They were, nevertheless, faced with difficult compromises, in particular by having to accept the consequences for public services of tighter levels of control on public spending and the reduction of the debt/gross national product ratio. While acute cuts in health and social services occurred during the second half of the 1980s, overall levels of social security benefits were preserved or improved in real terms (see Roche, 1997). The Irish welfare state was defended and with it the vision of Ireland as a social market economy in the new European order. Poverty, urban degradation and long-term unemployment remain major problems and affect a significant part of the constituency of trade unions.

In spite of the achievements of social partnership, unions have witnessed a progressive erosion of their membership base, rooted mainly in structural shifts in the composition of the workforce and changing employer strategies and postures at sectoral and enterprise levels. The trade union movement is becoming increasingly concentrated in the public sector and in more mature areas of the private sector. Union involvement in tripartism since 1987 cannot be linked in any empirically robust manner with declining density. At the same time, neither can it be said that neo-corporatism over much of this period delivered any specific supports to organization. By seeking such supports through a new mechanism for handling recognition disputes and to some extent through workplace partnership, unions in recent years have tested how far the boundaries of partnership could be extended to encompass the handling of contentious new areas.

During 1999, the last year of the then current tripartite agreement, a significant challenge to the continuation of social partnership arose from acute wage pressure, especially within the public services. Burgeoning economic growth, fiscal buoyancy, information coming to light of widespread tax evasion and low unemployment, had transformed the context of pay determination. Evidence can be found of substantial and widespread pay drift in the private sector. Here, it commonly takes the form of enhanced bonuses and conditions or payments linked to change and restructuring. Inter-company and inter-sectoral wage comparisons, traditionally the key features of pay dynamics in the private sector, are no longer pronounced, and the incidence of industrial disputes remains low. In the public services, the picture is very different. Relatively linked claims have re-emerged, resulting in pay increases for significant groups substantially higher than provided for under the regime of national pay agreements. Militant pay campaigns have been pursued by groups like the police and nurses, which had never before threatened or undertaken industrial action. In short, as the present national agreement expires, the continuation of social partnership is threatened by acute pressures of a traditional kind, rather than longer-term trends in the organizational base of unions, or resistance to the extension of union influence at workplace and company levels.

The Future

Could it be that the period from the late-1980s to the end of the 1990s will in retrospect be seen as both the pinnacle of trade union influence in Irish society and the beginning of a slide towards a progressive erosion of unions' organizational base? By working within the boundaries of social partnership, while attempting also to shift those boundaries in important respects, are

Irish unions colluding in their own gradual demise as an economy-wide economic and social institution? How well equipped are Irish unions to respond to the challenges they now must face? Two scenarios can be outlined in attempting to answer these questions.

The optimistic scenario for unions is that they will be able, based on their agreement to a new three-year social contract, to extend the boundaries of social partnership, to address the organizational challenges now faced and to halt or reverse nearly two decades of organizational decline. Because they remain a powerful economic and social institution, with a membership base widely dispersed across the private and public sectors, employers and governments will continue to find it expedient to negotiate with the trade union movement as a whole. The leverage available to unions will be such as to preserve and even further extend their influence over economic, fiscal and social policy. The centrality of unions could be further reinforced by Ireland's situation in a post-EMU European economy. Deprived of the capacity to use exchange rate policy or interest rates as levers of economic management, and facing a major trading partner, the UK, opting for the present to remain outside EMU, Irish competitiveness will increasingly pivot on the underlying dynamism of the economy's productive base and the flexibility of the labour market. The new economic order may thus be expected to increase the centrality of industrial relations to economic performance. What is more, the human resource and industrial relations policies associated with workplace partnership – in particular, gain-sharing and employee and union involvement in decision-making – may be best able to provide companies with the flexibility required to operate successfully in the new economic order. These policies could also provide companies with productivity-enhancing and profit-enhancing ways of responding to local wage pressures in a tight and dynamic labour market. In this scenario, unions will remain a major actor in the Irish political economy by finding new and creative compromises with employers and the state that serve further to institutionalize the partnership model in new economic and labour market conditions. Such a scenario points towards the development of a social market economy in which unions remain pivotal to economic and political governance.

The pessimistic scenario for unions is that the erosion of the membership base apparent since the mid-1980s will continue and that unions will not be able to halt declining density by extending the boundaries of social partnership. In this scenario there comes a point where it may no longer be critical for employers and the state to engage the entire trade union movement in national agreements. The movement may fragment, retaining strong pockets in the public sector and more traditional areas of the private sector. Wage pressures within these sectors may result in sectoral or company-level agreements with employers and the state. Entire areas of the private sector could simply slip outside the sphere of industrial relations and be governed by enterprise and workplace-level arrangements between management and employees. Should employers and governments no longer need to engage unions generally in economic and political governance, sectional and sectoral interests become more pronounced within the trade union movement.

The actual trajectory of Irish trade unions may turn out to be a good deal more circuitous than allowed for in these scenarios. There may be many negative trends and counter trends ahead and periods of years in which the long-run underlying direction of change will remain unclear. It would appear, however, that, even as they negotiate a fifth consecutive tripartite agreement, Irish unions have good reasons to be concerned about trends in their membership base.

Note

1. The 'DUES' series on trade union membership and density in Ireland, cited extensively in this chapter, was updated by Jacqueline Ashmore to 1995 (the latest year for which complete membership returns are available). Thanks are due to those who cooperated with the updating research. In particular, thanks to Trevor Mendez, Dermot Rafferty and the staffs of the Certification Offices in London and Belfast; to Martin Sisk and the staff of the Registry of Friendly Societies, Dublin; to Paula Carey of ICTU and to individual trade union officials who supplied information. Thanks also to the staff of the Labour Force Survey section of the Central Statistics Office. The work of Joe Larragy, Social Policy Analyst with the National Economic and Social Council, who collaborated on the original compilation of the Irish DUES series is also acknowledged with gratitude, as is Susan Neilson's excellent technical work in tabulating and graphing the data series. None of those who provided data or information bears any responsibility for the analysis and interpretation presented in the chapter. Nor do the views presented here reflect in any way the policy or outlook of the National Centre for Partnership.

References

Bain, G. and Elsheikh, F. (1976) *Trade Union Growth and the Business Cycle*, Oxford: Basil Blackwell.

European Industrial Relations Review (EIRR) 31 December 1999, p. 8.

Gunnigle, P., Morley, M., Clifford, N. and Turner, T. (1997) *Human Resource Management in Irish Organisations*, Dublin: Oak Tree Press.

Hardiman, N. (1987) *Pay, Politics and Economic Performance in Ireland 1970–1987*, Oxford: Clarendon Press.

Irish Business and Employers' Confederation (IBEC) (1998) *Guidelines for the Development of Partnership in Competitive Enterprises*, Dublin: IBEC.

Industrial Relations News (IRN) (1998) 'The Nolan judgement: Supreme Court overturns ruling', *Industrial Relations News*, **20**, 15–17.

Irish Congress of Trade Unions (ICTU) (1993) *New Forms of Work Organisation: Options for Trade Unions*, Dublin: ICTU.

Irish Congress of Trade Unions (ICTU) (1995) *Managing Change: Review of Union Involvement in Company Restructuring*, Dublin: ICTU.

Irish Congress of Trade Unions (ICTU) (1998) *Partnership in the Workplace: Guidelines for Unions*, Dublin: ICTU.

Katz, R. S. and Mair, P. (eds) (1992) *Party Organizations: A Data Handbook on Party Organizations in Western Democracies, 1960–90*, London: Sage.

McPartlin, B. (1994) 'The development of trade union organisation', in T. Murphy and W. K. Roche (eds) *Irish Industrial Relations in Practice*, Dublin: Oak Tree Press.

O'Brien, J. F. (1981) *A Study of National Wage Agreements in Ireland*, Dublin: Economic and Social Research Institute.

O'Connor, E. (1992) *A Labour History of Ireland*, Dublin: Gill and MacMillan.

Roche, W. K. (1992a) 'Modelling trade union growth and decline in the Republic of Ireland', *Journal of Irish Business and Administrative Research*, **13**, 86–102.

Roche, W. K. (1992b) 'The liberal theory of industrialism and the development of industrial relations', in J. H. Goldthorpe and C. T. Whelan (eds), *The Development of Industrial Society in Ireland*, Oxford: Oxford University Press in association with the British Academy.

Roche, W. K. (1994) 'British unions in Ireland: aspects of growth and performance', Working Paper IR-HRM, Nos 94–8, Centre for Employment Relations and Organisational Performance, Graduate School of Business, University College Dublin.

Roche, W. K. (1997) 'Pay determination and the politics of industrial relations', in T. Murphy and W. K. Roche (eds), *Irish Industrial Relations in Practice*, Dublin: Oak Tree Press, pp. 145–226.

Roche, W. K. (1998) 'Between regime fragmentation and realignment: Irish industrial relations in the 1990s', *Industrial Relations Journal*, **29** (2), 112–36.

Roche, W. K. and Larragy, J. (1990) 'Cyclical and institutional determinants of annual trade union growth and decline in Ireland: evidence from the DUES data series', *European Sociological Review*, **6** (1), 49–72.

Roche, W. K. and Turner, T. (1994) 'Testing alternative models of human resource policy effects on trade union recognition in the Republic of Ireland', *International Journal of Human Resource Management*, **5** (3), 721–53.

Roche, W. K. and Turner, T. (1998) 'Human resource management and industrial relations: substitution, dualism and partnership', in W. K. Roche, K. Monks and J. Walsh (eds), *Human Resource Strategies*, Dublin: Oak Tree Press.

Sheehan, B. (1996) *Crisis, Strategic Re-evaluation and the Re-emergence of Tripartism in Ireland*, Dublin: University College Dublin, unpublished M. Comm. thesis.

Sinnott, R. (1995) *Irish Voters Decide: Voting Behaviour in Elections and Referendums Since 1918*, Manchester: Manchester University Press.

Teague, P. (1995) 'Pay determination in the Republic of Ireland: towards social corporatism?', *British Journal of Industrial Relations*, **33** (2), 253–76.

Undy, R., Ellis, V., McCarthy, W. E. J. and Halmos, A. M. (1981) *Change in Trade Unions: The Development of UK Unions Since 1960*, London: Hutchinson.

Webb, S. and Webb, B. (1920) *Industrial Democracy*, London: Longmans Green.

6 UNIONS IN NEW ZEALAND: WHAT THE LAW GIVETH...

Raymond Harbridge, Aaron Crawford and Kevin Hince[1]

Introduction and Context

Unions in New Zealand have historically been creatures of the state. They operated under a system of state patronage in the period 1894–1991, and while their fortunes fluctuated according to the differing political, economic and social environments of that period, those fluctuations were not great as they retained patronage throughout. Hare (1946, p. 174) noted that in other countries the law facilitated the development of potentially strong spontaneous union movements. In New Zealand, however, the greater part of unions would not exist, he argued, if it were not for the state which called them into being as a prior condition to enforcing minimum wage rates. In 1991, New Zealand unions lost their patronage and their distinct legal status in employment law. In losing their patronage they lost their monopoly status, their exclusive rights to represent employees, their rights to compulsory union membership, and their rights to a collective bargaining framework that locked employers into a state-sponsored system of 'awards'. This chapter reviews the background and history of patronage and the effects of its removal on New Zealand unions.

In the private sector, the Industrial Conciliation and Arbitration Act of 1894 introduced a system of compulsory conciliation and arbitration to New Zealand as the primary mechanism of industrial regulation. Registration of unions (of both employers and employees) was a central feature of the system. The long title of the statute gave a clear statement of intent. It was '[A]n Act to encourage the formation of industrial unions and associations and to facilitate the settlement of industrial disputes by conciliation and arbitration.'

Registration bestowed upon a union the right to organize a specific category of workers, the right of recognition for bargaining purposes, and the right of access to a compulsory mechanism (Conciliation Boards and the

Arbitration Court) to determine and to enforce terms of settlements of industrial disputes on recalcitrant employers. Obligations of financial accountability and democratic operation counter-balanced these rights. Compulsory arbitration enabled weak unions to force recognition from strong employers. Non-union labour became increasingly less attractive to employers as awards emerging from the arbitration machinery were statutorily applicable to union and non-union employees alike. Further, the Arbitration Court, interpreting the intent of its enabling statute, began to insert a 'preference for unionists' clause in awards, as and when requested by union advocates.

Registration required the rules of a union, including a membership rule, to be lodged with and approved by the Registrar of Trade Unions. Each membership rule was required to show that a community of interest existed between potential members, and, as a result, membership rules often described specific occupations. Although plant or industry unions were not precluded by the registration provisions, a pattern of occupationally based unions emerged. The Registrar of Unions was prohibited from registering more than one union with the same coverage, thus eliminating competition between unions for members. Further, until 1936, the Registrar of Unions was not permitted to register unions on a national basis. New Zealand was divided administratively into eight geographical industrial districts and the Industrial Conciliation and Arbitration Act precluded the recognition of a union representing members in more than a single industrial district. Unionism prospered. That growth, however, was occupationally based and geographically fragmented.

Unsurprisingly the structure of collective bargaining arrangements followed that of union registration with awards typically negotiated on an occupational or industrial basis to mirror patterns of union organization. The award system established multi-employer bargaining as the mainstay of private sector industrial relations. Centrally negotiated awards set legally enforceable minimum wages and conditions that bound all relevant employers by virtue of the blanket coverage mechanism.

Until 1988, a separate set of institutional arrangements existed in the public sector. Occupational pay rates and other conditions of employment applied uniformly across the entire service. A mechanism of annual general adjustments was used to determine increases to public sector wage rates to ensure these remained broadly comparable with prevailing rates in the private sector. The State Sector Act of 1988 abolished this historical distinction between public and private sector industrial relations and brought the public sector under the same legislation (the Labour Relations

Act, 1987) and the set of institutions that governed the private sector.

Commencing in 1984, a programme of liberalization implemented by the fourth Labour Government had deregulated other markets leading to a decade of substantial and unprecedented economic and structural change in New Zealand. Many commentators have followed the transformation of the New Zealand economy over this period from one of the most regulated in the world to one of the least regulated (OECD, 1989 and 1990). Many have also commented on the exceptional pace of this change (Holland and Boston, 1992; Bollard, 1987).

The underlying basis for the changes that have transpired is the acceptance of supply-side economic theory as an alternative to traditional Keynesian approaches. The deregulation of various sectors of the economy was undertaken as part of a general economic policy shift. Two themes underpinned the deregulatory industry policies: sectoral neutrality of government regulation and intervention; and the promotion of competition (Galt, 1989).

These themes combined to ensure optimal allocation of economic resources in a (free) market environment. At the same time one must acknowledge more pragmatic considerations in the policies being pursued. The fiscal burden of industry protection maintained prior to 1984 was increasingly unsustainable in terms of both poor economic performance generally (resulting in part from poor investment decisions), and specifically in the increasing fiscal deficit and subsequent inflationary pressures associated with it (Galt, 1989). The programme of liberalization can be grouped into seven broad areas: fiscal; monetary; labour; industry; capital; international; and government. Such economic liberalization has had a significant impact on the levels and types of employment within New Zealand. The removal of protections for local industries has caused many to fail; others have used a variety of labour market flexibility techniques to survive.

The purposes of economic restructuring were twofold. First, restructuring was designed to reorientate New Zealand firms and enterprises towards being international businesses rather than providers to a domestic market and, second, it was designed to reform the public service. Its effects are clear. First, fewer people participated in the labour force in the period 1986–99, though participation has grown rapidly in the period 1994–9. Second, unemployment has grown and, despite recent reductions from the very high levels experienced in the early 1990s, remains double that experienced at the outset of the restructuring process. Third, notwithstanding this, overall employment has grown to levels in excess of that reported in 1986, and to its highest level ever in New Zealand's history.

This economic restructuring was initiated under the fourth Labour Government, which held office between 1984 and 1990. The election of a National (Conservative) Government in 1990, with policies of further deregulating the labour market, provides the context for a major change in the relationship between unions and the state.

Unions, the State and Political Parties

The Labour Government that provided the Labour Relations Act (and through it patronage of unions and a regulated labour market) lost office in October 1990. The incoming National Government repealed that statute, and implemented the Employment Contracts Act of 1991 (for an outline of the substantive content of the legislation see, *inter alia*, Anderson, 1991; Harbridge, 1993; Hince and Vranken, 1991). This government saw labour market deregulation as an integral part of the programme of economic liberalization that it was implementing. In October 2000, a new coalition government, which included the Labour Party, passed a new Employment Relations Act through parliament. This Act is briefly discussed at the end of this chapter, with a focus on the future of the New Zealand union movement. Some discussion in this section, nevertheless, centres around the Employment Contracts Act because it has had a radical impact on trade unions.

Part One of the Employment Contracts Act provided for freedom of association and gave employees the right to associate or not to associate with other employees for the purpose of advancing their collective employment interests. Membership of any employee organization was entirely voluntary, and discrimination in employment matters on the grounds of membership or non-membership of an employee organization was prohibited.

Part Two of the Act deals with issues of representation and bargaining arrangements. The Employment Contracts Act abolished the conciliation council mechanism, the Arbitration Court and the concept of an 'award'. All bargaining was to be towards an employment contract; a term that covers not only collective documents (previously known as awards or agreements) but also individual agreements, commonly known as contracts of service. Employers and employees were free to choose who would represent them in bargaining, and both the type of contract, individual or collective, and its contents, were a matter for negotiation. In fact the emphasis on individual contracts, and the lack of emphasis on collective bargaining, was such that the Employment Contracts Act, arguably, fails to meet the requirements of several International Labour Organization (ILO) conventions, particularly Conventions 87 (Freedom of Association and Protection of the Right to Organize), 98 (Right to Organize and Collective Bargaining) and 154 (Collective Bargaining).

The New Zealand Council of Trade Unions (NZCTU) took a complaint to the ILO in 1993 alleging the Act breached ILO conventions 87 and 98. The final report of the review committee upheld the NZCTU's complaint, concluding that:

> problems of incompatibility between ILO principles on collective bargaining and the Act stem in large part from the latter's underlying philosophy, which puts on the same footing (a) individual and collective employment contracts, and (b) individual and collective representation ... In effect the Act allows collective bargaining by means of collective agreements, along with their alternatives, rather than promoting and encouraging it. (ILO, 1995, p. 84; for further discussion, see Haworth and Hughes, 1995)

The Employment Contracts Act did not use the terms 'trade union' or 'trade unionism'. All sections of earlier legislation dealing with membership, ballots and elections within unions were deleted, and all exclusive rights previously accorded to unions were withdrawn. Whilst unions are free to play a role in industrial relations under the Act, they no longer had automatic and exclusive rights in the workplace. Exclusive rights to represent workers in collective negotiations and in processing grievances were two of the key rights abolished. Dependence upon registered trade unions, a characteristic of New Zealand industrial relations since 1894, was abandoned. The statute uses the term 'employee organisation', but such organizations are accorded neither registered status nor any of the historic rights that specifically pertained to trade unions.

In many ways, the Employment Contracts Act 1991 was the modern, legislative expression of antagonisms built up over time between conservative forces, especially rural conservatives, and trade unionism. Overt clashes of authority, especially on the waterfront, in 1913 and 1951, and in the mining and freezing industries typified this relationship (Roth, 1973). The issue of compulsory or voluntary union membership is another example. The first Labour Government introduced legislative compulsory unionism in 1936, whilst successive conservative (National) and Labour administrations made ideologically driven changes. As recently as 1983, a Conservative Government legislated for a voluntarist approach, whilst two years later, fulfilling an election promise to the union movement, the fourth Labour Government reinstated a form of compulsory unionism. The Employment Contracts Act's 'freedom of association' approach was then a natural progression.

Whilst strike action taken by unions was not deemed inconsistent with the presence of a Labour Government, there is no doubt that, as illustrated by the compulsory–voluntary unionism example, a more constructive relationship existed between unionism and the political wing of labour, the Labour Party. For example, lobbying was the basis of campaigns seeking a shorter working week, equal pay and restricted shop trading hours. Lobbying occurred regardless of government, but expectations were higher during periods of Labour Party power. In 1941, the Shop-assistants Union abandoned affiliation to the Labour Party when the Labour Government failed to keep a promise to constrain shop trading hours. The union did not reaffiliate until 1985.

By 1996, only four unions (of the 83 unions operating at that time) remained affiliated to the NZ Labour Party. Admittedly these were large unions and covered some 25 per cent of union membership. However, the decline in the number of unions affiliated, and the proportion of total membership involved, has been dramatic over the period since the mid-1980s.

Reflecting upon the longer historical pattern, Roth (1973, p. 154) asserted that it had become customary to speak of the two wings, industrial and political, of the labour movement. He noted further that the original constitution of the Labour Party made it possible for affiliated unions to dominate the party (assuming that unionists could be persuaded to vote in unison on contentious issues). This provision, as well as the relationship between the party organization and the parliamentary party, were under constant debate during the late 1980s and early 1990s. A split in the Labour Party itself and between groups of union leaders (the formation of the New Labour Party with more historically traditional labour policy positions) was a further reflection of reaction to the 'Rogernomics' economic programme of the Labour Government in the period 1984 to 1990. Currently, it does appear that links, informal and consultative, are being reforged between the NZ Council of Trade Unions and a Labour Party seemingly purged of the more extreme economic rationalist attitudes.

Ironically, this may not reflect anything exceptional in the tenuous relationship of political and industrial labour. Roth (1973, pp. 155–8) provides two illustrative union-sourced quotations. The first, from a union leader in the early 1900s: 'You will gain more in one day by job action than can be gained in a hundred years by political action.' The second quotation is an extract from a 1969 report to the NZ Federation of Labour Conference:

'The NZ Federation of Labour does not attempt to lay down how the NZ Labour Party, as the Government, shall administer the present capitalist system but organised steps can be taken to see that it operate less harshly under a Labour Government than under a National Government.'

Membership

Defining a 'union' was traditionally a simple matter in New Zealand. Private sector employee organizations that were granted registration as trade unions under the Industrial Conciliation and Arbitration Act of 1894, the Industrial Relations Act of 1973 or the Labour Relations Act of 1987 were by definition considered to be 'unions'. Public sector employee organizations that were recognized by the government as 'service organizations' prior to 1988 were not, however, officially listed or counted as trade unions; the data used in this chapter follows this established practice. After 1 April 1988, however, these public sector service organizations were given automatic registration under the Labour Relations Act of 1987, and this boosted the official numbers of unions and union members accordingly.

The passing of the Employment Contracts Act presents particular difficulties in defining a 'union'. The Act fails to provide for union registration and, accordingly, provides no definition or even description of what a 'union' might encompass. This is hardly surprising given that the Act does not use the word at any point. The Act marked a fundamental break with the state's historical interest in regulating the process of collective bargaining. The traditional recognition of unions and unionism and the special position held by trade unions in the system of industrial relations ended. The Office of the Registrar of Trade Unions was abolished, and with it the primary source of data collection on unionism in New Zealand.

We have adopted the international convention (see Visser, 1991) regarding professional and technical associations, considering them as unions where they undertake a bargaining function provided they show a degree of independence from employer control. A small number of single-firm enterprise unions have been included in our sample as unions – even though these unions fail the multi-employer test. Certain 'staff associations' have not been included in our register of unions as we are uncertain about the degree of independence between the association and the employer. In the absence of any official data, we have undertaken annual surveys of existing trade unions and employee associations to maintain a data series on the extent of unionism in New Zealand. We have modelled our surveys on those conducted by the former Registrar, but have included questions on gender and industry breakdown of membership, and on affiliations to other organizations. Unlike those of the former Registrar, our surveys are undertaken on an entirely voluntary basis. While a small number of unions consistently refuse to participate, most are willing to supply us with the information requested.

The data presented in Table 6.1 shows union membership in historical perspective. The data prior to the 1980s reports exclusively registered unions and their membership in the private sector. Investigations by the authors have been unable to unearth reliable data for public sector unions prior to that date. As indicated earlier, public sector service organizations were required to register under the Labour Relations Act as from 1 April 1988. Accordingly, the data from September 1989 is of all registered unions, whether public or private sector.

The data demonstrates the marked impact of the Employment Contracts Act on the level of union membership and on union density, with overall union membership in 1999 under half that of 1985. Union density, a measure of the number of union members as a proportion of the total employed workforce, has fallen from 43.5 per cent to 17.0 per cent over the same period.

The Registrar of Unions had not sought information about unions and their membership on an industry or a gender basis. Accordingly, there is no historical information available. Since December 1991, our survey has asked unions to indicate the number of women members as a proportion of total membership. Overall, in 1999, women made up 18 per cent of union members. This figure has remained relatively stable since 1991, leading us to conclude that men and women have left their unions at approximately the same rate.

In each survey we have undertaken since December 1991, we have asked unions to indicate the distribution of its membership by industry. The results of our first survey for the year to 31 December 1991 and the most recent survey are reported in Table 6.2. The data shows that while union membership has declined across all sectors, the fall has been far greater in some industries than in others. The number of union members employed in the agriculture, mining, building and construction, and retail, restaurant and accommodation sectors has fallen dramatically. A lower rate of decline of union membership is recorded for the manufacturing, transport, communication, finance, and public and community services sectors (the latter sectors including the core public services: teaching, nursing, police and fire service).

Table 6.1 *Unions membership and density, New Zealand, 1953–99*

Year	Unions	Private sector membership	Private and public sector membership	Density (%)
December 1953	412	290,149	n.a.	n.a.
December 1963	382	333,911	n.a.	n.a.
December 1973	309	427,692	n.a.	n.a.
December 1983	248	527,683	n.a.	n.a.
December 1985	259	n.a.	683,006	43.5
September 1989	112	n.a.	648,825	44.7
May 1991	80	n.a.	603,118	41.5
December 1991	66	n.a.	514,325	35.4
December 1992	58	n.a.	428,160	28.8
December 1993	67	n.a.	409,112	26.8
December 1994	82	n.a.	375,906	23.4
December 1995	82	n.a.	362,200	21.7
December 1996	83	n.a.	338,967	19.9
December 1997	80	n.a.	327,800	19.2
December 1998	83	n.a.	306,687	17.7
December 1999	82	n.a.	302,405	17.0

Notes

1: 'Unions' is private sector registered unions only for the period to 1985. From 1989 to May 1991 is for public and private sector registered unions. Since December 1991, data is reported from unofficial surveys of unions as reported by Crawford *et al.* (2000).

2: In reporting union density we have measured the surveyed level of union membership as a proportion of the total employed workforce as measured by the Household Labour Force Survey (Statistics New Zealand, 1998). This method of calculating density is likely to understate the 'true' density figure, as it makes no differentiation between full- and part-time employees, nor does it take account of the number of full- or part-time working proprietors included in the employed workforce figure. Thus, the denominator would tend to be overstated. At the same time, union membership is primarily reported on a full-time equivalent basis, thus understating the numerator.

3: As no reliable estimates can be made of public sector service organization membership prior to 1985, and as the Household Labour Force Survey was only commenced around that time, it is inappropriate to speculate on union density levels prior to 1985.

Sources: Department of Labour, *Annual Reports* (various years); Crawford, Harbridge and Walsh (1999).

Table 6.2   *Union membership by industry, New Zealand, 1991–9*

Industry	December 1991	December 1999	% decline 1991–9
Agriculture, fishing, hunting and forestry	14,234	1,265	91
Mining and related services	4,730	718	85
Manufacturing	114,564	65,172	43
Energy and utility services	11,129	4,574	59
Construction and building services	14,596	3,667	77
Retail, wholesale, cafes and accommodation	64,335	12,038	81
Transport, communication and storage	52,592	34,467	34
Finance and business services	32,219	17,420	46
Public and community service	205,925	162,905	21
Total	514,324	302,405	41

Source: Crawford *et al.* (2000).

The trend towards the concentration of membership in a handful of large unions is clearly visible. In 1981, the combined memberships of the ten largest unions (including the public sector organizations) represented approximately 43 per cent of total trade union members. By 1999, this figure had risen to 78 per cent. Notwithstanding the impact of the Labour Relations Act's '1,000 minimum member' provision, the largest ten unions' share of total membership remained relatively stable over the course of the 1980s. The marked increase in the level of concentration of membership evidenced by the data in Table 6.3 has occurred subsequent to the passage of the Employment Contracts Act of 1991.

Structure and Governance

The net result over time of the Industrial Conciliation and Arbitration Act, 1894, could be summarized as a rapid growth in the number of unions, a rapid growth in union membership, and a rapid increase in union membership as a proportion of the labour force. A further direct consequence, however, was a fragmented union movement comprising a few large but many small (or very small) unions. In 1953 there were 412 registered unions, but 353 had less than 1,000 members. Between 1953 and 1983, the number of unions slowly declined and average memberships slowly increased.

Table 6.3 *Union concentration in the ten largest unions, New Zealand, 1981–99*

Year	(A) Combined membership of ten largest unions	(B) Total union membership	(A) as a percentage of (B)
December 1981	298,976	691,856	43
March 1990	275,854	611,265	45
December 1999	234,405	302,405	78

Sources: Figures for 1999 were calculated from raw data obtained in Victoria University's annual survey of trade union membership, the results of which are reported in Crawford *et al.*, (2000). Data for 1990 were calculated from the Department of Labour (1990). Figures for 1981 were derived from several sources; private sector union membership was taken from the Annual Report of the Department of Labour (1982); data on membership in the larger public sector unions were obtained from Roth (1987, 1990), Simmonds (1983), and Smith and Shadbolt (1984); and the figure for total union membership in 1981 was taken from the Department of Labour (1986). This latter figure represents membership of all registered private sector unions and all public sector unions belonging to the Combined State Unions (CSU) and thus excludes some (smaller) public sector unions and those non-registered private sector unions.

However, as at December 1983, 67 per cent of unions (167) had less than 1,000 members and only 8 per cent of union membership. In fact 25 per cent of unions by number had less than 100 members and accounted for only 0.5 per cent of total membership. The Labour Relations Act, amongst other things, sought to change this pattern of union structure; in particular, it introduced the concept of a minimum of 1,000 members for registered unions. A more lasting impact of this Act was its provisions for state sector unions to join this already skewed governance structure.

Unions (termed 'service organizations') operated in the state sector for postal and telecommunications employees, teachers, nurses, police, fire-fighters, railway workers and core public servants. Such unions were not registered and were not (with two exceptions – postal/telecommunications and railways) subject to the compulsory unionism provisions that existed from time to time. Nevertheless, unionism prospered in the public sector and membership levels were high. The vertical spread of membership encompassed all levels of employees, including the most senior levels of the organizations. With the passage of the State Sector Act in 1988, service organizations were deemed registered under the Labour Relations Act and the Registrar of Unions was given the additional responsibility of applying that policy to recognized service organizations negotiating on behalf of employees of government departments, state-owned enterprises, and health and education services. The service organizations operating prior to these changes were, in general, larger than their private sector counterparts, averaging 7,400 members as compared with 2,100 members. Two very large service organizations dominated public sector unionism: the Public Service Association covering 69,700 members and the Post Office Union with 38,000 members.

The Labour Relations Act provided a legislative framework that brought about what, at the time, seemed to be a significant reshaping of the structure of unionism in New Zealand. Under the impetus of the Act, the number of unions continued to decline, reaching eighty by May 1991. Aggregate union membership, which had peaked at 683,006 in 1985, had declined to 603,118 by this date, and density, which was at 44.7 per cent in September 1989, declined to 41.5 per cent by May 1991. These latter changes were, it can be argued, in anticipation of the intention of legislative change and the introduction of the Employment Contracts Act in May 1991.

Historically, private sector unions in New Zealand affiliated to a single peak body, the New Zealand Federation of Labour. The Federation was formed in 1937 succeeding the 'Red Federation' (a group of anti-arbitrationist unions including miners and waterfront workers), which had been formed in the early 1900s. Public sector unions had affiliated to the Combined State Unions, formed in the 1960s. The NZCTU, the current dominant peak organization of unions in New Zealand, was formed in 1988. It was a merger of two peak bodies, the NZ Federation of Labour (predominantly blue-collar, private sector) and the Combined State Unions (public sector and with a dominance of white-collar, professional membership). The NZCTU has not developed as a strong centre in wage campaigns or on industrial issues, these remaining as key roles within individual unions. A public media face of unionism commenting on issues of the day, occasional crisis intervention and representation in international forums, have been the more noticeable aspects of the NZCTU's role. In fact, for several reasons, it can be argued that the status and authority of the NZCTU has been diminishing.

First, there has been a large decline in the absolute level of membership affiliation since foundation. Although the membership of NZCTU affiliates in 1999 was 77 per cent of total union membership (a modest decline from 87 per cent coverage in 1991) the large absolute decline in affiliated membership has meant reduced resources, financial and personnel, and induced a survival mode of operation. The data is detailed in Table 6.4.

Second, several significant unions, including the Waterfront Workers and Seamen, declined to join the NZCTU at the outset. Later, these unions

Table 6.4 *Union affiliations to NZCTU, 1991–9*

Year	NZ Council of Trade Unions		Trade Union Federation	
	Affiliate unions	Members	Affiliate unions	Members
December 1991	43	445,116	–	–
December 1992	33	339,261	–	–
December 1993	33	321,119	9	20,800
December 1994	27	296,959	11	23,198
December 1995	25	284,383	15	25,424
December 1996	22	278,463	17	22,055
December 1997	20	253,578	17	19,500
December 1998	19	238,262	17	18,012
December 1999	19	235,744	17	17,447

Source: Crawford *et al.* (2000).

created an alternative central body, the NZ Trade Union Federation (TUF), attracting more left-of-centre, ideologically class-based unions as a core. Although the TUF is small in size, with affiliated unions representing just 7 per cent of total union membership, it has provided an additional, often more militant voice.

Third, the focus of the Employment Contracts Act on the decentralization of industrial relations has highlighted a profile for individualized, localized campaigns rather than centralized action. At the same time, the political position of the National Party Government and of national level employers, the New Zealand Employers Federation, has been to downplay tripartite involvement of the social partners in discussion or consultation on industrial, economic and social issues of the moment. Whilst formalized tripartism has rarely been part of the prescription, informal consultative processes at top level had been a consistent feature of industrial relations in New Zealand for many years, at least until the mid-1980s.

Finally, there is a widely perceived significant failure of leadership of the NZCTU in the aftermath of the introduction of the Employment Contracts Bill in October 1990, and its subsequent enactment. The NZCTU had sought to lead a rationalization of the trade union movement. Planning documents were developed, 'The Need for Change' and 'Strategies for Change' (NZCTU, 1989), search conferences and seminars were held and the appearance of a consensus strategy emerged. However, implementation has been in the hands of individual unions and change has been minimal. Individual union organizational strategies have, where such existed, inevitably taken precedence.

Orientation and Strategies

This section considers the strategies adopted by the New Zealand trade union movement in response to the various challenges it faced in the 1990s. Strategies operate at a number of levels and in pursuit of a number of goals. At the broadest level of strategy, the union movement in New Zealand has had to consider its very future in this country. This has been driven not only by the introduction of hostile legislation, but also by global trends (particularly the increasing speed of capital movement and the globalization of production) which have seen trade union membership decline in many Western economies.

The New Zealand Council of Trade Unions' 1994 Search Committee Report gathered together a wide range of representatives from affiliated unions and considered the goals of the union movement and the strategies needed to achieve these goals. The report identified the goal for the trade union movement as the establishment of membership-driven, democratic, well-resourced and well-managed unions that would:

- organize the maximum number of workers

- enhance collective values through effective organization and education of workers

- have an industry focus

- value diversity

- work for inter-union and international solidarity

- have an effective political voice in the community

- have a positive public image (NZCTU, 1994).

These proposed strategies focus on the political and organizational goals of unionism and give little consideration to the traditionally central industrial or economic goals of the union movement (nothing in the above quote, for instance, deals explicitly with collective bargaining). This is indicative of the NZCTU executive's distancing itself from the business union model in favour of a wider political role (see Douglas, 1998; NZCTU, 1996). As part of this political role, the NZCTU has sought to campaign on a programme of alternate policy proposals, part of which was its 1998 proposals for industrial relations law reform embodied in a Workplace Relations Bill (NZCTU, 1998).

Opposition to the NZCTU's direction amongst non-affiliated unions led to the formation of the Trade Union Federation in 1993. The new Federation criticized the NZCTU for being politically conservative and out of touch with the union rank and file, and explicitly positioned itself as a more militant, grass-roots organization (Gay and MacLean, 1997). Consequently, the TUF have adopted a more 'direct action' approach, organizing and supporting public protests against various government policy proposals. While some unions not originally part of the federation have subsequently affiliated to the TUF, they still represent only a small (but vocal) proportion of organized labour.

While the pursuit of political goals generally tends to be the domain of peak bodies, individual unions have been highly visible participants on specific single-issue campaigns; for example the Engineers Union's campaign against changes to the Accident Compensation and Rehabilitation Insurance scheme, and the Post Primary Teachers' Association's campaign on education policy. These campaigns have sought to challenge the direction of government policy on particular issues and mobilize public opinion.

The traditional support of the Labour Party as a vehicle for advancing labour's political interests has largely broken down. During the post-war period, and particularly after the 1951 waterfront lockout and Labour's subsequent electoral defeat, the links between political and industrial wings of the Labour movement weakened. The union movement focused largely on industrial goals and was able to obtain significant advances in wages and conditions for members under National (Conservative) governments of the day, without the same obligations to moderate their actions as they may have felt when a Labour government was in office (Roth, 1973). These attachments were further weakened as a result of the impacts on union constituencies of the industrial and economic policies pursued by the Fourth Labour Government (1984–90). The NZCTU made one bid to negotiate a social contract (the 'Compact') with Labour in 1988, but faced strong opposition from some affiliates who distrusted the Labour Government. Employer groups refused to participate in the process, and the eventual document was far more general than hoped at the outset (Harvey, 1992). Currently just a handful of unions (four) remain affiliated or partially affiliated to the Labour Party.

Securing improvements to the wages and conditions of employment of their members has always been a key industrial goal of trade unions. Collective bargaining with employers has been the traditional strategy for furthering this goal. Under the award system, all bargaining was under-pinned by compulsory state-sponsored arbitration of unsettled disputes of interest. Thus, unionism in New Zealand developed according to the needs of the award system, with collective bargaining, as typically understood, largely circumscribed by arbitrationist approaches. Collective bargaining continued under the Employment Contracts Act, but its structure changed dramatically. Multi-employer bargaining has virtually disappeared. Legal prescription under the Act on the means available to unions for obtaining multi-employer contracts, as well as the ideological opposition to multi-employer agreements amongst employer groups (the traditional role of which was to coordinate such arrangements) mean there is unlikely to be any immediate resurgence of multi-employer bargaining under the new legislative framework introduced in late 2000. Despite this, collective bargaining remains an important role of unions and is still a key organizing tool in most – including those unions moving away from traditional models of organization (see Oxenbridge, 1997).

Official statistics on work stoppages show that the number and extent of strikes has declined over recent years. To some extent this is a continuation of a longer-term trend, but also, more importantly, it is due to the reducing collectivization of the workforce under the Employment Contracts Act, rather than a conscious policy decision on the part of unions to abandon the strike weapon. The data highlights the fact that an increasing proportion of organized conflict is occurring in the public sector where unionism levels have remained relatively high.

The greater legalism of the Employment Contracts Act, and the focus on individual rights meant that personal grievance claims by members demanded a proportionally greater share of increasingly scarce union resources. During the tenure of this legislation, a number of unions embraced new approaches based around the recognition of alternate methods of furthering aspirations and improving the working conditions of members. These examples are innovative in the New Zealand context in that they transcended the traditionally narrow preoccupation of unions with addressing issues of wealth distribution, while ignoring issues of wealth generation. This narrowness can be attributed to the award system's restrictions of the scope of matters unions were allowed to negotiate over – unions were limited to negotiating on a narrow range of 'industrial' matters, leaving 'non-industrial' matters largely to managerial prerogative.

The Public Service Association – to criticism from some quarters – has entered into 'Partnership' arrangements with some employers with the aim of developing an ongoing relationship between the employer, the staff and their union around the identification and progression of their joint interests (Dale *et al.*, 1998). The New Zealand Engineering Union has been active in initiating workplace reform programmes. The basis of this approach is that the job security of its members relies on New Zealand manufacturing being internationally competitive, and that manufacturing enterprises (and New Zealand industry, more generally) face a stark choice between high-skill/high-wage or low-skill/low-wage production paradigms. Consequently, issues surrounding training have been high on the union's bargaining agenda (NZEU, 1991). The New Zealand Dairy Workers Union has also been involved in the reforms of the New Zealand Dairy industry, entering a process of award restructuring which initially maintained multi-employer bargaining. However, this industry contract lapsed in 1997 and was replaced by a series of enterprise or company collectives (Law, 1998).

Ensuring the continuing viability of trade unions has been a key imperative of the adjustment to the industrial relations regime of the 1990s. Attempts to reform union organization away from their occupational basis towards an industry focus preceded the Employment Contracts Act (NZCTU, 1989). Amalgamations and mergers have been the primary means adopted to this end. Typically, the first amalgamations after 1991 were defensive actions in response to rapid falls in membership amongst some unions resulting from legislative change. More recent proposals have taken more strategic and longer-term views, with restructuring still aimed at rationalizing unions along industry lines. There have been, for example, ongoing discussions between four key unions – the Association of Staff in Tertiary Education, the Association of University Staff, the Public Service Association, and the Tertiary Institutes Allied Staff Association – over the establishment of a single tertiary education sector union (AUS, 1998).

The most significant merger, however, in terms of size was the formation of the 'super-union': the New Zealand Engineering, Printing and Manufacturing Union. This was a result of the merger of the Printing, Packaging and Media Union (itself a result of the 1995 merger between the Printing and Related Trades Union and the Journalists Union) with the Engineers Union. In contrast, there are also examples of unions separating from earlier mergers, essentially ones of convenience required by the '1,000 members' rule of the Labour Relations Act, 1987.

Membership levels remain of primary importance for union survival. Under the award system, registration provided each union with a protected pool of members and monopoly rights of representation. With the removal of these protections, and the additional problems associated with the shift to voluntary membership, the spectre of inter-union raiding of members has emerged. As well as maintaining existing memberships, unions face the challenge of recruiting new members and organizing new enterprises. New Zealand unions traditionally had little call to mount organizing drives, being able to rely instead on the compulsion of the award system, and consequently few unions devoted resources to this aspect of union operation (see Harbridge and Honeybone, 1996). 'Innovative' recruitment strategies such as those adopted by the Engineers Union – for example, discounted pay TV and airfares offered to new members – have been viewed with suspicion in some quarters (Gay and MacLean, 1997). A number of other unions have followed suit and sought to provide a range of non-industrial services to both retain existing members and attract new ones. The centrality of recruitment strategies to unions operating in New Zealand during the 1990s has certainly hit home. Much effort, however, has been concentrated on the already organized sectors of the labour force, with inter-union rivalries increasing as a result. Unions have not had a great deal of success in organizing greenfield sites, where employers have been able to use the legislation to refuse entry on to the site.

The State of the Unions and The Future

As this chapter reports, union membership in New Zealand has fallen dramatically (by more than half) since 1985. Union density has decreased from 43.5 per cent to 17 per cent in 1999. The legislative change of 1991 is undoubtedly the dominant force behind this radical turnaround in union fortunes. Deprived of their external legitimacy and their legislatively enforced membership base, unions have had to turn to the business of recruitment and retention of members; issues that, given compulsory unionism, traditionally did not require attention.

Almost without exception, the breakaway, boutique unions operate solely as bargaining agents. They do not have a link with other groups in 'campaigns', either industrial or political. The larger unions (Engineers, Public Service Association, Financial Sector Union) have become more focused on a business model of operation, from the titles of positions (Chief Executive Officer, Manager) to the basis of restructuring operations. The Public Service Association has adopted a business agent model of the organization, with field operatives, each with a span of responsibility determined by a package of contracts.

A real change in the focus of activity towards the workplace has occurred, and action at this level has become the norm. There has been a diffusion of task from the national level that was prevalent under the award system, to the local level. This necessitates greater membership involvement, with assistance from field agents. This was a fundamental change from the 1970s and 1980s although it did tend to replicate the on-the-job activity of the second-tier over-award bargaining that occurred in sectors of the manufacturing and construction industry at that time.

The fall in the number of unions that took place as a result of the Labour Relations Act's requirement for a minimum of 1,000 members initially continued under the Employment Contracts Act. Recently, however, the number of unions has increased as small unions emerge or re-emerge. Individual unions have responded with different levels of vigour to the dramatically different environment in which they find themselves. By and large, their strategies have not, as yet, been obviously effective. It remains to be seen whether they will revive. At the present time, unions as a whole in New Zealand are struggling. Given that the removal of external legitimacy has been the vital factor in union decline, it is arguable that the reversal of this decline can only come about with the restoration of such legitimacy.

Multi-employer bargaining in New Zealand has effectively collapsed. Unions operating in the private sector, with its many small employers, were always particularly dependent on multi-employer bargaining. The New Zealand Employers' Federation, the body that coordinated the employers' side of multi-employer bargaining, has encouraged employers to move to single-employer and individual negotiation. Given this collapse, and without unions adequately resourced to bargain individually with every small employer, the outlook for private sector reunionization is bleak.

With a few exceptions, a significant trend towards 'staff associations' or single workplace/employer unions has not emerged. Perhaps more importantly, unions simply no longer have any institutionalized workplace presence. Employees are able to join unions, but employers could simply refuse to negotiate with them if they so choose. Under the Employment Contracts Act, there was no 'free-loading', for the conventional remedies for such activity – compulsory unionism or some form of closed shop – are not available under that statute. Aggressive and effective recruitment by unions can go some way to combating the problem of free-loading. Other challenges for unions to overcome, if they are to prosper, are the growth of individualism and the need to reorientate in the deregulated environment.

External legitimation by a new government offers some prospect. 'Fairness' in labour market matters was a major plank in the Labour Party's 1999 electoral campaign. A coalition Labour/Alliance Government – formed following the election of November 1999 – introduced an Employment Relations Bill to parliament in March 2000. The explanatory note stated (p. 2):

> In order to address the issues underlying its objectives, the Bill therefore promotes the voluntary organisation of employees via unions and collective

> bargaining as the best means of addressing power imbalances, while giving individuals the choice as to how their terms and conditions are negotiated, either individually or collectively ... In particular, the Bill requires employers and unions to conduct their collective relationships in good faith ... In a bargaining context, however, good faith will not require the parties to conclude collective agreements or specify particular outcomes, recognising that these are for the parties themselves to determine and that the most effective means for settling problems is by voluntary agreement between the parties.

Specifically, the Bill promoted the collective organization of employees by relegitimizing unions and providing for their registration. Registration will require satisfying the Registrar of Unions that the union is democratic and independent of employers, and has appropriate rules. Union membership itself will be sufficient to authorize representation of members. Unions will be given access to workplaces for bargaining, representation and union business including recruitment. Further, a statutory entitlement to paid union meetings and paid employment relations education will exist. New employees are specifically catered for. For the first 30 days of employment, new employees who are not union members but whose work falls within the coverage of an existing collective agreement, will be employed on those terms and conditions of the applicable agreement. After the 30-day period, if the employee has not joined the union, the employee may agree with his or her employer to any changes in terms and conditions. Strikes and lockouts are allowable provided the parties have been negotiating for at least 40 days, and strikes in support of multi-employer agreements are specifically allowable.

The Bill was passed in October 2000. Unions are again legitimized in New Zealand and will be able to meet some of the conditions for union renewal. Unions will have a largely uncontested workplace environment, will be able to undertake inclusive bargaining, and will have a powerful constraint against 'free-loading' – failure to join will disenfranchise the employee from the benefits of the collective agreement, allowing the possibility of an employer offering inferior terms and conditions. All this, however, is likely to operate in a modern environment that is largely free of multi-employer bargaining. Small employers are unlikely to be troubled by the new arrangements – medium and large employers may be. It can be expected that union penetration, density and membership will rise, but to what levels? Given the broad changes in New Zealand society during the 1990s, including industry restructure, changes in work patterns and employer attitudes towards unionism, the increases may not be very significant. Unionism is certainly unlikely to reverse the declines of the 1990s.

New Zealand has traversed a system of industrial relations that for the best part of a century, until the 1990s, promoted state-sponsored collectivism, unionism and bargaining. For a decade, the pendulum swung towards deregulation, promoting individualism and delegitimizing unions. This has had devastating consequences for the trade union movement. In the first year of the new millennium, the pendulum is now certain to swing back, not to the all-embracing system of compulsory conciliation and arbitration, but to a system that relegitimizes unions and promotes collective bargaining. How successfully the pendulum will drift to the centre after a decade of radical labour market deregulation, remains to be seen. The challenges still loom very large for the New Zealand union movement.

Note

1. The research upon which this chapter is based was funded by a research grant from the Public Good Science Fund administered by the Foundation for Research, Science and Technology (FRST Contract: VUW F903). The research team has been led by Raymond Harbridge, Aaron Crawford and Pat Walsh, and most recently has included Ross Nelson and Natalie Shennen.

References

Anderson, G. (1991) 'The Employment Contracts Act: an employer's charter', *New Zealand of Journal of Industrial Relations*, **16** (2), 127–42.

Association of University Staff (AUS) (1998) 'A new union for the new millennium?', *AUS Bulletin*, June, **38**, 1.

Bollard, A. (1987) 'More market: the deregulation of industry', in A. Bollard and R. Buckle (eds) *Economic Liberalisation in New Zealand*, Wellington: Allen & Unwin.

Crawford, A., Harbridge, R. and Walsh, P. (1999) 'Unions and union membership in New Zealand: annual review for 1998', *New Zealand Journal of Industrial Relations*, **24** (3), 383–96.

Crawford, A., Harbridge, R. and Walsh, P. (2000) 'Unions and union membership in New Zealand: annual review for 1999', *New Zealand Journal of Industrial Relations*, **25** (3), 291–302.

Dale, C., Prior, M. and Chambers, D. (1998) 'Manukau City Council & Public Service Association: In Pursuit of Joint Interests and the Challenge of an Industrial

Partnership, Paper presented to IIR 12th Annual Industrial Relations Conference, 11–12 March 1998, Auckland.

Department of Labour (various years) *Annual Report of the Department of Labour*, Wellington: Department of Labour.

Douglas, K. (1998) 'What Lies Ahead?', *Employment Today*, Jan/Feb, **38**, 8–9.

Galt, D. (1989) 'Industry and trade policies', in S. Walker (ed.) *Rogernomics: Reshaping New Zealand's Economy*, Auckland: Centre for Independent Studies.

Gay, M. and MacLean, M. (1997) 'Six years hard labour: workers and unions under the Employment Contracts Act', *California Western International Law Journal*, **28** (1), 45–64.

Harbridge, R. (ed.) (1993) *Employment Contracts: New Zealand Experiences*, Wellington: Victoria University Press.

Harbridge, R. and Honeybone, A. (1996) 'External legitimacy of unions: trends in New Zealand', *Journal of Labor Research*, **27** (3), 425–44.

Hare, A. (1946) *Industrial Relations in New Zealand*, Wellington: Whitcombe and Tombs.

Harvey, O. (1992) 'The unions and the government: the rise and fall of the compact', in J. Deeks and N. Perry (eds) *Controlling Interests: Business, the State and Society in New Zealand*, Auckland: Auckland University Press.

Haworth, N. and Hughes, S. (1995) 'Under scrutiny: The ECA, the ILO and the NZCTU complaint 1993–1995', *New Zealand Journal of Industrial Relations*, **20** (2), 143–62.

Hince, K. and Vranken, M. (1991) 'A controversial reform of New Zealand labour law: The Employment Contracts Act 1991', *International Labour Review*, **130** (4), 475–93.

Holland, M. and Boston, J. (eds) (1992) *The Fourth Labour Government: Politics and Policy in New Zealand*, (2nd edn), Auckland: Oxford University Press.

International Labour Organization (1995) *Case No. 1698, Final Report of the Committee on Freedom of Association on the Complaint Against the Government of New Zealand Presented by the New Zealand Council of Trade Unions*, Geneva: ILO.

Law, M. (1998) 'Mopping up after spilt milk: a survey of union members in the dairy industry', in R. Harbridge, C. Gadd and A. Crawford (eds) *Current Research in Industrial Relations: Proceedings of the 12th AIRAANZ Conference*, Wellington, New Zealand, 3–5 February 1998, pp. 212–20.

New Zealand Council of Trade Unions (NZCTU) (1989) *Strategies for Change: Challenges for the Trade Union Movement of Today*, Wellington: New Zealand Council of Trade Unions.

New Zealand Council of Trade Unions (1994) *Unions Organising for the Future: Report of the NZCTU Search Conference and Responses Developed as a Result of the NZCTU Executive Planning Exercise*, Wellington: New Zealand Council of Trade Unions.

New Zealand Council of Trade Unions (1996) *NZCTU Election Policy 1996*, Wellington: NZCTU.

New Zealand Council of Trade Unions (1998) *Workplace Relations Bill Information and Education Kit*, Wellington: NZCTU.

New Zealand Engineering Union (1991) *Strategies for the Future: The Engineers Union Blueprint for Continued Development*, Wellington: New Zealand Engineering Union.

OECD (1989) *Economic Surveys: New Zealand*, Paris: OECD.

OECD (1990) *Economic Surveys: New Zealand*, Paris: OECD.

Oxenbridge, S. (1997) 'Organising strategies and organising reform in New Zealand service sector unions', *Labor Studies Journal*, **22** (3), 3–27.

Roth, H. (1973) *Trade Unions in New Zealand, Past and Present*, Wellington: A. H. & A. W. Reed.

Roth, H. (1987) *Remedy for Present Evils: A History of the New Zealand Public Service Association from 1890*, Wellington: NZPSA.

Roth, H. (1990) *Along the Line: 100 Years of Post Office Unionism*, Wellington: NZ Post Office Union.

Simmonds, E. (1983) *NZEI 100: An Account of the New Zealand Educational Institute, 1883–1983*, Wellington: NZEI.

Smith, M. and Shadbolt, Y. (eds) (1984) *Objects and Outcomes: New Zealand Nurses' Association 1909–1983: Commemorative Essays*, Wellington: NZ Nurses' Association.

Statistics New Zealand (1998) *Household Labour Force Survey*, Wellington: Government Printer.

Statistics New Zealand (various years) *New Zealand Official Yearbook*, Wellington: Government Printer.

Visser, J. (1991) 'Trends in trade union membership', in *Employment Outlook*, Paris: OECD, pp. 97–134.

7 AMERICAN UNIONISM AT THE START OF THE TWENTY-FIRST CENTURY: GOING BACK TO THE FUTURE?

Paul Jarley

Introduction and Context

American unions entered the twentieth century as a rather insignificant social force. Largely craft-based and concentrated in the cities of the northeast, American labour's mainstream ideology of 'pure and simple business unionism', attracted workers at a slow but steady pace. From a membership base of just over 3 per cent of the nation's workers in 1900, organized labour's ranks grew to just under 12 per cent by 1920 (Troy and Shefflin, 1985), but the 'roaring twenties' proved to be a cruel decade. Rising real wages spawned worker apathy. The federal courts struck down or gutted legislative efforts to provide unions with even limited rights and generally facilitated employer efforts to defeat unions with a combination of suppression (for example, yellow dog contracts, 'the American Plan', and injunctions) and substitution strategies (for example, Welfare Capitalism, company unionism) (Sloane and Whitney, 1997, pp. 70–1). Unimaginative and complacent union leaders failed to meet these challenges. By 1929, organized labour had lost one-third of its membership and 'appeared to have a superb future behind it' (Sloane and Whitney, 1997, p. 71).

Debates about the proper path to union revitalization brought division and rivalry in the 1930s. Division came not so much over the ideology of business unionism, but over the wisdom of recruiting semi-skilled and unskilled workers into organized labour's ranks. The traditional, craft-based American Federation of Labor (AFL) largely ignored semi-skilled and unskilled workers in the new mass-production industries and worked to suppress industrial unionism. Suppression led to division and an eventual reversal of AFL policy after semi-skilled and unskilled workers seeking relief from the dismal terms and conditions of employment that accompanied a general economic collapse began to flock to the more socially-oriented Congress of Industrial Organizations (CIO). Mired in the Great Depression, a desperate national government also turned to industrial unionism in the hope of reviving the economy and improving workers' lives (Kochan, Katz and McKersie, 1986, p. 26). New federal legislation embraced collective bargaining as the preferred method for wage determination. By the end of the decade, worker demand for representation, new legislation and open competition among unions from rival federations for the same workers helped make membership soar. The union movement was transformed into a powerful economic and social force.

The 1940s and 1950s brought the institutionalization of collective bargaining and 'job control' industrial unionism. Wartime imperatives necessitated a government-enforced truce in labour–management hostilities and normalization of industrial relations activities through the promulgation, refinement and extension of both the War Labor Board and National Labor Relations Board rulings. The end of the Second World War brought strikes and more restrictive federal legislation concerning union activities, but the general principles governing industrial relations interactions remained unchanged (Kochan, Katz and McKersie, 1986, p. 33). Sustained consumer demand for mass-produced American goods continued to provide a munificent environment where unionism flourished. Employer efforts to roll back negotiated wage and benefit gains continued on-and-off throughout the 1950s, but an increasing number of employers turned to a policy of accommodation: buying labour peace by yielding to union demands for more generous terms and conditions of employment. The institutionalization process continued and appeared to be strengthened by the merger of the rival peak trade union federations into the AFL–CIO in the mid-1950s. At the time of the newly created federation, aggregate union membership accounted for about one-third of all non-agricultural, and 25 per cent of total, employment.

The character and goals of American unions and the legislation that regulates labour–management relations have exhibited remarkable stability since the 1950s. Yet, union membership and influence have wavered. The decline was slow at first, almost imperceptible. Disclosures of corruption and undemocratic practices in unions such as the Teamsters eroded public support and brought new legislation regulating internal union activities in the late 1950s. Employment shifts from union strongholds in manufacturing to poorly organized service industries; falling win rates in union representation elections; new government legislation protecting individual rather than collective employment rights; and the emergence of a non-union model of employee relations that stressed individual employee development and growth (Kochan, Katz and McKersie, 1986) all contributed to a levelling off of private sector union membership. Only a dramatic rise in public sector unionism kept aggregate union membership growth from falling sharply behind employment increases through much of the 1960s and 1970s.

The early 1980s saw the malaise in aggregate union membership turn to full-blown crisis. Pressure from international and domestic non-union competition combined with industrial restructuring and an economic recession to produce massive job loss in the union sector (Voos, 1994). Legal and illegal efforts on the part of employers to remain non-union intensified (Kochan and Weinstein, 1994; Meyer and Cooke, 1993) and the absolute number of union members began to fall sharply. Unionized employers demanded and received wage and benefit concessions. Non-union wage and fringe benefit increases began to outpace their union counterparts (Kochan and Katz, 1988, p. 378). Formal and informal centralized bargaining structures crumbled as employers shifted the locus of negotiations to the shop floor amid concerns about managerial flexibility (Katz, 1993). Job control unionism and the union's role at the shop floor were threatened by new work-organization principles imported from the non-union sector (Piore, 1991). Rather than instigating changes in employment practices, unions now grudgingly acquiesced to them. Changes in government philosophy only exacerbated these problems. Deregulation increased competition in key industries (Voos, 1994). A conservative Republican administration blamed unions for the decline in national industrial competitiveness. Government enforcement of federal labour laws was relaxed and labour's political message found few supporters.

Today, American unionism finds itself in much the same state it was in at the end of the 1920s. Private sector union density has returned to single digits. Public sector union density has avoided such a free-fall, but union power is again becoming a localized phenomenon, restricted to a few industries, occupations and regions of the country. With few exceptions (for example, the United Postal Service strike of 1997), unions appear to have been on the losing end of the most visible strikes of recent years (for example, Caterpillar, the Detroit Free Press). Survival in the face of fierce employer opposition, government indifference and low worker-instrumentality perceptions are again the issues of the day. Just as in the early days of the twentieth century, debates about the relative efficacy of legal enactment versus self-help, of the virtues of cooperation versus confrontation with employers, and how best to convince workers that unions can improve their everyday lives fill the halls of organized labour. Dissatisfaction with traditional approaches has produced the first successful challenge to the presidency of the peak federation in almost eighty years. The reformers hope to reverse labour's fortunes by adopting a new 'organizing model of unionism' that in some ways represents a return to the principles and practices embraced by craft and occupational unions in the early days of the American Federation of Labor.

Too much can be made of the parallels. Today, government exhibits legislative indifference, more than judicial hostility. No union leader is advocating abandoning industrial unionism where it still has even a toehold, and public sector unionism is a much stronger force than it was in the 1920s. Yet, few would dispute that American unionism is again on the verge of becoming an insignificant social force. There is serious concern among scholars and labour practitioners that American unions will fade into obscurity in the first few decades of the present century.

Detailing the precarious position of American labour facing the new millennium and union efforts to turn the tide using both very old and new methods are the primary subjects of this chapter.

The State, and Political Parties

American unions have been first and foremost private associations of workers that seek better terms and conditions of employment for their members within the capitalist system through direct workplace negotiation with employers (Barbash, 1984). Founded on American workers' 'job consciousness', not 'class consciousness', the AFL's pragmatic 'business unionism' had, by 1920, clearly triumphed over more reformist (for example, the Knights of Labor) and revolutionary alternatives (for example, the Industrial Workers of the World) (Dulles, 1966). The AFL's voluntarist tradition combined with a broad-based American consensus favouring a classic liberal socioeconomic philosophy to sharply limit government's role in setting employment terms. The Great Depression and the CIO's broader vision of unions as social-change agents led to greater acceptance of government intervention. The Second World War even brought some crude experiments with 'corporatist-style' arrangements such as the creation of the War Labor Board. Yet vestiges of the pre-war ideologies and traditions endured and interacted with post-war government policy to maintain a decentralized industrial relations system focused on workplace-level bargaining. The contemporary American system lacks both the ideological orientation and centralized structures necessary to effectuate tripartite management of the economy or industrial relations, and the legal system continues to focus much more on the process of labour–management interaction than on substantive outcomes.

None of this is meant to suggest that American unions are merely apolitical bargaining agents or that workers join unions solely for economic reasons (Fiorito, 1987). On the contrary, American unions engage in both electoral and legislative politics, but the bulk of these actions are complements to rather than substitutes for bargaining activity. Political action in support of wider social objectives is a secondary concern that sometimes generates controversy even among union members (Delaney and Masters, 1991).

Unlike most of the countries discussed in this volume, the mainstream American labour movement has never developed lasting formal ties with a political party (Bok and Dunlop, 1970, pp. 384–405). The primary reasons given for this American exceptionalism include: the lack of a feudal tradition; the attainment of universal male suffrage prior to the advent of national unionism; the absence of a parliamentary system of government; the pragmatic anti-socialist views of early AFL leaders; and a belief in voluntarism (Bean, 1985, p. 26). Although more active in the electoral process today than in the early days of the AFL, American unions have at least formally held to the pragmatic business unionism approach of 'rewarding one's friends and punishing one's enemies' regardless of party affiliation. Endorsements are granted to candidates from either party on a case-by-case basis by evaluating their comparative records on issues of primary importance to labour.

This pragmatic view of electoral politics has not produced balanced endorsements of candidates from the two major political parties or prevented union leaders from taking active roles in party politics. Today, the AFL–CIO and many, but not all, national unions routinely endorse and support through voluntary member contributions and other means Democratic Party candidates for national political office. Endorsements of state and local candidates are less one-sided, but for much of the last fifty years organized labor has 'operated as a pressure group, ideologically, if not organizationally, allied with the Democratic party, but steadfastly eschewing an independent labor party track while maintaining institutional autonomy' (Masters and Jones, 1999, p. 300).

Union electoral efforts complement other traditional interest-group tactics designed to influence government policy. The AFL–CIO and a majority of national unions employ lobbyists to provide information to legislators on issues of interest to unions and workers generally (Delaney and Masters, 1991, p. 322). More recently, the AFL–CIO has experimented with 'issue ads'

– television and radio commercials designed to influence and mobilize public opinion on issues currently being debated before Congress, state legislatures, or during election campaigns (Masters and Jones, 1999, pp. 300–1). In sum, unions have attempted to influence government policy by a two-track strategy designed to elect sympathetic candidates to office and then to lobby them through conventional means much like any other interest group (Masters and Jones, 1999, p. 301).

Somewhat ironically, conventional wisdom suggests that unions have been relatively more successful in those areas where they support legislation of benefit to workers generally (for example, worker health and safety, minimum wage) than in areas of primary interest only to unions and their members (for example, changes in union recognition procedures). Although sorting issues along these lines can be difficult, there is little doubt that unions have failed in their efforts to amend federal labour relations law in ways that would significantly increase union effectiveness. In fact, the bulk of federal labour relations law was passed in the period between 1935 and 1959. Although it can be argued that court interpretation has narrowed the scope of protected union activity over time, the basic character and philosophy of the law has remained largely unchanged since the late 1950s.

Consistent with organized labour's historic interest in collective bargaining, the focus of American labour relations law is on the creation, maintenance and loss of bargaining rights, not worker association *per se*. Under federal law, organizations composed of workers that do not bargain or otherwise deal with, or seek to deal with, employers over wages, hours and conditions of employment are not 'labour organizations.' Such organizations operate outside of the regulatory framework. To be a 'union' in the United States, an organization must be, or seek to be, the bargaining agent for a group of employees in negotiations with their employer.

The dominant legislative framework is the Labor Management Relations Act (LMRA). The LMRA covers virtually all non-supervisory private sector employees outside of airlines, agriculture and the railroads. Airline and railroad employees are governed by the Railway Labour Act (RLA). Agricultural workers are not covered by any federal legislation. Public sector labor relations law is more diverse and has been subject to greater change. Each of the fifty states has legislation, executive orders, or judicial decisions covering its own state, county and municipal employees. Most federal government employees are covered by the Civil Service Reform Act of 1978.

Some details have important implications for the scope and power of the labour unions that operate under a statute, but the basic approach and key concepts driving these laws are largely the same. In general, labour organizations must establish *majority support* among the workers in a well-defined *bargaining unit.* The bargaining unit is a group of jobs that by their very nature employ workers with sufficient community of interests to be covered by a single collective bargaining agreement. Without the mutual agreement of both the union and the employer (or employers), the bargaining unit is typically limited to a group of employees at a single business location, with units composed solely of production and maintenance personnel and units limited to office clerical employees each considered presumptively appropriate. After both the union and the employer have simultaneously conducted campaigns designed to win workers over to their point of view, majority support is typically determined by the results of a government-supervised election among incumbents employed in the bargaining unit. Should a majority favour having a union represent them in negotiations with their employer, that union is awarded *exclusive bargaining agent* status for *all* members of the bargaining unit. Only the union can try to negotiate a collective contract with the employer covering the wages, hours and conditions of employment for all bargaining-unit members. Outside of the sports and entertainment industries, members of the bargaining unit rarely negotiate individual contracts and where they do, any such contract cannot be inconsistent with the collective agreement. Exclusive bargaining-agent status also brings with it a *duty of fair representation*, meaning the union must not discriminate in the pursuit of bargaining-unit member interests on the basis of union membership.

This duty of fair representation is significant because under federal law a vote for union representation is not equated with a vote for union membership. Subject to the negotiation of a union shop agreement with the employer that requires all bargaining-unit employees to pay union dues as a condition of employment, individuals are free to join or not join the union as they see fit. In addition, since enactment of the LMRA in 1947, states have had the right to pass legislation outlawing union shop provisions. Twenty-one so-called 'right-to-work law' states have outlawed the union shop for private sector employees and most states do not permit such arrangements in contracts covering state and local government workers, nor does the federal government in the case of its own employees.

It is also important to recognize that, under American law, majority status only brings with it an employer obligation to negotiate in good faith with the union. It creates an employer *duty to bargain*, not a duty to agree to any of the union's demands. This distinction is especially important in the private sector where many unions do not achieve first contracts. For example Pavy (1994) reports that fifty per cent of unions established in 1987 did not have a first contract after five years. The duty to bargain persists so long as the union continues to have majority support among bargaining-unit employees, but employers are free to unilaterally implement final offers where they are at an impasse with the union. Within very broad parameters, the scope and terms of any agreement are left to the parties themselves and their willingness to engage in strikes, lockouts and other forms of economic pressure in pursuit of their objectives. In contrast, many, but not all, public sector employees are legally prohibited from striking and contract disputes between the parties are ultimately either submitted to some third party for resolution (referred to as interest arbitration) or resolved through legislative action. In both the public and private sector, any agreement that is achieved represents a legally enforceable document and either party can sue in court for breach of contract.

Initially, these legal principles merely codified much of the character of the unions that operated in the middle decades of the twentieth century. Today, these rules also serve as significant constraints to organized labour's growth and evolution. Conceived of as local workplace bargaining agents, contemporary American unions continue to derive their legitimacy, legal recognition and economic power from their ability to achieve and maintain majority support among groups of workers on the shop floor. This requires union organizers to convince adequate numbers of workers that collective bargaining will improve the employment conditions offered by their employer sufficiently to merit paying the costs of forming and maintaining a union. Cultivating such union instrumentality perceptions encourages treating workplace issues in distributive terms, and given the exclusive bargaining-agent principle, not only puts the union in direct conflict with the employer but also pits employees who desire union representation against those who do not. Thus, American unions are always born out of workplace conflict. Where unions achieve legal recognition, survival requires that they continually show a majority of bargaining-unit employees that they remain effective bargaining agents worthy of financial and in-kind support. Where they fail to achieve or lose majority support, the concept of exclusive bargaining-agent status precludes minority unionism (with a limited exception of consultation rights for most federal employees). Even where substantial minorities of workers support unionization, they are effectively denied union representation and, in most instances, any real motivation for union membership.

PAUL JARLEY

Membership

Perhaps no single indicator better summarizes the health of a labour movement than membership change. Virtually all union activities directly or indirectly contribute to membership change, either by helping to attract new members or to retain old ones (Fiorito, Jarley and Delaney, 1995, p. 623). Outside of the building trades and longshoring, union membership is more a collective than individual decision. As alluded to earlier, to be eligible for membership most workers must either have a job in a bargaining unit represented by a union or convince a majority of their coworkers in a bargaining unit to support union representation. In reviewing the numbers presented below, keep in mind that the vast majority of bargaining units were formed years ago and that many of these bargaining units are covered by contracts that include a union shop provision. Thus, the vast majority of people who have entered or left the ranks of organized labour over the last few decades did so not because they made a conscious decision to seek or drop union membership but because they merely accepted or lost a job covered by a union contract. Table 7.1 reports both US union membership and density figures for selected years since 1900. As noted in the introduction, American unionism was a very modest force at the turn of this century, with less than a million members. Membership advanced in the first two decades, but retreated sharply in the 1920s, totalling just over 3.4 million workers or 6.8 per cent of total employment in 1930. The golden age of American unionism occurred between 1936 and 1956. During that time, membership increased by over 400 per cent and union density went from just 7.4 per cent to 25.2 per cent of total employment. Union density peaked in 1956, but membership continued to grow until about 1980, then fell sharply. In just five years between 1980 and 1985, aggregate membership fell by 24 per cent. It fell by only another 1.5 per cent in the last half of the 1980s and has experienced some small fluctuation in the 1990s. Yet, despite modest net increases in 1993, 1994, 1998 and 1999, it is still lower in 1999 than it was in 1990. Membership as a percentage of total wage and salary employment stood at just 13.9 per cent in 1999. Factoring in the 1.7 million non-union workers in bargaining units represented by a union in that year yields a contract coverage figure of around 15.5 per cent of total employment in 1999.

These aggregate figures mask important variation in density levels and change by sector, industry, occupation and region. As Table 7.2 reports, private sector union membership as a percentage of private sector non-agricultural employment fell almost 8 percentage points between 1980 and 1985, and has continued to drop, albeit at a slower pace. By 1999, private

Table 7.1 *Aggregate US union membership and total density, 1900–99*

Year	Membership	Total density (%)
1900	932	3.3
1910	2,169	5.9
1920	4,823	11.7
1930	3,401	6.8
1935	3,728	6.7
1940	8,717	15.5
1950	14,267	22.3
1956	17,490	25.2
1960	17,049	23.6
1970	19,381	22.6
1976	19,634	20.3
1980	22,366	20.9
1985	16,996	18.0
1990	16,740	16.1
1991	16,568	16.1
1992	16,390	15.8
1993	16,598	15.8
1994	16,748	15.5
1995	16,360	14.9
1996	16,269	14.5
1997	16,110	14.1
1998	16,211	13.9
1999	16,477	13.9

Sources: see Masters (1997, p. 44) and US Bureau of Labor Statistics (2000).

sector union density was just 9.4 per cent. Within the private sector, all seven industrial classifications experienced large declines, with traditional union strongholds experiencing double-digit losses in union density between 1980 and 1999: transportation and public utilities (−22.5 percentage points); mining (−21.5 percentage points); manufacturing (−16.7 percentage points); and construction (−12.5 percentage points). Public sector unionism, on the other hand, increased slightly over the same period, gaining about 2.3 percentage points. By 1999, seven million union members were employed in the public sector compared to 9.4 million in the private sector. American unionism is becoming a public sector phenomenon. Overall, union density is highest in the government sector (37.3 per cent) followed by transportation and public utilities (25.5 per cent) and construction (19.1 per cent). The service, wholesale and retail, and finance and insurance industries all have density rates below 6 per cent.

Table 7.2 *Density by industry, USA, 1980–99*

Industry	1980	1985	1990	1999
Mining	32.1	17.3	18.0	10.6
Construction	31.6	22.3	21.0	19.1
Manufacturing	32.3	24.8	20.6	15.6
Transportation and public utilities	48.0	37.0	31.6	25.5
Wholesale and retail trade	10.1	7.2	6.3	5.2
Finance and insurance	3.7	2.9	2.5	2.1
Service	8.9	6.6	5.7	5.5
Private sector (no agriculture)	22.3	14.6	12.1	9.4
Government	35.0	35.8	36.5	37.3

Sources: see Masters (1997, p. 48) and US Bureau of Labor Statistics (2000).

An examination of density by occupation (Table 7.3) underscores the increasing importance of public sector unionism, as well as the persistent weakness of unions in the growing retail and service occupations. Protective service occupations, the bulk of which are found in the government sector, exhibit the highest union-density figure (38.2 per cent). Three other occupational groups (transportation and moving, machine operators, and craft) exhibit density rates above 20 per cent. These jobs are easily characterized as blue collar. In contrast, three white-collar occupations (sales; executive, administrative and managerial; other services) exhibit single-digit density rates, with sales occupations being the least unionized (4.1 per cent). Over the ten-year period, no group showed an increase in union density and the rank order of occupations by union density remained largely unchanged. Despite membership losses, the locus of union activity remains in blue-collar occupations.

Union densities by selected demographic groups are presented in Table 7.4. Men continue to exhibit higher rates of unionization than women, but the decline since 1985 for women has been much less pronounced than for men. The same can be said for the differential between part-time and full-time employees. Part-time union density remains lower but has been the more stable. Blacks continue to exhibit higher-density rates than whites or hispanics, but the differences in union density by race have also narrowed substantially since 1985. The relationship between union density and worker age is an inverted 'u' shape. It tends to rise until about age 55 and declines thereafter. A comparison of union density by age in 1999 and 1985 shows that the relationship between density and age has remained basically the same over this time frame.

Table 7.3 *Density by occupation, USA, 1985–99*

Occupation	1985	1990	1999
Executive, administrative and managerial	6.5	6.0	5.6
Professional specialty	22.5	21.4	19.7
Technicians	11.8	11.5	11.0
Sales	6.0	5.0	4.1
Administrative support	13.5	13.6	12.2
Protective services	39.2	38.9	38.2
Other services	10.8	9.9	8.5
Craft	28.5	25.9	22.4
Machine operators	34.1	27.1	20.5
Transportation and moving	33.5	28.6	22.8
Handlers	26.1	23.1	18.9
Farming, forestry, and fishing	5.5	4.9	5.8

Source: US Bureau of Labor Statistics (1986–2000).

Table 7.4 *Density by selected personal characteristics, USA, 1985–99*

Characteristic	1985	1990	1999
Age			
16–24	7.9	6.4	5.7
25–34	18.2	14.0	11.9
35–44	23.9	20.2	15.2
45–54	25.5	22.3	19.8
55–64	25.0	21.6	17.8
65+	9.8	8.9	8.1
Gender			
Male	23.0	18.8	16.1
Female	13.8	11.7	11.4
Race			
White	18.0	15.5	13.5
Black	25.9	21.1	17.2
Hispanic	n.a.	14.8	11.9
Employment status			
Full-time	21.5	18.1	15.5
Part-time	7.3	7.0	6.9

Source: US Bureau of Labor Statistics (1986–2000).

Finally, Table 7.5 summarizes union density by state. These figures show considerable variation in density across states, ranging from almost twice the national average in Hawaii (27 per cent) to just 4 per cent in North Carolina. Density rates tend to be highest in the northeast, Pacific Coast, and Great Lakes states and lowest in the southeast and southwest parts of the United States. Many of these latter states have passed 'right-to-work' legislation rendering union shop provisions in collective bargaining agreements unenforceable. Most striking is the change in state union-density figures from 1983 to 1998. In 1983, 22 states had union-density rates of at least 20 per cent. By 1998, only six could make that claim. The change at the bottom of the distribution is even more pronounced. In 1983, only four states had union-density rates below 10 per cent. In 1998, 19 states failed to exhibit double-digit union density. Two states, North and South Carolina, had density figures at or below 5 per cent.

Table 7.5 *Union-density rates by state, USA, 1983 and 1998*

Union density	1983	1998
Greater than 30%	2	0
Between 29.9% and 20.0%	20	6
Between 19.9% and 10.0%	24	25
Less than 10%	4	19
Union density	20.1	13.9

Source: Troy and Sheflin (1985) and Hirsch and Macpherson (1999).

Together, these figures show that the typical union member of today is more likely to be female, a racial minority, and to work in the public sector than was true in years past. The data suggests a more inclusive labour movement, but the key point is that it is much smaller than previously. All told, the numbers suggest that unionism has again become a localized phenomenon, with a significant presence in just a few industries, occupations and geographic regions. Private sector unionism is in a very bad way, with density below 10 per cent and falling. Many industries that were once traditional union strongholds have experienced declines in density of almost 50 per cent since 1980. Any membership gains in private sector growth industries such as the service sector have failed to keep pace with expanding employment. Few states have maintained union-density rates above 20 per cent and many have dropped below 10 per cent, seriously limiting organized labour's ability to act as a significant political force at the state and local level.

Structure and Governance

The lone peak trade union federation is the AFL–CIO. The Federation's basic structure is presented in Figure 7.1. Its 68 national and international union affiliates are comprised of roughly 50,000 local unions totalling about 13 million members. Another 30 or so local unions remain directly affiliated with the AFL–CIO because no national union affiliate has been given jurisdiction over their members. The AFL–CIO maintains a number of departments to service the needs and coordinate the activities of its national union affiliates, as well as 51 state central bodies that perform similar functions for its members' local unions and almost 600 local central bodies formed by the AFL–CIO to help local unions coordinate activities within their communities.

Affiliation with the AFL–CIO is voluntary. Approximately three million union members are represented by one of about 40 independent national unions, including the National Education Association, the nation's largest union (Robinson, 1992). Most of the unaffiliated national unions represent government or white-collar employees and many have less than 25,000 members. About 1,500 local unions are not affiliated with any higher-level organization (Jacoby and Verma, 1992). These independent local unions tend to operate on an enterprise basis, representing the employees of a single company or plant.

By international standards, the AFL–CIO is weak. The national unions that formed the AFL were dissatisfied with what they saw as excessive centralized control exercised by the Knights of Labor (Dulles, 1966, p. 161). They created an organization based on the principle of national union autonomy and gave the AFL virtually no control over the affiliates. The CIO, having created several of its affiliates, exercised more control over them than did the AFL (Herman, 1997, p. 81), but the merged federation's constitution requires affiliates to abide by only a few general rules. AFL–CIO member unions must promise to remain free of corruption and Communist influences, practice non-discriminatory policies, refrain from raiding the membership of other affiliates, and submit jurisdictional disputes over work assignments to binding arbitration. They also pay membership dues on a per capita basis, but the Federation controls only about one per cent of total US union resources (AFL–CIO Executive Council, 1996b). The only power the AFL–CIO has to enforce compliance with these rules is expulsion from the organization; a power it has used sparingly and with limited effect over the years. The Federation has no authority to replace national union officers, change their rules or dictate their policies or actions. Affiliates are also free to withdraw from the Federation at any time.

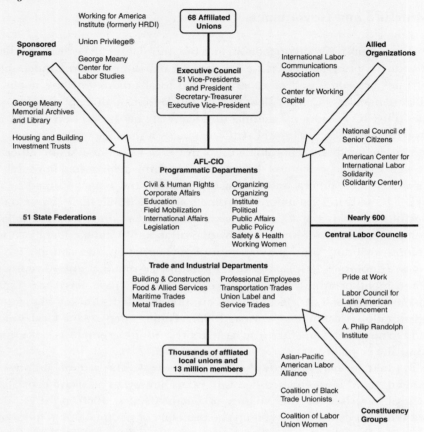

Figure 7.1 *AFL–CIO structure*
AFL–CIO homepage: www.aflcio.org/about/meet_work.htm

Nonetheless, the AFL–CIO is not powerless and its role and influence varies across the set of activities common to all labour movements in English-speaking countries. A primary role has always been to pursue the common political interests of its affiliates and workers generally. The AFL–CIO plays a key role in setting organized labour's political agenda, devotes considerable financial and in-kind resources to help endorsed candidates win public office, lobbies law-makers to influence legislation, and sponsors radio and television ads designed to influence public opinion and voters on key issues. The Federation also plays an important role in organizing. In their early days, the AFL and the CIO focused on creating new national unions. Today, organizing assistance focuses on helping established unions recruit new members through research on the organizing process, training programmes designed to improve organizer effectiveness, and coordination of multi-union organizing campaigns in specific communities or industries. In other areas, the AFL–CIO's influence and activities are more muted. The Federation does not engage in collective bargaining with employers. Through its various departments, it does offer venues where unions operating in the same industry or with the same employers can coordinate their goals and activities, but it is the participating national unions that determine the scope and substance of any coordinated effort. The AFL–CIO does get involved in industrial disputes, but only by invitation and typically to provide technical, moral and financial support to a union locked in a prolonged battle with an employer. Boycott actions, assistance in comprehensive campaign planning and execution, and special financial assessments to support strikers often accompany AFL–CIO involvement.

The true power centres of the American labour movement are the national unions. Nationals set bargaining, organizing and political goals, collect revenues, and devise and implement policies. They also exercise supreme authority over the affairs of their locals. Historically, local unions created national unions and submitted to their authority in order to coordinate activities and gain control over geographically expanding labor (Ulman, 1966, pp. 150–2) and product markets (Andrews, 1936). Today, the scope of the labour and product markets in which the national union operates still goes a long way towards explaining the degree of operational control national unions exercise over their locals, especially in bargaining matters (Hendricks, Gramm and Fiorito, 1993). For example, some national unions must approve all locally negotiated collective bargaining agreements; others do not. Some leave organizing largely to local officials (for example, business agents in construction unions), while others employ national union staff for this activity.

National unions vary considerably in size, jurisdiction and internal organization. The largest union, the National Education Association, claims more than two million members, mostly teachers. Others unions, such as the Major League Umpires Association, have less than one hundred members. Larger unions and those with more heterogeneous memberships tend to have more complex internal structures (for example, more functional departments, coordinating councils, and caucuses for members with similar interests) to accommodate their members' more diverse needs and interests (Jarley, Fiorito and Delaney, 1997).

Both the number and internal structure of national unions have been greatly affected by the general decline in union membership over the last two decades. In an effort to maintain membership levels and revenues, many national unions expanded their jurisdictions (Seeber, 1984), sometimes without adequately considering whether workers from these new sectors shared sufficient interests with workers in their historic jurisdiction (Chaison and Dhavale, 1990). Although few nationals would qualify as true general unions willing to admit anyone regardless of industry or occupation (for example, the Teamsters), many have become multi-industrial (for example, United Auto Workers) or multi-occupational/craft organizations (for example, Service Employees Union).

Such jurisdictional expansion has often come through merger activity. The AFL–CIO has been in favour of union mergers since its founding in 1955. More recently, a report by its Committee on the Evolution of Work (1985, p. 30) hinted that elements within the Federation were especially concerned that national unions with less than 50,000 members were incapable of adequately servicing members or operating as effective bargaining agents. However, the Committee merger recommendations were never fully implemented by the Federation and it has remained characteristically passive in the merger process. The Federation offers encouragement and technical assistance, but ultimately defers to national union autonomy over merger decisions. Nevertheless, the number of national unions has declined more rapidly than membership in recent years, almost entirely as a result of mergers and absorptions.

Chaison (1996, pp. 17–50) convincingly argues that the poor prospects for membership recovery through other methods, such as organizing and employment growth in unionized firms, have pushed several national unions into voluntary mergers. Coincident with the dramatic decline in union membership that began in 1980, there has been an appreciable upswing in mergers. Between 1980 and 1994, the USA experienced 57 union mergers; an average of 3.8 mergers per year compared to just 2.5 per year from 1956 to 1979 (Chaison, 1996, p. 25). The vast majority of the post-1980 mergers (91 per cent) involved larger unions absorbing smaller ones. Fewer political hurdles must be overcome in absorbing a small union than in amalgamating with an organization of similar size. Yet the popularity of absorptions also reflects the primary incentives behind merger activity in the post-1980 period: large unions seeking quick membership fixes, financial stability and a means of spreading risk through diversification are courting small unions with limited resources and growth potential with offers of job security for officers and staff, and promises of better service to their members.

More recent evidence suggests that the merger wave is continuing. From 1992 to 1997, 18 AFL–CIO affiliates have merged (Parks, 1997, p. 16). Three unions were especially active over this period. The United Food and

Commercial Workers added 155,000 members through four mergers. The Steelworkers completed two mergers involving 116,000 members and the Service Employees added 40,000 members through various merger activities. Absorptions remain the more popular merger type, but some, such as the 85,000-member Retail, Wholesale and Department Store Union's decision to join the United Food and Commercial Workers, involve unions of significant size. Significant amalgamations have also been completed or are in the process of completion. The merger of the International Ladies Garment Workers Union with the Amalgamated Clothing and Textile Workers to form the Union of Needletrades, Industrial and Textile Trades in 1995 involved two unions in the apparel industry that had experienced significant declines in membership over the years. Amalgamations among larger unions appear to be motivated by a desire to match increases in employer size, diversification and sophistication (Parks, 1997). Yet the recent experiences of the American Federation of Teachers and the National Education Association, as well as the drawn-out proposed three-way combination of the Auto Workers, Machinists and Steelworkers shows that the political obstacles to such unification efforts remain robust.

Another emerging trend involves national union efforts to grow by affiliating independent local, regional or state labour organizations (Chaison, 1996, pp. 41–5). Rationales and approaches seem to vary a bit by union. Some, such as the American Federation of State, County and Municipal Employees, strategically target independents in geographic areas where they lack a presence but believe the area is ripe for traditional organizing efforts. The new affiliate serves as a base to launch organizing campaigns. Others, such as the United Food and Commerical Workers, absorb 'neighbours' in an effort to increase membership while simulta-neously holding down administrative costs. The primary motivation for affiliation by the independent union appears to be changes in their environment that threaten the historic balance of power between them and the employers in their jurisdiction. Protection against membership raids by other AFL–CIO affiliates appears to be another motivation.

Such affiliations may be one factor contributing to an increase in the percentage of union members represented by AFL–CIO unions. In 1975, 64 per cent of all union members were represented by an AFL–CIO affiliate. By 1995, that number had increased to 79 per cent. Another factor has been the decision of some large independent national unions to seek shelter within the Federation during difficult times. The most notable examples involve the reaffiliations by the Auto Workers in 1981, the Mineworkers in 1989 and the Teamsters in 1997.

An outside observer examining these trends might conclude that the American labour movement is becoming increasingly centralized. With almost all major unions affiliated with the AFL–CIO, its power would appear to be enhanced. In addition, as just discussed, mergers have placed more union members under the control of a small number of national unions. Masters (1997, p. 66) notes that at the time of the AFL–CIO merger in 1955, the top 28 unions accounted for 54 per cent of all union members. By the mid-1980s, that figure had stabilized at about 80 per cent. Appearances can, however, be deceiving. Recall that respect for national union autonomy gives the AFL–CIO little direct influence over national unions. The degree of control exercised by national unions over their constituent elements varies, making it difficult to generalize. Merger and affiliation agreements often preserve much of the absorbed unions' autonomy, creating mini-federations rather than fully integrated organizations. The breakdown of centralized bargaining structures in many industries during the 1980s, employer efforts to shift bargaining to the shop floor, and union efforts to increase members' participation in union affairs discussed below, have also worked to shift the locus of decision-making down to the local level. These developments may have mitigated much, if not all, of the effects of mergers on centralization of decision-making.

Strategies

The decentralized structure and governance of the American labour movement has conditioned its response to the contemporary environment. Over the last fifteen years or so, the AFL–CIO has taken an increasingly proactive leadership role in assessing problems and developing solutions, but it remains, on most issues, an advisory body. The Federation has established task forces, issued reports, developed new technical expertise, and on occasion, even offered affiliates matching funds to undertake new initiatives. All of this activity, however, merely provides national unions with an analysis of labour's common problems and an incentive structure for adopting specific solutions. Each affiliate is free to reject any or all of the Federation's agenda and develop its own response to what it perceives as its unique situation. Unions operating outside of the Federation seem even more likely to develop and implement alternate strategies. Early survey evidence on national unions' uneven adoption of the Committee on the Evolution of Work's (CEW) 1985 report recommendations (Jarley, Delaney and Fiorito, 1992) underscores the potential pitfalls of generalizing from AFL–CIO activities to the American labour movement as a whole. Recognition of the variance across national unions in their control over local unions adds further reason to be cautious about any such generalizations.

In reality there has been, and continue to be, a variety of responses to contemporary conditions, with some actions engendering greater inter-union coordination than others. That said, AFL–CIO initiatives do reflect, in at least general terms, the preferences of the national union coalition that comprises the Federation leaderships' power base. The size of this coalition and the AFL–CIO's publicity machine make its activities the single most identifiable and important set of responses to current events. The Federation's superior ability to disseminate information about its initiatives throughout the labour movement also increases the likelihood that its successful innovations will eventually be adopted (and adapted) by most national unions. None of this is to suggest that AFL–CIO actions and policies are superior to those espoused by dissident unions; only that at any point in time, AFL–CIO-endorsed approaches are likely to be those most widely adopted and its reform programme most indicative of the general, short- to medium-term direction of future change. It is for these reasons that the Federation's actions are given special attention throughout this section.

In the early 1980s, American unions were largely in a state of denial. Membership declines and concession bargains were seen as primarily the result of transitory economic and political forces. Recovery from deep economic recession and a change in government were expected to go a long way towards curing labour's ills (for a more detailed discussion, see Kochan and Katz, 1988, pp. 43–8). The basic strategy was to try to hold the line in bargaining with employers, while engaging in political activities to unseat 'Reagan Republicans' and enact labour law reform that would 'fix' the problems in the regulatory system. Proposed changes focused on facilitating organizing at non-union workplaces and increasing penalties on illegal employer activity. Labour did not seek radical revisions that would redefine its role; only changes meant to restore the balance of power in conventional labour–management relations. In general, the last fifteen years have seen a broader approach as political stalemate, the continued decline in union density, and a new AFL–CIO leadership combined to revive interest in organizing, force serious discussions about internal reform and promote experimentation across many union activities. The basic elements of labour's contemporary strategy are now reviewed and contrasted with the approach of the late 1970s and early 1980s.

PAUL JARLEY

Politics

Politics has remained the most stable dimension of union strategy. Unions continue to endorse and offer financial and other in-kind forms of support to pro-union candidates, most of whom are Democrats, while working to defeat anti-union candidates most of whom are Republicans. Union financial political contributions have increased substantially since 1980, but remain far behind the dollars flowing to their corporate and trade association counterparts (Masters, 1997, pp. 121–3). Just how many election outcomes have hinged on union support or opposition is difficult to judge. Few candidates have made labour relations reform a focal issue in their election campaigns. Rank-and-file union members generally vote for the candidates endorsed by their unions (Delaney and Masters, 1991, p. 332), but such endorsements are frequently used by opponents to label candidates as serving 'special interests'. Delaney and Masters (1991, p. 326) report that union-endorsed candidates did win a majority of Congressional elections from 1978 to 1988, but because many union-endorsed candidates were incumbents, it is difficult to separate out the effects of such endorsements from those of incumbency.

What is clear, is that these electoral activities have not significantly shifted the balance of power in Washington to organized labour's advantage. Consistent with the experience of much of the 1960s and 1970s, union-backed bills of value to workers generally, such as increases in the minimum wage, protection against discrimination based on disability, and unpaid leaves for family medical reasons, were enacted into law during the late 1980s and early 1990s. Labour has also been largely successful in defeating employer attempts to roll back existing union rights, but it has failed to pass legislation that would extend or strengthen those rights (Delaney and Schwochau, 1993, p. 283). Divided government and public apathy continue to produce political stalemate. The Dunlop Commission experience is a case in point. AFL–CIO support of Bill Clinton's successful presidential campaign was rewarded with the appointment of a blue-ribbon panel to recommend changes in industrial relations law in 1993. The Commission's final report, issued in 1995 after Republicans gained control of Congress, failed to generate much support and even drew considerable criticism from the AFL–CIO. Ultimately, it was used by Republicans seeking to relax the law's prohibition of company-dominated labour organizations. The Republican-sponsored legislation, known as the TEAM Act, eventually passed Congress, but was vetoed by President Clinton.

Political stalemate at the national level has encouraged both unions and

employers to seek legislative change at the state level. Both parties believe that victory in one state can be used to generate momentum for its initiatives in other states and nationally. Recent initiatives include union efforts to bar employers from using strike replacement workers and employer efforts to require that each union member give annual written permission before any of their dues money can be used for political activities. Although these initiatives have yet to produce a significant victory for either side, considerable resources have been flowing to these activities. For example, it has been reported that $7.5 million out of the $28 million the AFL–CIO had targeted for political activity in 1988 was used in just three states to defeat ballot initiatives designed to restrict union political activity (Edsall, 1988). Some of the remaining money went to influence key local races for political office (Edsall, 1998). The growing importance of local politics is also illustrated by a new AFL–CIO's '2000 in 2000' initiative designed to encourage 2,000 union members to run for government office in the year 2000 (Hall, 1998).

This initiative is a natural outgrowth of the AFL–CIO's long-standing desire to have more friends in office. It is not an attempt to end labour's historic relationship with the Democratic Party. In contrast, a few national unions, including a couple of AFL–CIO affiliates, have moved to form an independent Labor Party (White, 1998). Frustrated by an inability to advance a pro-union political agenda and outraged by key Democrats' support for the North American Free Trade Agreement (NAFTA), the party held its first convention in 1998. Third parties have received more attention in the USA in recent years, but the infant Labor Party has been largely ignored by the general public, not to mention the country's largest unions, although some locals from a variety of national unions have affiliated (White, 1998). The party failed to have any significant impact on the AFL–CIO's endorsements and contributions to candidates from established parties for the year 2000 elections.

The dim prospects for national legislative reform have also forced American unions to look inward. Public acknowledgment by the AFL–CIO that union resurgence required changes in union policies and practices, not just legal reform, came in 1985 with the CEW's second report. Since that time, the Federation has increased its efforts to provide greater leadership in promoting national union reform and inter-union coordination, while simultaneously encouraging greater grassroots activity through policies designed to decentralize union decision-making and mobilize the membership. Many of these activities started under former President Lane Kirkland, but have increased dramatically since a group of large, reform-minded unions ousted the old guard and elected John Sweeney to the AFL–CIO presidency in 1995.

Organizing

By far the most dramatic change in union policy and activity has centred on efforts to revitalize organizing. The decline in private sector organizing activity and success is well documented. From the mid-1950s to the mid-1960s, unions won about 60 per cent of representation elections supervised by the National Labor Relations Board (NLRB). By 1981, that number had steadily fallen to just 45 per cent. NLRB-supervised election activity remained fairly constant during the 1970s, but the bottom dropped out, starting in 1982 when unions made 40 per cent fewer election petitions than in 1981 (Rose and Chaison, 1996, pp. 84–5). From 1975 through to the end of 1981, unions averaged 7,191 NLRB election petitions per year and gained representation rights for 157,397 workers annually. From 1982 to 1992, unions averaged just 3,346 election petitions per year and gained representation rights for only 73,992 workers annually. Thus, on average, both NLRB election activity and the number of workers gained through such activity declined by more than 50 per cent. Although it has been noted that some unions attempted to achieve recognition from employers without the assistance of the NLRB during this period (Chaison and Dhavale, 1990, p. 372) it is clear from the figures noted above that private sector organizing had fallen off sharply. Comparable data on public sector organizing activity does not exist, but what sketchy information is available suggests that the low win rates and curtailed organizing activity that characterized the private sector during the 1980s and early 1990s were not experienced by public sector unions. Public sector union membership grew by almost 14 per cent in the 1980s (Masters, 1997, p. 48) and comprehensive data on public sector organizing activity in 1991 and 1992 reveals that unions won more than 85 per cent of the representation elections conducted over that two-year period (Bronfenbrenner and Juravich, 1995).

AFL–CIO's efforts to promote organizing began under Lane Kirkland. The CEW (1985, pp. 27–9) report encouraged unions to improve their selection and training of organizers and to experiment with a number of new strategies to improve organizing effectiveness. These recommendations led to the creation of the Organizing Institute in 1989. The Organizing Institute selects, trains and places union organizers in paid jobs with one of the sixteen unions that directly participate in the programme. However, while the union win rate in NLRB-supervised representation elections rebounded from its historic low in the early 1980s, the number of elections continued to fall, suggesting that unions were becoming more selective in choosing organizing targets.

Estimates suggest that when Sweeney took office in 1995, most unions devoted less than 5 per cent of their annual budget to organizing (Bernstein, 1995; AFL–CIO, 1998). Unions won just over 50 per cent of elections in 1995, with the total number of LMRA election petitions falling below 3,000. Running on a platform to make organizing the primary priority, the Sweeney administration has challenged affiliates to devote 30 per cent of their resources to organizing and achieve a minimum average annual growth rate of 3 per cent per year. To help achieve these goals, the Organizing Institute was expanded into a new Organizing Department with a much broader mission and a new $20 million matching fund designed to encourage multi-union organizing campaigns in growth industries of strategic importance to the labour movement (AFL–CIO Executive Council, 1996a). Prior to this expansion, organizing was 'the weak sister' in a Department of Organizing and Field Services.

Perhaps somewhat paradoxically, increased participation by the AFL–CIO in assisting national union organizing efforts has resulted in greater local union and rank-and-file involvement in organizing. The sheer size of the task and the financial constraints placed on many unions by declining member-ship has placed a premium on finding creative, cost-efficient ways to enhance organizing effectiveness. One strategy is to eliminate unnecessary duplication by centralizing research, development and training functions at the Federation level. Another is to exploit the potential voluntary efforts of the membership and pro-union workers in non-union firms. Even fairly modest participation by rank-and-file workers in organizing would dwarf the work that could be achieved by paid union staff.

Decentralization of organizing activity was further enhanced by both union and academic research suggesting direct worker participation in the organizing process increases the likelihood of union success (see, for example, Bronfenbrenner, 1997). Falling union density, job losses in the unionized sector, and a shrinking union/non-union wage differential, have undermined unions' ability to appeal to workers in purely financial terms. The search for new themes has brought an emerging emphasis on the issues of dignity, fairness and empowerment through self-directed collective action. These social themes have received considerable attention in recent organizing campaigns involving low-wage and immigrant workers such as janitors, field hands and garment workers, and seem to have struck a chord with some workers and progressive community-based groups.

PAUL JARLEY

Internal Reform

The result has been a systematic AFL–CIO campaign to replace the traditional 'service model' of unionism with an 'organizing model'. This new model is still developing and various unions are in different stages of its implementation, but its basic elements are easy to detail. Rather than view union members as passive consumers of services delivered by paid union leaders and staff, the organizing model stresses the fulfilment of member goals through self-help. Members are to be given the knowledge, skills and decision-making authority to take responsibility for their own, and the union's, development and growth. Rather than solving members' problems for them – the essence of the service model – the organizing model seeks to educate workers on how to collectively solve problems for themselves (Grabelsky and Hurd, 1995, p. 100). In other words, the organizing model seeks to mobilize members to pursue collective goals by giving them a greater sense of ownership in their union. This philosophy also fosters an organizing model because recruitment and internal organizing activities are seen as the primary means by which workers gain dignity and influence over their lives. As noted earlier, local unions have also been challenged to devote 30 per cent of their resources to organizing and a recent AFL–CIO report suggests that 150 local unions now devote 10–20 per cent of their resources to organizing, and that another 150 increased their organizing budgets in 1997 (Parks, 1998, pp. 10–11).

This change in philosophy requires very different organizational structures at both the local and national union level. Local unions gain greater control over goal setting and must build democratic structures that encourage member participation and mobilization. Such decentralized systems should also allow for greater experimentation. National union offices no longer focus on the development and enforcement of uniform standards across locals, but are redesigned to serve as resource centres to promote the achievement of local objectives. National administrative structures provide specialized services that support coordinated independence among locals through information collection and analysis, innovation generation and diffusion, and the provision of expert advice. The AFL–CIO Organizing Department has been charged with assisting unions interested in effectuating such changes in their structures and activities (AFL–CIO Executive Council, 1996b).

Coalition Building

Renewed interest in recruiting new members and local political action has also brought an emphasis on coalition building. The contemporary importance of coalition building can be traced to early corporate campaign experiences where alliances with local religious and civil-rights-based organizations helped bring moral and political pressure to bear on employers involved in organizing and bargaining disputes with unions representing low-wage workers (Jarley and Maranto, 1990). Since that time, unions have moved to strengthen ties with a variety of progressive American organizations, as well as international labour federations and foreign-based unions. International labour contacts have been primarily used to help pressure multinational corporations locked in labour disputes with US unions; one example was a series of rolling strikes by European unions against Belgian-based Delhaize in support of the United Food and Commercial Workers' campaign against Delhaize's American subsidiary Food Lion, (see Jarley and Maranto, 1990). There have also been some efforts to use international labour coalitions to oppose multinational trade agreements, such as NAFTA, and call attention to human rights and labour abuses by American companies operating in the Third World (Nissen, 1998). On the domestic front, the Federation and many national union affiliates have moved to reinvigorate old alliances such as the Leadership Conference on Civil Rights, and institutionalize new ones with the founding of such organizations as the Campaign for America's Future and the Jobs with Justice Coalition. These domestic coalitions have been used in efforts to promote labour's political agenda, defeat a variety of conservative legislative initiatives, and provide structure and support to affiliated community-based groups.

At the local level, community-based organizing is reflected in such initiatives as 'Union Cities' and 'Union Summer'. Union Cities is a new initiative designed to help AFL–CIO city centrals increase labour's relevance in community affairs (Hall, 1997). The eight-step programme focuses on building community outreach programmes, creating alliances to influence local economic development strategies, and grass-roots lobbying and political-action committees to build power at the local government level that can be used to promote organizing activities. The Union Summer programme was launched in 1996 and is modelled after the civil-rights movement's Freedom Summer of 1964, when large numbers of students went to the southern United States to register black voters (Cooper and Parks, 1996, p. 16). Young interns spend four weeks getting hands-on experience in union, community and political organizing in communities where the

AFL–CIO hopes to increase labour's presence. Both of these programmes provide vivid examples of how labour's political, organizing and coalition-building efforts are all interrelated and tied to efforts to build 'organizing-driven' unions. Members are being given the power to help set local union agendas over a broad range of issues and are being asked to volunteer their time to build community-based power that will help them achieve their goals.

Bargaining and Confrontational Tactics

Because bargaining goals and tactics remain the exclusive province of national unions and their affiliated locals, it is difficult to generalize about the course of union-bargaining strategy, yet it can be stated with some certainty that this is the area where unions have remained the most reactive. In the early 1980s, employers were on the offensive. Two deep economic recessions at the start of the decade combined with public policies designed to fight inflation and reduce the scope of government brought soaring unemployment and massive job loss, especially in such traditional union strongholds as durable goods manufacturing and construction (Voos, 1994, pp. 10–11). Deregulation of key industries and government efforts to integrate the USA into the world economy increased both domestic non-union and foreign competition for many unionized private sector employers (Voos, 1994, pp. 9–10). Cuts in federal transfer payments, lower tax revenues generated by a stagnant economy, and fears of tax-payer revolts placed similar strains on state and local government budgets (Chandler and Feuille, 1994, p. 540). Both firms and governments responded to these changes by seeking labour-cost relief. Some firms literally ran from their collective bargaining agreements, relocating their operations. Some governments achieved similar results through privatization of public services. Those who did not or could not run, often sought and obtained wage, fringe benefit and work rule concessions from unions through threats of job loss, work relocation and use of strike replacements. Still other employers sought productivity enhancements through joint labour-management cooperation and employee involvement schemes. These latter two strategies placed an emphasis on the negotiation of local agreements tailored to local conditions, and centralized bargaining structures consequently crumbled (Katz, 1993). Real wages fell (US Bureau of Labor Statistics, 1997) and unionized workers' nominal compensation increases began to lag behind those of non-union workers (US Bureau of Labor Statistics, 1998).

In the 1990s, concession bargaining in the form of lower wage and fringe benefit levels has largely ceased and unionized workers' wages remain well above those of non-union workers (US Bureau of Labor Statistics, 1999). Nevertheless, the most common themes of the day such as outsourcing, use of contingent workers and productivity improvement primarily reflect management interests, and unions have struggled to find effective responses. Voos (1994, p. 5) observes that some unions have essentially settled on a modern version of productivity bargaining: trading changes in work rules and employee participation in productivity-enhancing efforts for job security and better financial terms than management would otherwise offer. As for the AFL–CIO, it has come around to endorsing some forms of employee involvement and encouraged unions to get involved in these changes in order to ensure that they are not completely shut out of work re-organization and strategic firm-decision-making (AFL–CIO Committee on the Evolution of Work, 1994). Implementation of this agenda, however, has been sporadic and generated controversy and opposition from the rank-and-file (see Katz and McDuffie, 1994, pp. 210–12). Unions have typically participated only where they have been able to gain promises from employers to end hard-ball bargaining tactics and take neutral stances in union organizing drives at their non-union plants (Voos, 1994, p. 17).

Not only are employers continuing to set much of the bargaining agenda; unions also seem increasingly reluctant to engage in work stoppages to support their positions at the bargaining table. Data from the US Bureau of Labor Statistics (1999) reveals that work stoppages among workers in major collective bargaining units (those with 1,000 or more workers) are way down. In 1980, 187 work stoppages idled 795,000 workers. In 1997, the number of stoppages involving such units hit an all-time low of 29, idling 339,000 workers. In 1998, there were only 34 stoppages involving 387,000 workers. There appears to be growing experimentation with other forms of confrontation. Such strike substitutes include in-plant strategies designed to slow production and maintain union-member solidarity while working without a contract, and corporate campaign activity to escalate conflicts beyond workplaces and into corporate boardrooms, government regulatory hearing rooms, and the printed and electronic media (Jarley and Maranto, 1990).

Current State of the Unions

A quick look at just membership numbers suggests that contemporary American unions are worse off in the late 1990s than they were at the start of the decade. Unions have lost about half a million members since 1990. Such figures, however, tell only part of the story. The decentralized nature of American unionism, and of industrial relations generally, permits considerable variation across workplaces and entire sectors of the economy. For example, although private sector unionism continued to struggle during this decade, public sector unionism posted small increases in both membership and density. Union mergers may also have created more powerful organizations better able to service members despite the problems associated with increased membership heterogeneity and internal political considerations that place limits on efficiency gains. Even the decline in aggregate membership takes on a slightly different meaning when evaluated against the experiences of the early 1980s. The 1990s may not have brought reversal, let alone resurgence, but the free-fall has stopped and given unions the opportunity to regroup. Sixteen million union members can still be a formidable force.

It is this recognition that lies at the heart of much of the AFL–CIO's strategy for resurgence. AFL–CIO efforts to lead and coordinate affiliate political activities, build ties with community groups, and promote an organizing model of unionism have generated considerable interest and activity among unions. It has also given the American labour movement some much-needed direction and a sense of control over its future. Progress to date has been slow but, to be fair, much of the AFL–CIO programme is relatively new and the explosive growth unions experienced in the middle of the century may still contribute to unrealistic expectations about the pace of any contemporary turnaround. Employers spent at least the first 30 years under federal labour law looking for ways to reclaim hegemony in union–management relations. They eventually succeeded, not by enacting major changes in the legislative framework or through a highly coordinated response by some peak employer association, but rather through decentralized experimentation and diffusion of successful practices across firms over time. Can unions slowly turn their fortunes around using a similar approach?

Future

Anyone charged with predicting the future direction of the American labour movement would do well to remember the experience of George Barnett. In his Presidential Address before the 1932 meeting of the American Economic Association, Barnett noted: 'I see no reason to believe that American trade

unionism will . . . become in the next decade a more potent social influence.'
His prediction proved to be a very bad one. Yet, as a fellow prognosticator
faced with the possibility of experiencing a similar fate, I must point out that
Professor Barnett's prediction was based on a solid assessment of the facts.
The past is often the best predictor of future performance and American
labour's recent past is one of misfortune. A boom economy, low union
instrumentality perceptions among workers and the public generally, a
hostile judicial system, employers' experiments with welfare capitalism and
company unionism, and William Green's uninspired leadership of the AFL,
all contributed to falling union membership in the 1920s. History strongly
suggested that economic depression would only worsen labour's lot. No one
could have foreseen how the scope and consequences of the Great
Depression, the rise of industrial unionism, the Second World War, and
America's economic hegemony in the war's immediate aftermath, would
help transform organized labour into a powerful social force.

There are many striking parallels between labour's experiences of the
1920s and those of the last two decades. After a deep recession in the early
1980s, a vigorous economy, falling union instrumentality perceptions,
aggressive employer anti-union human resource policies, and uninspired
union leadership, all conspired to keep union density heading downward
towards pre-1930 levels in the private sector. Things again look very bleak.
The dire circumstances of the 1920s gave way to unprecedented growth in
the 1930s, but that scenario is not likely to be repeated. A very strong case can
be and has been made (Lipset, 1986, p. 445) that it was the period from 1935
to 1955 that was the aberration from the typical American experience. In
most decades of the twentieth century, union membership changes failed to
keep pace with employment growth. The conditions that existed between
1935 and 1955 are not likely to reappear and many are beyond organized
labour's control. Changes in production technology, consumer demand and
global competition have undermined the logic of job-control unionism
(Piore, 1991). For these reasons alone, the return of industrial unionism on a
large scale is highly unlikely.

Labour's fortunes are not, however, simply the product of exogenous
forces. A departure from the craft union model, a commitment to organize
what many unionists saw as the unorganizable, and the use of new
confrontational tactics such as the sit-down strike all contributed to
organized labour's rise during the 1930s. The actions of contemporary
American unions will play a similar role in determining their fate. In the
immediate term, organized labour seems committed to allocating a higher
percentage of its resources to organizing, building coalitions with community

groups, and decentralizing its internal structures in an effort to extend and refine its 'organizing model' of unionism. Unionism is to be rebuilt from the bottom up, one work-site at a time. Pursuing this strategy may very well create some 'union cities' but only in industries where production must occur locally such as services, trade and government. Without sufficient national union density and coordination across work locations, unions remain especially vulnerable to capital flight. Employers will move to 'non-union cities' or pressure unions into providing employment terms similar to those found elsewhere. Perhaps by coincidence, perhaps not, many of the organizing drives recently touted by the AFL–CIO target workers in industries where capital flight is difficult and employment is expanding most rapidly, such as in the service sector. Many of these work-sites are small. Each organizing victory adds only a few members and may require the creation of regionally based general locals to make servicing such workers economically viable.

Ultimately this strategy may produce enough union members to maintain financially sound organizations with some measure of political and economic clout in specific communities, but it is unlikely to return organized labour to a position of national prominence. A union movement made up largely of relatively low-paid, low-skilled private sector workers and government employees is unlikely to play a leading role in determining employment conditions for workers generally. Such a strategy is also likely to yield gains too slowly to maintain a long-term political consensus among union leaders that it should continue. At current levels, just holding density constant requires unions to net 310,000 to 320,000 new members per year. Sustaining this level of annual recruitment would be an impressive achievement for a movement that has achieved this mark only twice in the last 20 years. Even at this pace, it would take unions approximately 20 years just to return total union membership to the level that existed in 1980! It is doubtful that union leaders and members would continue to allocate resources to organizing just to achieve these results.

It seems that a different approach is required. One modest alternative approach can be found in the American sports and entertainment industries where unions use their majority status to negotiate uniform minimum terms and conditions of employment with employers. Individuals and their agents are then free to negotiate contracts that augment and supplement the collective agreement. Such an approach may appeal to many employees, especially white-collar workers, who may desire a collective safety net in such areas as health and safety, retraining and dismissal, without the impediments to individual advancement often associated, rightly or wrongly, with unionism. Excluding wage items from such collective agreements or establishing fairly modest minimum conditions might also reduce employer resistance to unionization, making organizing less costly. Negotiating minimums that reduce employer resistance to unions while simultaneously providing workers with sufficient benefits to encourage membership is no small task and is made more difficult in markets where low union density makes it impossible to standardize even minimum terms across a broad set of employers. Yet, such an approach has been successfully implemented in a few, albeit atypical, industries, and experimentation along these lines can be conducted without the need for labour law reform.

More radical suggestions typically require American unions to abandon the principle of majority representation and focus on building regional employee associations on an occupational basis. The details of what Strauss (1995, p. 345) has characterized as these 'somewhat fuzzy' proposals vary in their particulars. For example, Rogers (1995) argues that unions should attempt to control regional labour markets through supply-side mechanisms that offer training, job placement, and career development, services to employees, as well as human resource services to employers (such as staffing assistance, provision of temporary employees, assistance in establishing and maintaining grievance systems) who agree to abide by community-endorsed employment standards achieved through local political action. Other proposals (Masters, 1997) see the establishment of more workplace-based minority unions that would enforce individual legal rights on the job and enter into bargaining agreements with specific employers over a variety of members' concerns.

These more radical proposals have been inspired by survey research that suggests enormous growth potential in meeting the unmet demand for various forms of employee representation among non-union workers (US Commission on the Future of Worker–Management Relations, 1994). Majority status requirements are seen as an obstacle to trade union growth because only about 25–30 per cent of non-union survey respondents typically express an interest in traditional forms of unionism. Yet, recruiting just half of these employees (many of whom work at locations where a majority of workers do not support union recognition) into organized labour's ranks would more than double union membership. The main weakness of such proposals, especially those that suggest some type of employer recognition of a minority organization, is that they would probably require changes in prevailing labour law. Some reformers (for example, Freeman and Rogers, 1993; Kochan, 1994) have gone so far as to suggest that the law be amended to require employers to establish European-style works councils where a significant percentage of employees (30–40 per cent) requested such an organization.

An even more radical option, but close to the one suggested by Rogers (1995), would be to forgo the creation of local collective organizations and offer direct, work-related services to individual workers. Such services might include information that could be useful in individual salary negotiations with employers, bargaining-agent services, legal counselling on employment-related matters, worker training, and political lobbying efforts in support of professional or occupational objectives. This approach would probably not require changes in existing labour law since many of the services would not involve 'dealing with the employer' and those that might are on behalf of a single worker and therefore not 'collective action' within the meaning of American labour law. The most obvious negative is that by treating workers' individual needs, these organizations would lack any capacity to act collectively at the workplace level and might find it difficult to build a stable membership among heterogeneous groups of workers who are little more than passive consumers of organizational services.

The options detailed above are not mutually exclusive, nor are they completely incompatible with the maintenance of majority status and exclusive bargaining rights in already organized units. There may even be some synergies associated with a multi-faceted approach. Proposals to require works councils or form workplace-based employee associations where majority status is not yet possible are in part motivated by public sector union experiences that demonstrate the utility of such organizations as stepping-stones to full-blown unionism (Ichniowski and Zax, 1990, pp. 205–6). Contingent workers and other types of non-traditional employees – for example, those engaged in production out of their homes – have little opportunity to form traditional unions and may only be effectively serviced by some form of regionally based unionism (Cobble, 1994). In addition, managerial and supervisory employees may find some collective mechanism for addressing their common concerns to their employer in a non-confrontational manner. These employees have not had a federally guaranteed right to organize since 1947, but contemporary law does not prevent supervisors or managers from forming unions, nor does it prevent employers from voluntarily recognizing them. Even modest success in developing forms of employee representation that appeal to these untapped groups could translate into many more union members.

Ironically, contemporary reform proposals frequently recall earlier days. As Strauss (1995, p. 345) notes, several proposals stress a form of occupational unionism that bears many similarities to the craft unionism of the 1920s, while works councils share a number of attributes with company-dominated unions. Back in the 1930s, the latter was outlawed, while the former was branded reactionary and inferior to industrial unionism.

Whether these more radical proposals can and will be implemented is another matter. Frankly, I doubt it. Any reforms requiring significant change in federal labour law will have to overcome the political stalemate that has existed in Washington for many years. Until there is an end to 'divided government' and renewed interest in industrial relations reform by the general public, the prospects for legislative change remain dim. Even if such an opportunity did arise, unions seem reluctant to back away from notions of majority status and exclusive representation rights. Even the Dunlop Commission's rather modest reform recommendations concerning employee participation programmes drew significant criticism from the AFL–CIO. Unions seem unwilling to risk further erosion in their traditional base on the promise of reaching many more workers with some untested alternate form of representation. Their resistance to change is consistent with organizational science research that notes organizations have great difficulty implementing radical reform (Tushman and Romanelli, 1985). Truly radical change often requires new organizations. The AFL–CIO schism of the 1930s is a case in point. To blossom, industrial unionism had to break free of the AFL. Contemporary union growth through radical change and rival unionism would really be a case of 'going back to the future', but the more likely scenario is that unions will continue to engage in modest structural reforms while pumping more and more money into organizing with only modest results. Such actions may guarantee pockets of unionism well into the next century, but without unexpected changes in the environment they are unlikely to bring a general resurgence.

References

AFL–CIO (1998) Homepage on Union City Initiative, http://www.aflcio.org/unioncity/goal1.html.

AFL–CIO Committee on the Evolution of Work (1985) *The Changing Situation of Workers and Their Unions*, Washington DC: AFL–CIO.

AFL–CIO Committee on the Evolution of Work (1994) *The New American Workplace: A Labor Perspective*, Washington DC: AFL–CIO.

AFL–CIO Executive Council (1996a) *AFL–CIO Organizing Fund Guidelines for Assistance and Support*, Executive Council Statements, http://www.aflcio.org/estatements/feb96/ecguide.html.

AFL–CIO Executive Council (1996b) *Building Power for Workers by Organizing*, Executive Council Statements, http://www.aflcio.org/estatements/feb96/ecguide.html.

Andrews, J. (1936) 'Nationalization', in J. R. Commons *et al.*, *History of Labour in the United States*, Vol. 2, New York: Macmillan, pp. 3–194.

Barbash, J. (1984) *Elements of Industrial Relations*, Madison, WI: University of Wisconsin Press.

Bean, R. (1985) *Comparative Industrial Relations: An Introduction to Cross-national Perspectives*, London: Routledge.

Bernstein, A. (1995) 'Can a new leader bring labor back to life', *Business Week*, July 3, 87.

Bok, D. and Dunlop, J. (1970) *Labor and the American Community*, New York: Simon & Schuster.

Bronfenbrenner, K. (1997) 'The role of union strategies in NLRB certification elections', *Industrial and Labor Relations Review*, **50**, 195–211.

Bronfenbrenner, K. and Juravich, T. (1995) *Union Organizing in the Public Sector: An Analysis of State and Local Elections*, Ithaca, NY: ILR Press.

Chaison, G. (1996) *Union Mergers in Hard Times: The View from Five Countries*, Ithaca, NY: Cornell University Press.

Chaison, G. and Dhavale, D. (1990) 'A note on the severity of the decline in union organizing', *Industrial and Labor Relations Review*, **43**, 366–73.

Chandler, T. and Feuille, P. (1994) 'Cities, unions, and the privatization of sanitation services', *Journal of Labor Research*, **15**, 53–72.

Cobble, D. (1994) 'Making postindustrial unionism possible', in S. Friedman, R. Hurd, R. Oswald and R. Seeber (eds) *Restoring the Promise of American Labor*, Ithaca, NY: ILR Press.

Committee on the Evolution of Work (1985) *The Changing Situation of Workers and Their Unions*, Washington, DC: AFL–C10.

Cooper, M. and Parks, J. (1996) 'What I did on my summer vacation', *America@Work*, **1**, 15–17.

Delaney, J. and Masters, M. (1991) 'Unions and political action', in G. Strauss, D. G. Gallagher and J. Fiorito (eds) *The State of the Unions*, Madison, WI: Industrial Relations Research Association, pp. 313–46.

Delaney, J. and Schwochau, S. (1993) 'Employee representation through the political process', in B. Kaufman and M. Kleiner (eds) *Employee Representation: Alternatives and Future Directions*, Madison, WI: Industrial Relations Research Association, pp. 265–304.

Dulles, F. (1966) *Labor in America: A History*, (3rd edn), New York: Crowell.

Edsall, T. (1988) 'Grass-roots organizing tops TV ads in AFL–CIO political agenda', *Washington Post*, May 20, p. A-3.

Fiorito, J. (1987) 'Political instrumentality perceptions and desires for union representation', *Journal of Labor Research*, **8**, 271–90.

Fiorito J., Jarley, P. and Delaney, J. (1995) 'National union effectiveness in organizing: measures and influences', *Industrial and Labor Relations Review*, **48**, 613–35.

Freeman, R. and Rogers, J. (1993) 'Who speaks for us? Employee representation in a nonunion labor market', in B. Kaufman and M. Kleiner (eds) *Employee Representation: Alternatives and Future Directions*, Madison, WI: Industrial Relations Research Association, pp. 13–80.

Grabelsky, J. and Hurd, R. (1995) 'Reinventing an organizing union: strategies for change', *Proceedings of the Forty-Sixth Annual Meeting*, Madison, WI: Industrial Relations Research Association, pp. 95–104.

Hall, M. (1997) 'The road to union city: eight ways to rebuild the labor movement in our communities', *America@Work*, **2**, 15–17.

Hall, M. (1998) '2000 in 2000' *America@Work*, **3**, 15–18.

Hendricks, W., Gramm, C. and Fiorito, J. (1993) 'Centralization of bargaining decisions in American unions', *Industrial Relations*, **32**, 367–90.

Herman, E. (1997) *Collective Bargaining and Labor Relations*, Saddle River, NJ: Prentice Hall.

Hirsch, B. and Macpherson, D. (1999) *Union Membership and Earnings Data Book*, Washington DC: Bureau of National Affairs.

Ichniowski, C. and Zax, J. (1990) 'Today's associations, tomorrow's unions', *Industrial and Labor Relations Review*, **43**, 191–208.

Jacoby, S. and Verma, A. (1992) 'Enterprise unions in the United States', *Industrial Relations*, **31**, 137–58.

Jarley, P. and Maranto, C. (1990) 'Union corporate campaigns: an assessment', *Industrial and Labor Relations Review*, **43**, 505–24.

Jarley, P., Delaney, J. and Fiorito, J. (1992) 'Embracing the Committee on the Evolution of Work report: what have unions done?, *Proceedings of the Forty-Fourth Annual Meeting*, Madison, WI: Industrial Relations Research Association, pp. 500–11.

Jarley, P., Fiorito, J. and Delaney, J. (1997) 'A structural contingency approach to democracy and bureaucracy in U.S. national unions', *Academy of Management Journal*, **40**, 831–61.

Katz, H. (1993) 'The decentralization of collective bargaining: a literature review and comparative analysis', *Industrial and Labor Relations Review*, **47**, 3–22.

Kochan, T. (1994) 'Principles for post-New Deal employment policy', in C. Kerr and P. Staudohar (eds) *Labor Economics and Industrial Relations*, Cambridge, MA: Harvard University Press, pp. 646–71.

Kochan, T. and Katz, H. (1988) *Collective Bargaining and Industrial Relations*, (2nd edn), Homewood, IL: Irwin.

Kochan, T. and Weinstein, M. (1994) 'Recent developments in U.S. industrial relations', *British Journal of Industrial Relations*, **32**, 483–504.

Kochan, T., Katz, H. and McKersie, R. (1986) *The Transformation of American Industrial Relations*, New York: Basic Books.

Lipset, S. (1986) 'North American labor movements: a comparative perspective', in S. Lipset (ed.) *Unions in Transition: Entering the Second Century*, San Francisco: ICS Press. pp. 421–54.

Masters, M. (1997) *Unions at the Crossroaods: Strategic Membership, Financial, and Political Perspectives*, Westport, CT: Quorum Books.

Master, M. and Jones, R. (1999) 'The hard and soft sides of union political money', *Journal of Labor Research*, **20**, 297–328.

Meyer, D. and Cooke, W. (1993) 'U.S. labor relations in transition: emerging strategic and company performance', *British Journal of Industrial Relations*, **31**, 531–52.

Nissen. B. (1998) 'Alliances across the border: the U.S. labor movement in the era of globalization', Paper presented before the 1998 Work, Employment, and Society Conference, Cambridge, England.

Parks, J. (1997) 'Marriage for muscle', *America@Work*, **2**, 16–19.

Parks, J. (1998) 'Organizing: either we do it or we fail', *America@Work*, **3**, 8–11.

Pavy, G. (1994) 'Winning NLRB elections and establishing stable collective bargaining relationships', in S. Friedman, R. Hurd, R. Oswald and R. Seeber (eds) *Restoring the Promise of American Labor*, Ithaca, NY: ILR Press, pp. 110–21.

Piore, M. (1991) 'The future of unions', in G. Strauss, D. Gallagher and J. Fiorito (eds) *The State of the Unions*, Madison, WI: Industrial Relations Research Association, pp. 387–410.

Robinson, J. (1992) 'Structural characteristics of the independent unions in the U.S. revisited', *Labor Law Journal*, **43**, 567–75.

Rogers, J. (1995) 'A strategy for labor', *Industrial Relations*, **34**, 367–81.

Rose, J. and Chaison, G. (1996) 'Linking union density and union effectiveness: the North American experience', *Industrial Relations*, **35**, 78–105.

Seeber, R. (1984) 'The Expansion of National Union Jurisdictions, 1955–1982', unpublished manuscript, Ithaca, NY: New York State School of Industrial and Labor Relations.

Sloane, A. and Witney, F. (1997) *Labor Relations*, (9th edn), Upper Saddle River, NJ: Prentice Hall.

Strauss, G. (1995) 'Is the New Deal system collapsing? With what might it be replaced?', *Industrial Relations*, **34**, 329–49.

Troy, L. and Sheflin, N. (1985) *U.S. Union Sourcebook: Membership, Finances, Structure Directory*, West Orange, NJ: Industrial Relations Data and Information Services.

Tushman, M. and Romanelli, E. (1985) 'Organizational evolution: a metamorphosis model of convergence and reorientation', in L. Cummings and B. Staw (eds) *Research in Organizational Behavior*, Volume 7, Greenwich, CT: JAI Press, pp. 171–222.

Ulman, L. (1966) *The Rise of the National Union: The Development and Significance of its Structure, Governing Institutions, and Economic Polices*, Cambridge, MA: Harvard University Press.

United States Bureau of Labor Statistics (1986–2000) *Employment and Earnings*, Washington DC: Government Printing Office.

United States Bureau of Labor Statistics (1997) BLS News no. 75, *Productivity & Costs*, Washington DC: Government Printing Office.

United States Bureau of Labor Statistics (1999) 'Major Work Stoppages Involving

1,000 or more Employees' Internet site data from series: http://stats.bls.gov/news-release/wkstp.to1.htm.

U.S. Commission on the Future of Worker–Management Relations (1994) *Report and Recommendations*, Washington DC: Government Printing Office.

Voos, P. (1994) 'An economic perspective on contemporary trends in collective bargaining', in P. Voos (ed.) *Contemporary Collective Bargaining in the Private Sector*, Madison, WI: Industrial Relations Research Association, pp. 1–24.

White, J. (1998) 'Midweek perspectives: the Labor Party speaks up for the American dream, *Pittsburgh Post-Gazette ONLINE*, Wednesday, 11 November.

8 CONCLUSION: THE STATE OF THE UNIONS

Gerard Griffin and Peter Fairbrother

Over the last two decades trade unions in many countries have experienced a 'time of profound change' (Olney, 1996, p. 2). Many analyses of unionism during this period have used words such as 'crisis', 'challenge' and 'transition' in their titles to indicate the nature and character of these developments (see, for example, Edwards *et al.*, 1986, Leisink *et al.*, 1996, Lipset, 1986). While some union movements have retained a marked presence in the economy (see ILO, 1998; Galenson, 1998), the conclusion that unions overall are in some difficulty is not in question. The key issue is whether this is a long-term development and, if so, what will be the consequences for the union form of organization, especially in industrialized countries? Alain Touraine has argued that 'movements such as unionism have a life history: infancy, youth, maturity, old age and death' (1986, p. 157). Are we witnessing, in a significant number of countries, an old-age union movement on the way to its deathbed? Or are these unions suffering something like a mid-life crisis in their maturity? Or is a declining aggregate union membership only one factor in this process? We cannot, of course, in this chapter reflect on these questions for the worldwide union movement. Rather, we focus on such issues for our chosen countries. We draw together recent developments within the six trade union movements, commencing with a consideration of union membership trends and patterns of institutional reorganization, policies and practices focusing on the bases of membership representation and organizational structures, and relationships with the state and political parties. We then assess their current state of play, particularly their strategies, and we speculate as to the immediate future prospects of trade unionism in these mainly English-speaking countries. Both our analysis and prognosis are somewhat cautious and pessimistic: unions have struggled on virtually all dimensions of analysis over the past two decades and their prospects for revival are not immediately apparent.

The Question of Membership

A number of trends emerge from a comparison of membership data across the six countries: first, there has been a decline in membership density in all countries over the 1980s and 1990s; second, unionism in the public sector has emerged as the mainstay of most union movements; third, traditional differences in gender-based density have decreased; and fourth, there has been a concentration of membership into a smaller number of unions. Taken together, these aspects of change point to a major recomposition of union membership in these countries.

Focusing initially on density, the experiences of the six countries over the past two decades vary widely, from decimation in Australasia to slight, but worrying, declines in Canada and Ireland. Density rates in New Zealand have dropped from 43.5 per cent in 1985 to 17.0 per cent in 1999. Between 1990 and 1999, there was a 41 per cent decline in density. In short, unionization rates have plummeted towards USA levels. Much of this decline has been attributed to the effect of the Employment Contracts Act of 1991. Changes to the New Zealand industrial relations system introduced in the Employment Relations Act, 2000 raise the possibility of at least halting, if not reversing, this dramatic decline. Density rates in Australia have declined at a not much less frenetic pace: from 49 per cent in 1982 to 40 per cent in 1992 to 26 per cent in 1999. Over the period 1992 to 1999, density declined by an average of two percentage points each year. Worryingly for the union movement, there is no indication that this rate of decline is slowing. While it is outside the scope of this chapter to analyse the reasons for these declines (see Griffin and Svensen, 1996, for such a discussion), the obvious point must be made that these massive drops in density have occurred in the two union movements – Australian and New Zealand – that most relied on the state for guaranteed memberships.

Trade union density in Britain also dropped dramatically during the 1980s and 1990s. Following a decade of growth during the 1970s – that saw density reach 55.8 per cent in 1979 – membership dropped to 46 per cent by 1987 and to 30 per cent in 1998. Some relief may, however, be in sight: the 1998 data was effectively unchanged from the 1997 figures.

The data in the remaining three countries also offer some hope to their union movements. Following a sharp decline in membership during the 1980s, the rate of decline in the USA slowed significantly during the 1990s. An optimist could point to the increase in absolute membership in some years during the 1990s and be particularly hopeful about the 1998 and 1999 absolute increases. Such an individual could advance the argument that the emphasis of the US union movement on organizing during the latter half of the 1990s is now paying dividends. The pessimist could simply note that an overall density rate of less than 14 per cent remains abysmal. Canadian data shows a growth in union density during the first half of the 1980s decade, followed by a decline in the second half. During the 1990s, absolute membership remained fairly steady with density declining slightly. Nevertheless, the 32.3 per cent density rate for 1999 compares favourably with that of its southern neighbour, a difference much speculated on in the literature (see, for example, Rose and Chaison, 2000). Murray hints in the chapter on Canada that a significant challenge lies ahead of the Canadian union movement to maintain its relative success. The Irish union movement can also claim a degree of membership success. A decline during the 1980s was followed by growth, both in absolute membership and density during the first half of the 1990s. The lack of continuous and reliable data for the late 1990s is unfortunate. However, using the data on ICTU affiliate membership, Irish union density remains significantly higher than that found in the other five countries.

Overall, union membership declined in all countries other than Canada during the 1980s; in most cases, these declines were very heavy. During the 1990s, membership in Australia, Britain and New Zealand continued to decline heavily while the other three countries had much less significant declines. Visser (1990) has suggested that union movements should be judged as lightly unionized if their density is 30 per cent or less, medium unionized if their rate is between 31 and 50 per cent, and heavily unionized if density is greater than 50 per cent. Based on this criterion, in 1980, three of our six countries were heavily unionized (Australia, Ireland, UK), two were in the medium category (Canada and New Zealand) while only the USA fell into the low-density grouping. By the late 1990s, Australia, New Zealand and the UK had joined the USA in the low-density category while Canada was struggling to remain in the medium category. Only Ireland, with its location in the upper echelons of the medium category, had any pretence to being a union movement with significant membership density.

Public sector membership is now at the core of all six union movements. For the five countries for which data is available (New Zealand is the exception) public sector density is higher than private sector density; indeed in four of the countries the difference is very significant, ranging up to over 50 percentage points for Canada. Data for the USA best exemplifies this divergence between private sector and public sector density: in 1980, private sector density was 22 per cent while the public sector figure was 35 per cent. By 1998, the private sector rate had fallen to 9.5 per cent while the public sector figure had actually risen to 37.5 per cent. Applying the low/medium/ heavy categorization to public sector density results in a late 1990s' classification of two countries in the medium category (USA and UK) and three in the top category (Australia, Canada and Ireland). Given the relatively low level of decline of union membership in the 'public and community service' industry classification in New Zealand (see Table 6.2) it is highly likely that public sector rates in that country would fall into the medium-density ranking. The implications of this swing away from private sector unionism towards public sector unionism have not yet, arguably, surfaced to any great extent. They are, however, likely to do so in the not-too-distant future.

Two further membership trends can be identified from the country chapters. First, there has been a decrease in the traditional gap between male and female density rates. A number of factors have, no doubt, contributed to this narrowing difference, including the increased participation of females in the workforce and the gradual, if slow, spread of females into traditional male industries. However, a key factor is also that male density has been declining at a faster rate than female density. Second, and not surprising given the numbers of mergers over the past two decades, in all countries there has been an increasing concentration of membership in the largest ten unions. The most dramatic illustration of this trend comes from New Zealand: in 1981 some 43 per cent of all unionists were members of the ten largest unions; the equivalent 1999 figure was 78 per cent.

Overall, union membership has declined in all countries, dramatically in some; the public sector is now a key stronghold of the union movement; there has been a concentration of membership in a small number of key unions; and gender-based density differences have narrowed. The outcome is a situation where trade union movements have and are being pushed to re-examine the institutional bases for membership recruitment and representation.

The Question of Recruitment and Organization

During the 1980s and 1990s, union movements began to address the question of recruitment and the organizational arrangements that might be most appropriate to the changed conditions of these decades. In most countries, the key driver behind this questioning was, of course, the declining membership levels identified above. How were unions to respond to this decline? It is possible to identify four interrelated dimensions of change, all found in most, if not all, six trade union movements. First, there has been huge institutional change through a wave of union mergers. Second, and partly related, the membership constituency for many unions has broadened significantly. Third, membership recruitment has become a top priority. Fourth, the power, influence and role of union federations have decreased while those of individual unions have increased.

During the 1980s and the 1990s, there has been a massive wave of trade union mergers in all six countries. The dimensions of the change can be illustrated by Australian and British data. In the former, the total number of unions dropped by more than half over the first five years of the 1990s decade, from 295 in 1990 to 142 in 1995. In Britain, a similar decline, but over a lengthier period, occurred: the 454 unions in existence in 1979 had decreased to 238 by 1998. A wide range of factors that can influence the extent of union mergers has been identified in the literature. These factors are usually divided into external influences, such as the political, economic and legal environment, and internal factors such as leadership, finance and changing membership (see Chaison, 1996; Waddington, 1995). Clearly, the relative importance of these factors can and will vary over time and between countries. However, given the patterns of declining membership, particularly during the 1980s, a strong case can be argued that this factor was a key driving force behind the merger wave. Regardless of such debates, what is indisputable is that the various union movements restructured themselves dramatically through an extensive merger process during the last two decades of the twentieth century; many of these movements had not previously experienced such a radical restructuring.

All of these mergers broadened considerably the membership bases of trade unions and, inevitably, created some strange bedfellows. For example, what is to be made of the Manufacturing Science Finance union in Britain; Services, Industrial, Professional and Technical Union in Ireland; or Communications, Electrical, Electronic, Energy, Information, Postal, Plumbing and Allied Services Union of Australia? Equally, a number of absorbing unions retained their existing title post-merger but expanded considerably the scope of their membership. In addition, even when a union did not partake in the merger frenzy, many, as a competitive response, started to recruit outside their traditional domain. For example, in Canada, the Steelworkers now recruit service sector employees as indeed does the Iron and Steel Trades Confederation in Britain, while in the USA the Teamsters have a long history of recruitment outside the transport industry. All of this activity means that traditional descriptors of unions as 'craft' or 'industrial' are, in many cases, no longer relevant. Union structure is now something of a hotchpotch. Based on titles, there would appear to be a large number of craft unions. In reality, the old approach of including 'allied' workers within their ambit has been expanded enormously and few, if any, genuine craft unions remain. Equally, many unions that traditionally recruited within one industry are now more correctly described as multi-industry or multi-occupational unions. Few have yet made the transition to general unionism, although some unions, such as descendants of the Transport and General Workers' Union in Ireland and Britain come close to this category. In many ways, these large, multi-occupational unions, with their divisional structures covering non-related memberships, are the equivalents of business conglomerates. The least amount of institutional change seems to have occurred within 'professional' unions, covering employees such as nurses, teachers and engineers. In most cases, such unions appear to have maintained their separate identity; where mergers have occurred, they usually have involved mergers of organizations of unions covering the same memberships but in different geographical locations.

Membership recruitment and organizing activities have been elevated to the top tier of union policies and priorities. This is a new and challenging experience for some union movements, particularly those in Australia and New Zealand, that, traditionally, had membership strongly encouraged if not guaranteed by the state. In other countries, such as Britain and the USA, these new recruitment priorities had to contend with employer attitudes and frequently hostile legislatures. The most overt demonstration of this new emphasis on recruitment was the formation of formal organizing structures, usually under the aegis of federations. The AFL–CIO's Organizing Institute was established in 1989. This was followed by similar structures, explicitly based on international experience, in Australia in 1994 and in Britain in 1997. Neither Canada nor New Zealand followed this trend but, in both countries, policies and resource allocation indicate the high priority of recruitment strategies. Ireland is an outlier in this development, with discussions on organizing and recruitment still in an early and uneven stage.

The roles of federations traditionally varied within the six countries. As a generality, the Canadian and USA federations had little power, with the national affiliates wielding authority within those countries' union movements. In contrast, and concurrent with the increased incorporation of unions into the polity from the 1950s onwards, federations in the other four countries started to accumulate some limited degree of power. Usually this was based on the moral authority conferred on these bodies in their role of representatives of organized labour interacting with the state. The periods of social contracts involving Labour Party-based governments saw the zenith of federation power. In at least one country, Australia, the federation dominated its affiliates during the period of such institutional arrangements (see Griffin, 1994). Concomitant with the move away from macro-level bargaining and the disentanglement of the state from labour market institutions, the roles of federations in Australia, Britain and New Zealand have become much less central and more akin to the roles of their Canadian and USA counterparts. Only in Ireland, with its maintenance of the corporatist approach, does the federation, the Irish Congress of Trade Unions, wield some significant level of moral authority. Yet, even given this centralized institutional arrangement, the roles of affiliates are still dominant. Overall, within five of the countries power clearly lies within individual unions rather than at federation level.

Within individual unions, establishing the locus of power is rather more difficult. In the USA, Canada and Ireland, national-level unions appear to retain their dominance. In the other three countries, some devolution of power has probably taken place within the newly formed large conglomerate unions towards the divisional level. Equally, in these countries some unions with a history of branch autonomy, perhaps based on geographical divisions as in the Australian states, have probably retained much of that autonomy. In general, however, the key sphere of influence within these countries is probably also the national level.

Overall, the 1980s and 1990s saw major organizational and policy changes within the six countries' trade union movements. Survival through new or replacement membership, either through mergers or organizing, has been the top priority for many unions. In this scramble, niceties such as traditional demarcation lines no longer apply. Federations in most of the six countries have recognized this new reality and have attempted to provide a framework to reduce inter-union conflict. However, the pithy Canadian federation description of this approach – use it or lose it – best captures the view that if a union with formal coverage is unable to sign up potential members then some/any other union should be allowed, and even encouraged, to attempt to do so.

The State and Political Parties

To understand the complexity of the relationship between the state and trade unions some historical perspective is necessary. In general, and throughout much of the nineteenth century, the state usually treated the nascent union movement with, at best, extreme suspicion and, more frequently, outright hostility buttressed by legislation prescribing union membership and/or any collective activities. By the start of the twentieth century, this relationship had evolved, in a number of countries, into a position of wary acceptance. Over the next few decades, the state gradually came to accept, through legislation, the legitimacy of trade unions. The Second World War saw full union recognition by all arms of the state, followed, over succeeding decades, by a degree of incorporation by these states of trade unionism. By the 1970s, most union movements in most industrialized societies held secure, apparently guaranteed positions of power in their societies.

This, of course, is a broad-brush description of state–union relations and many exceptions can be found. Indeed, the experiences of some of the six countries studied in the present volume fall outside these parameters. The Australian state, for example, went from strong opposition to unionism in the early 1890s to enshrining extensive union rights in legislation in 1904, while in the USA, state recognition arguably did not arrive until 1935. Neither does this description differentiate between the not infrequently differing and contradictory actions and policies of the various arms of the state, such as the judiciary and the legislature. Overall, however, in most industrialized economies, state policies towards trade unions gradually evolved from overt hostility to at least broad acceptance, particularly by the social democratic governments in these countries. By the 1970s, many states had reached an accommodation with trade unions: few questioned the legitimacy of union involvement in economic, social and political activity and most conferred a key role on unions in these areas. The period of social contracts in countries such as the UK, during the second half of the 1970s, and Australia, during the 1980s, was the apex of union involvement in the polity.

This form of union 'political economism', to use Hyman's (1994) term, was, however, relatively short-lived in English-speaking countries. The analysis in the six chapters highlights a major change in state–union relations in each country during the last two decades of the twentieth century. Crucially for our purposes, the sharp deterioration in the international economy that followed the boom years of the Keynesian decades led to a major questioning of both the dominant economic paradigm and the pluralist political ideology that underpinned the role of unions. The growth of the 'new right' philosophy, with its demands, among other things, for the dominance of markets and a roll-back in the role of the state, quickly gained a remarkable ascendancy (for one example, see Pusey, 1991). The role of unions and the legitimacy of existing labour market structures were debated and attacked. Two of the countries studied in the present volume emerged as the leaders of this trend. Under Prime Minister Thatcher and President Reagan, state–union relationships quickly deteriorated in Britain and the USA. In the former, a series of laws were passed throughout the 1980s and early 1990s that attacked the power base of unions, while in the latter a series of related judicial appointments and legal decisions during the 1980s reflected the changed political realities. In both cases, the legitimacy of trade unionism was challenged and questioned, usually supported by strident political rhetoric.

In the Australasian countries, the election of Labour Party governments in the early 1980s held out the prospect of an ongoing cordial state–union relationship. In New Zealand, however, the 'reformist' agenda of the Lange Government quickly resulted in significant deregulation of labour markets in 1984 and 1987 through legislation that, arguably, provided the necessary groundwork for the radical Employment Contracts Act of 1991. This Act, introduced by a new Conservative government, placed New Zealand at the forefront of labour market experimentation. Individual contracts of employment became the centrepiece of the employment relationship and traditional collectivist provisions such as multi-employer bargaining were proscribed. This legislation decimated the labour movement. In Australia, the 1983 negotiation of a social contract between the union movement and a new Labor government saw a return to a centralized wage-fixing system with a key role for unions, particularly for the Australian Council of Trade Unions. The Accord, as the agreement was termed, technically lasted until 1996. However, from 1987 onwards, significant elements of the centralized system were gradually eroded. In 1991, a system of enterprise bargaining was introduced and was extended in 1993 to non-unionized workplaces. As in New Zealand, an incoming Conservative government built on these changes to legislate more radical laws, with a number of anti-union provisions.

In Canada, law and political interaction at the provincial level plays a key role in union–state relations. In general, when Conservative governments have held power, the legislatures have passed laws either attacking the roles of unions or advancing the theme of individual employment relationships. For example, in 1995, in Ontario, the Province with the largest population, a new Conservative government repealed existing, more union-friendly laws that had been introduced by the New Democratic Party (Rose and Chaison, 2000).

Only in Ireland has a collectivist, centralized form of corporatist union–state relationship remained. At the beginning of the 1980s, such a development seemed highly unlikely. Influenced by the same economic factors and political ideology that influenced change in other societies, the

Irish system of industrial relations swung abruptly away from its traditional centralized form of bargaining towards the workplace. In the late 1980s, however, influenced by poor economic indicators, a 1960s/1970s-style social partnership involving employers as well as unions and the state was introduced. Buttressed by significant economic growth (see Barry, 1999), successive three-year partnerships, the latest titled *Partnership 2000*, have been negotiated in the Celtic Tiger.

The gradual improvement in state–union relationships throughout the twentieth century, discussed earlier, was far from smooth and continuous. Advancements in social incorporation tended to occur most frequently when Social Democratic/Labour Parties have held political office. Such a trend was obviously not unexpected given that, in many countries, unions and Labour Parties referred to themselves as the industrial and the political wings respectively of the labour movement. Accordingly, during the 1980s, a not unexpected strategic reaction of union movements faced with hostile Conservative governments was simply to await the re-election of their political allies. What has been the impact of Social Democratic/Labour governments on state–union relationships during the 1980s and 1990s? In brief, this impact has been limited and, from the union perspective, disappointing. The experiences of unions with, for example, a Labour government in New Zealand, a Democratic Party President in the USA and a New Democratic Party government in Canadian Provinces such as British Columbia and Saskatchewan, pointed to new dimensions in the Labour government–union relationship. For a number of reasons, but primarily economic, governments seemingly sympathetic to unions were unlikely, often unwilling and usually unable, to return to the arrangements existing prior to the election of the Conservative government. The 1997 election of a Labour government in the UK, the first such government since 1979, saw remarkably few changes to the prevailing labour law and government ethos. Similarly, in Australia, much of the changes to labour markets, union power and membership took place while the Labor Party held political power. Overall, a Labour government may negate some of the sharpest, anti-union provisions in legislations introduced by Conservative governments – as appears likely to happen with the Employment Relations Act, 2000 in New Zealand. In English-speaking countries, however, strong state support for trade unionism has disappeared.

Overall, the strategic lesson for trade unions is clear: at the turn of the twenty-first century, even when Labour Parties comprise the legislative arm of the state, labour law and public policy is likely to remain neutral towards the collective concept of trade unionism. At best, only some small measures of support could be reasonably anticipated. Accordingly, in five of the six countries covered, unions must rely on their own resources to survive, rather than expect the state, guided by a Labour government, to guarantee such survival. Such a lesson is not, of course, any news to the union movement in the USA. Recent interest by, for example, Australian and British unions in the strategies of USA unions, particularly approaches to membership organizing, indicates that these union movements are now beginning to accept this harsh reality. Even in the sixth country, Ireland, the debate within the union movement around *Partnership 2000* points to the realization that macro-incorporation does not necessarily guarantee membership at the individual firm level, particularly in multinational firms.

Strategies for Union Futures

It is possible to identify three core phases of union strategy during the last two decades of the twentieth century. The first phase was, typically, a defensive, 'wait it out' approach; the second an institutional, restructuring phase; and the third, a focus on organizing and recruiting. We do not argue that these three phases are necessarily independent, sequential phases or that each phase was of equal importance in all six countries. For example, some limited restructuring inevitably took place during, and as part of, the defensive phase. We do contend, however, that these phases can be found to a greater or lesser extent in all six countries.

The initial, defensive strategy of most union movements in the early 1980s is readily understandable. Since the 1930s, the union movements in all six countries had, generally, been on an upward trajectory in both the economy and the polity. Despite the occasional setback, union power and influence, both industrially and politically, were increasing and membership was steady if not growing. In this scenario, a policy of riding out what were likely to be the temporary setbacks occasioned by the election of Conservative governments had much to commend it. After all, governments themselves had initially adopted traditional policies towards the changed economic climate from the mid-1970s onwards. Thus, unions resigned themselves to having to await the departure of President Reagan in the USA and Prime Minister Thatcher in the UK. Exclusion from the corridors of power was expected to be temporary.

As the 1980s progressed, as labour laws were changed, as political structures and advisory councils were dismantled, as membership numbers plummeted and as neo-liberalism gained the intellectual hegemony, this defensive strategy began to be questioned, albeit in hesitant and uneven ways in some countries, such as Britain. With the election of Social Democratic Parties in Australia, New Zealand, some of the Canadian provinces, and as part of a coalition government in Ireland, it became apparent that such governments would, at best, diffuse and delay somewhat the impact of market forces on workers and union members. In the new globalized environment, the powers of such governments to pursue union-friendly policies were self-circumscribed. For unions, the waiting strategy became self-evidently non-viable. In the second stage, unions began to look at the question of union recruitment and retention. Committees of inquiries were established, usually by federations and less formally by larger individual unions, study tours were undertaken, sometimes research was commissioned and, inevitably, a swathe of new policies was proposed. In brief, a general view emerged, no doubt fuelled by declining membership levels, that trade unions needed to reposition themselves, particularly through restructuring, to deal more adequately with the new environment of the 1980s. While such a task would be difficult, it offered the prospect of stemming the decline in membership, particularly through the additional organizing muscle gained through the economies of scale potential. This second union-strategic phase resulted in a massive wave of union mergers, usually during the second half of the 1980s and the first half of the 1990s. Union structure, as discussed above, was transformed in all six countries. However, this institutional restructuring was uneven and often implemented in contested ways. The results were varied, at best slowing the rate of membership decline and, at worst, having no impact on the haemorrhaging of membership in countries such as Australia, New Zealand and Britain.

Spurred by this continuing decline, a third and complementary set of strategies was investigated, focusing explicitly on questions relating to recruitment and the bases of representation. In this search, union movements began to explore the previously neglected dimension of international experience, particularly in those three countries where institutional restructuring had little impact on membership levels. Somewhat ironically, given that its membership density was the lowest of all six countries, union experience and strategy in the USA became the focus of attention. The role of the Organizing Institute, and the philosophy of organizing generally, was keenly analysed. The Australian union movement was so impressed that, in 1994, it established an equivalent unit, Organising Works, within its federation and attempted to inculcate the organizing philosophy throughout the movement. Subsequently, the TUC in Britain drew on the experiences of both the Australian and USA union movements to guide its approach to membership campaigning and, to a more limited extent, the bases of membership representation within unions. Overall, during the second half of the 1990s, union organizing – a type of back-to-the-future policy – became the third dominant strategy in virtually all of the six union movements. The possible exception is Ireland, where membership density, underpinned by the centralized wage-fixing system, remained viable. Yet even here, as discussed in Chapter 5, decreasing density in multinational companies has raised concerns and organizing strategies are being given more attention.

These three strategies are not, of course, the only strategies discussed and implemented within sections of the union movements in the six countries. For example, at the individual union level, many unions now offer a very wide range of non-industrial services, ranging from discounted shopping and travel to financial and legal advice. More importantly, at the macro-level, the strategy of social movement unionism – linking and forming alliances with other social groupings – to be found in North America has a number of union adherents. To date, this strategy has had little impact in the other four countries, possibly because unionism has not perceived itself traditionally as 'just another pressure group' or because the conception of unionism based on waged work remains strong. Until relatively recent times it was not unusual, for example, for federations in Australasia to refer to their conferences as 'the worker's parliament'. Such a view effectively precluded equal partnerships with other social movements. Accordingly, social-movement unionism has remained a second-tier choice for many unions. Advocacy of such initiatives is linked to the recognition that the union movement can no longer achieve its goals and policies without support from these other groups. Despite some rhetoric, such a dramatic changed way of thinking has, to date, had little influence outside North America. Within that continent it remains a minority influence. Finally, the point should be made that the traditional political strategy of affiliation to a social democratic political party remains intact in some countries but has been severely downgraded in importance in others. Unions in Australia, Ireland and the UK remain, by and large, affiliated to their Labour Parties, although the Labour Party in the UK has explicitly downplayed this relation. In contrast, only four New Zealand unions retain affiliation, while the experiences of some Canadian unions with NDP provincial governments has led to some disillusionment about this political strategy. In the USA, the 'reward-your-friends, punish-your-enemies' strategy is still pursued; however, while no unions are formally affiliated, the bulk of union financial contributions still flow to the Democratic Party.

At the start of the new century, trade unions cannot be accused of policy or strategic sclerosis. After a slow start, a number of initiatives were adopted and implemented over the past two decades. The issue, of course, is whether these measures will prove successful.

Back to the Future

We opened this book with the remark that trade unions face an uncertain future. Based on the assessment of the six countries covered in this book, it is difficult not to be pessimistic about the future of trade unionism in at least the majority of these countries. This is not, of course, to argue that unions are irrelevant and will disappear, or, to revert to Touraine's (1986) terminology, that they are nearing the death category. Rather, it is realistic to recognize that, in most predominantly English-speaking societies, the roles, powers and influences of trade unions have declined dramatically during the 1980s and 1990s, raising questions about the form that trade unionism may take in the early twenty-first century. In line with the observation in the first chapter about the bases of trade unionism in capitalist economies, it can be expected that the transformation of unionism presently under way will continue. In these six countries, however, there seems little short-term prospect of any immediate reversal of the trends outlined above. The political and economic decline is all the more remarkable given that, during the preceding three decades, unions in these countries were either ensconced in the decision-making process of the polity or were key players in determining the employment relationship.

Inevitably, both the extent of the decline and the prospects for union renewal vary between national union movements. The prospects for renewal are, of course, contested and could apply to a number of union dimensions, such as recruitment, organizational structure and practice, finances, the bases for new leaderships and the boundaries of unionism (see Fairbrother, 2000, pp. 17–22 and 324–37). More generally, the question facing unions is how, and under what circumstances, to reassess the way they organize and operate given the conditions that they now face? In view of the analysis in Chapter 1, it is likely that the debates about the union form will continue for the foreseeable future. Inevitably, in the light of increasing political marginalization and membership decline, past forms of unionism will continue to be questioned and it is possible that new forms of unionism, such as internationally based unions, may emerge.

Drawing on membership data as the most widely utilized measure of union decline, the Irish trade union movement is best placed to face the challenges of the future. Based on a return to a corporatist-type wage-fixing system and a supportive public policy, Irish trade unions appear more appropriately grouped with Scandinavian union movements rather than their predominantly English-speaking counterparts. Yet, as outlined by Roche and Ashmore in Chapter 5, union leaders are uneasy with the anti-union policies apparently being followed by the increasing number of multinational companies operating in the services and information technology sectors. Corporatist, macro-level policies may not survive micro-level management strategies.

The USA labour movement lies at the other end of the spectrum. With membership declining since the 1950s, the outlook is bleak. With the exception of a handful of states – more than 50 per cent of all unionists live in just seven states – and industries, unionism is largely irrelevant in the private sector. The public sector and a recent (1998 and 1999) stabilization of absolute membership numbers provide a beacon of hope for the future. Nevertheless, in view of the tight labour market – particularly the historically low rate of unemployment – this outcome is far from satisfactory. Currently, the extremely patchy presence and role of unions in the USA may be the pointer to the future roles of unions in other countries.

Such a future appears highly likely in the two Australasian countries. In New Zealand, simple survival has been the dominant theme during the 1990s. One of its largest unions became insolvent; others simply disappeared. The remaining unions now represent 17 per cent of the workforce. The election of a Labour Government in 2000 holds out some hope for New Zealand unions. Notwithstanding our earlier comments about the limited roles of social democratic governments the foreshadowed replacement of the stridently individualistic, anti-union Employment Contracts Act should give the union movement some succour. Realistically, however, it faces a massive task to regain even a limited part of its former membership, power and influence. The Australian union movement is only slightly better off than its trans-Tasman cousin. Membership decline shows no sign of slowing and, among other adverse factors, such as a massive swing to casual and part-time work, the current federal government is constantly attempting to pass legislation that would restrain union activities and restrict organizing. Fortunately for Australian unionism, and unlike the unicameral New Zealand parliament, the Conservative government does not control the Senate, the upper house of parliament, which has, to date, refused to pass such legislation.

The experiences of trade unionism in the UK can be bracketed with those of their antipodean counterparts. Indeed, in one of those statistical quirks, the declining UK union-density rates track the equivalent figures in Australia. Overall, the role, powers and membership of UK unionism have declined dramatically. Further, the election of a Labour Government in 1997 seems to have had a limited impact on these trends. Some unions have now begun to question the previous boundaries of unionism, either looking to the community or exploring the potential of international unionism. Also, as in the USA, some potential signs of membership stabilization, particularly in regions such as Wales, can be discerned. Overall, however, the immediate future predominantly remains bleak.

The remaining union movement, that of Canada, has survived the tribulations of the past two decades in relatively reasonable shape. Crucially, it has retained much of its membership support and density, and has done so in an environment of employer opposition and occasional hostile state governments and public policy. It also, however, faces significant challenges, and the massive effort put into organizing remains a priority.

The experience in Ireland and, to a lesser extent, Canada shows that it is possible for unions movements to survive well and to continue to play an important role in determining the broad industrial relationship. Neither shows any signs of approaching old age. In the other four countries, some individual unions do indeed play significant roles in some industry sectors and/or regions; in other industries and regions, frequently the majority, trade unionism plays little if any role. Overall, in a macro-sense, unions have been relegated to the status of just one of a number of competing pressure groups.

Where do unions go from here? Some previous analyses of union decline have concluded with an optimistic view of the future (see Edwards *et al.*, 1986). However, based on two decades of decline and our review of the current status of trade unionism in six countries, such a view seems, overall, unwarranted. A major obstacle to adopting an optimistic outlook is that, of the many policies and strategies being discussed or followed within trade unions, virtually all have been tried before. In the mid-1980s, a former President of the AFL–CIO, in rebutting a pessimistic view of the future of US unionism, listed 'substantial progress' being made by US unions in:

- organizing and collective bargaining

- communicating with its members and the general public

- providing new services and benefits for existing members

- mobilizing community support

- strengthening its internal structure. (Kirkland, 1986, p. 401)

Many of these policies have a familiar ring to them, so there is clearly continuity with the past. We do recognize, however, that there have been difficulties and problems with implementing previously espoused policies. For example, union officials in a number of countries traditionally paid lip-service only to organizing strategies. Obviously, though, there is a significant difference between spending 3 per cent and 30 per cent of budget on organizing. Equally, it could be claimed that the particular clustering of problems facing unions, and the union policy experimentation that is taking place (particularly drawing on international example), has not been seen before. Accepting these provisos, we still tend towards a pessimistic view of the future in the short term.

Are unions, then, powerless to control their own destiny, as some commentators imply? Must they simply await the return of the long-term business cycle with its favourable environmental conditions (see Kelly, 1998)? Our discussion above indicates that unions are trying to be much more proactive; in particular, they are focusing on the question of membership recruitment and the appropriate organizing strategies in attempting to secure the future. Regini (1992) has argued that trade unions have had a set of three main relationships over the past few decades: with the state, with employers and with their members. Looking to the future generally, it seems to us that this last element – the position and place of membership and associated representational arrangements – is the key both to explaining the declining role of unions in the late twentieth century and exploring whatever possibilities exist for union renewal and revival in the twenty-first century. We do not wish to argue that the other two relationships are unimportant; the impact of state restructuring as well as the legislative role of the state, for example, is well documented. Neither do we wish to assert an automatic correlation between membership density and union power. We are aware, for example, that controlling supply of labour and/or regulation of job-entry qualifications were key sources of power for craft unionism. Equally, it is difficult to envisage a significant variation in union power in, say, one of the Scandinavian countries resulting from increasing density of five percentage points. Nevertheless, we hold that the significant shift of most of the countries studied towards the lightly unionized end of the continuum discussed earlier has had devastating impacts on these union movements. Put simply, just as the growth of unionism during much of the twentieth century allowed unions to wrest influence and legitimacy from other power groupings in society and the polity, so the decline of membership has facilitated the transfer away from unionism of their authority. In response, unions have focused on the question of retention and recruitment, and, albeit tentatively and in uneven ways, begun to consider the bases and forms of representation.

If the goal is universally agreed, the strategies to achieve this goal are contested. Should the traditional political strategy of supporting social democratic parties and influencing their policies be continued? Should unions adopt the social movement option of forming links, alliances and even partnerships with other groups in the polity? Should unions devote resources to international structures and activities given the role of supranational organizations such as the World Trade Organization in an increasingly globalized world? The clear central thrust in five of the countries – the possible exception being Ireland where the political/corporatist approach is attractive – is to focus primarily on organizing and retaining membership. The other strategies are not being neglected. Social movement unionism, for example, has its adherents in Canada and the USA, while in Britain possibilities such as a partnership with employers or a regulatory role for the European Union holds attraction for some sections of the union movement. The core focus, however, is on membership in general and, in particular, ensuring that this membership is generated through, and guaranteed by, the activities and strengths of the union movements themselves.

Given the experiences of the past two decades, it is difficult to fault this current strategic priority. Will it be successful? In the immediate short term, there is likely to be little or limited success, and contestation about the appropriateness of particular approaches. Realistically, that is probably all that can be expected. A likely medium-term scenario is that trade unions will survive, and perhaps even flourish in specific segments of the economy such as the public sector, large organizations, skilled areas of manufacturing and specific areas of the service sector. For the long term, the key choice is for workers themselves. In the past, despite employer and state opposition, workers chose to establish, to join and to participate in trade unions. So long as segments of workers perceive the necessity of trade unionism, the concept and philosophy will survive and experiments in the form that unionism takes will continue.

References

Barry, F. (ed.) (1999) *Understanding Ireland's Economic Growth*, New York: St Martin's Press.

Chaison, G. (1996) *Union Mergers in Hard Times: The View from Five Countries*, Ithaca: ILR Press.

Edwards, R., Garonna, P. and Todtling, F. (eds) (1986) *Unions in Crisis and Beyond: Perspectives from Six Countries*, Dover: Auburn House.

Fairbrother, P. (2000) *Trade Unions at the Crossroads*, London: Mansell.

Galenson, W. (1998) *The World's Strongest Trade Union: The Scandinavian Labor Movement*, Westport: Quorum.

Griffin, G. (1994) 'The authority of the ACTU', *Economic and Labour Relations Review*, **5** (1), 81–103.

Griffin, G. and Svensen, S. (1996) 'The decline of Australian union density: a survey of the literature', *Journal of Industrial Relations*, **38** (4), 505–47.

Hyman, R. (1994) 'Changing trade union identities and strategy', in R. Hyman and A. Ferner (eds) *New Frontiers in European Industrial Relations*, Oxford: Blackwell, pp. 108–39.

ILO (1998) *World Labour Report 1997/8*, Geneva: ILO.

Kelly, J. (1998) *Rethinking Industrial Relations: Mobilization, Collectivism and Long Waves*, London: Routledge.

Kirkland, L. (1986) 'It has all been said before', in S. M. Lipset (ed.) *Unions in Transition: Entering the Second Century*, San Francisco: ICS Press, pp. 393–404.

Leisink, P., Van Leemput, J. and Vilrokx, J. (1996) *The Challenges to Trade Unions in Europe: Innovation or Adaption*, Cheltenham, UK: Edward Elgar.

Lipset, S. M. (ed.) (1986) *Unions in Transition: Entering the Second Century*, San Francisco: ICS Press.

Olney, S. (1996) *Unions in a Changing World: Problems and Prospects in Selected Industrialized Countries*, Geneva: ILO.

Pusey, M. (1991) *Economic Rationalism in Canberra: A Nation-building State Changes its Mind*, Melbourne: Cambridge University Press.

Regini, M. (1992) *The Future of Labour Movements*, London: Sage.

Rose, J. and Chaison, G. (2000) 'North American unionism in the 21st century: the prospects for revival', Mimeo, June.

Touraine, A. (1986) 'Unionism as a social movement', in S. M. Lipset (ed.) *Unions in Transition: Entering the Second Century*, San Francisco: ICS Press, pp. 151–76.

Visser, J. (1990) *In Search of Inclusive Unionism*, Deventer: Kluwer.

Waddington, J. (1995) *The Politics of Bargaining: The Merger Process and British Trade Union Structural Development, 1892–1987*, London: Mansell.

INDEX

amalgamations *see* mergers
American unions
  affiliations 217, 218
  American Federation of Labor 200,
    203, 204, 213
  American Federation of Labor-
    Congress of Industrial Organization
    11, 75, 109, 112, 201, 213–18, 228
    '2000 in 2000' initiative 221
    coalition building 225–6
    Committee on the Evolution of
      Work 218, 221, 227
    organizing 222, 223, 243
    Organizing Department 223, 224
    Organizing Institute 11, 222–3, 243,
      249
    political activity 204–5, 220, 221
    strategies 218–19
  bargain, duty to 206–7
  bargaining tactics 226–7
  bargaining unit 206, 208
  business unionism 200
  centralization 218
  coalition building 225–6
  collective bargaining 201, 205, 226
  concession bargaining 226–7
  confrontation tactics 227
  Congress of Industrial Organization
    201, 203, 213
  corruption 201
  Democratic party 204
  dues 213, 221
  electoral activities 214, 220
  exclusive bargaining agent 206
  fair representation, duty of 206
  federations 243, 244
  free trade treaties 100
  general unions 216
  historical development 200–3
  industrial unionism 200–1
  institutionalization 201
  international labor coalitions 225–6
  job control 201

jurisdictional expansion 215–16
Knights of Labor 203, 213
Labor Party 221
lobbying 214
majority support 205–6
membership 208–12
  age 210, 211
  decline in 100, 200, 202, 215, 227–8,
    240
  density 208–12, 230, 239
  growth in 201, 202
  private sector 202, 206, 212, 228
  public sector 202, 209, 228, 240–1
  race 210, 211, 212
  women 210, 211, 212
mergers 216–17, 218, 228, 242
national unions 215–16
North American Free Trade Agreement 221
political parties 204–5, 221
politics 214, 220–2, 228
recruitment and organization 214–15,
  222–3, 225–6, 230, 243
Service Employees International
  Union 81
strategies 218–27
structure and governance 213–18
Union Cities 225
union membership 4
Union Summer 225–6
Wagner Act 95
arbitration
  Australia 22, 28–30, 41, 44–5
  New Zealand 177, 178, 191
  see also conciliation
Australian unions
  Amalgamated Metal Workers Union 39
  amalgamations 39–41, 42, 45–7
  anti-union legislation 8
  arbitration system 22, 28–30, 41, 44–5
  Australian Council of Trade Unions 5,
    11, 25, 38–9
    authority 42–3

Australian Industrial Relations
    Commission 29, 30, 35, 42, 50–1
centralization of power and authority
    41
closed shops 27
Communist Party 23
conservative political parties 23, 24
contracting-out 27
de-mergers 49
decision-making process 41–2
Democratic Labor Party 23
enterprise bargaining 25, 26, 30, 43,
    50, 51
enterprise flexibility agreements 43, 49
enterprise unions 26, 49
federal legislation 26–7
federations 244
historical development 21–3
indexation of wages 25, 30
individual contracts 26, 28, 30, 49
industrial action, restrictions on 26, 28
Industrial Relations Reform Act 1993
    26, 49
internal reform 224
Labor Party 23, 24–5, 30, 49, 247
Liberal/National coalition parties 23–4
market-orientation 46
membership 30–5, 36
    crisis in 46–8, 51–2
    decline in 4, 22–3, 28, 32, 34–5,
        46–8, 240
    density 22, 31–4, 48, 239
    minimum size 26
    public sector 27, 241
    Queensland 28
    Western Australia 28
mergers 39–41, 42, 45–7
Metal Trades Federation 38
multi-unionism 36–7, 46
New South Wales 28
non-union agreements 49
number of unions 35, 36
officials, restrictions on 26, 49
Organising Works 11, 47, 249
organizing model of unionism 47
orientation and strategies 43–8, 50–1
participation rate 42
political parties 23–5
preference clauses, prohibition of 27,
    28
Prices and Incomes Accord 25, 50
Queensland 28

recruitment and organization 46–7,
    48–9
secret ballots 24
South Australia 28
state legislation 27–8
strategic unionism 39
structure and governance 35–43
Tasmania 28
Victoria 28
Western Australia 27–8
Workplace Relations Act 1996 26–7,
    49–50

British unions
branches 70
British-based unions in Ireland 152,
    154, 160
centralized organization 84, 85, 87
collective bargaining 64, 72
conferences 70
Conservative governments 57, 60–1,
    63, 73, 80, 247
corporatism 59–60, 61
elections 70
European Union legislation 78–81
general unions 243
historical development 56–7
incomes policies 60
individual contracts 61
industry pay settlements 72
industry-level bargaining 72–3
joint consultative committees 56
Labour governments 60, 247
Labour Party 8, 56–7, 60, 61–2, 80, 83,
    84
legislative changes 61, 62, 63
managerial unionism 86
manufacturing unions 82
marginalization of 57, 61, 81
membership 62–9, 154
    black workers 69
    decline in 63–9, 84, 240
    density 63, 239
    part-time workers 75
    public sector 60, 63, 65, 68, 85, 241
    right to 63
    women 68–9, 75
    young people 75, 76
mergers 72, 78, 242
militant unionism 86
minimum wage 62

modernization 84
national bargaining 72–3
national executives 70
national pay settlements 72
neo-liberal interventionist state 60–1
neo-liberal stakeholders 61–2
New Labour 57, 85
new management 82–3
New Unionism 76, 81
orientation and strategies 76–83
participative unionism 86
patterns of unionism 70–3
political parties 56–7, 60
pressure-group model 74
privatization 78–9
professional unionism 86
recognition 63, 75, 81
recruitment and organization 75, 76, 77, 81, 82, 249–50
renewal process 86–8
service-model unionism 73
sex discrimination 79–80
shop-steward model 59, 75, 76, 77, 84–5
Social Contract 60
social partnership 86
structure and governance 70–6
Trades Union Congress 5, 56, 72, 73–6, 81, 82, 83
    relaunch of 75
    Special Review Committee 74–5
    TUC Strategy 74
transfer of undertakings 80
utilities 79, 85, 88
voluntarist tradition 58–9
wage restraint 60
'winter of discontent' 60
Works Councils 80

Canada
    mergers 121
Canadian unions
    accountability to members 97
    affirmative action 122
    Alberta 103, 127
    amalgamations 121
    appropriate bargaining unit 95–6, 107
    British Columbia 97, 100, 103
    business unionism 99, 116, 125, 129
    Canadian Labour Congress 95, 108, 109–11

Catholic unions 94
central labour bodies 108
certification election 96, 128
certification unit 96, 107, 108
Communist Party 118
conciliation 97
congresses 108
dealing 'in good faith' 96–7
decentralization 96, 98, 108, 113
democratization 125
dues 96, 99, 101
economic restructuring 129–30
exclusive bargaining 95–6
federations 108, 243, 244
free trade treaties 100
general unions 113, 120, 130
historical development 94–5
imposition of agreements 97
industrial action 97, 99
international affiliations 108
international unions 94, 108, 111–12
judiciarization 98
labour congresses 109–11
legal framework of collective representation 95–8
Manitoba 100, 103, 127
membership 95, 100–7, 127–8, 133
    cards 96
    decline in 113
    density 95, 103, 106, 239, 240
    distribution of 103–7
    diversity of 122–3
    growth in 100–1, 102, 103, 112
    measurement of 101–2
    participation 122–3
    public sector 95, 105, 120, 126, 240, 241
    right to 95
    trends 100–3, 132
    unemployed members 101
    women 104, 121–2
    young people 106–7
mergers 112, 121, 242
national union organizations 108
neo-liberalism 126, 133
New Democratic Party 95, 99–100, 118, 126, 131, 247
Newfoundland 103
North American Free Trade Agreement 100
objectives and ideology 115–18, 129–32

Ontario 97, 99, 100, 103, 125, 126, 127
Parti Québécois 118, 127
philanthropy 100
political action 99–100, 125–7
private services sector 105, 120, 122
Québec 94, 103, 108, 109, 110, 118,
    120, 124–5, 127, 130
recognition as majority agent 95–6
recruitment and organization 119–21,
    128, 129, 132, 243
Saskatchewan 100
selective diversification 120
servicing 123
Social Contract legislation 126
social movement unionism 99, 117–18,
    125, 126, 127, 131–2
social unionism 99, 117, 125–6, 130–1
strategic responses 118–27
strikebreakers, prohibition on use 97
structural reform 121
structure 107–14
unfettered diversification 120–1
union locals 108, 113–14
wage restraint 126
worker participation 125
workplace change 124–5, 128–9, 130
capital mobility 9
case studies 13–14
closed shops
    Australia 27
    Ireland 140
Communist Party
    Australia 23
    Canada 118
comparative studies 12–13
conciliation
    Canada 97
    Ireland 139
    New Zealand 177, 178, 191
    see also arbitration
confederations 4, 108, 243–4
cyclical view 11

DUES Project 145

federations 4, 11, 108, 243–4

general unionism 243
    Canada 113, 120, 130
    Ireland 152, 243
    United Kingdom 243

United States 216
globalization 9, 76

incomes policies 4
    Australia 25, 50
    Canada 126
    Ireland 143–4
    United Kingdom 60
International Confederation of Free
    Trade Unions 3
international unions 11
    Canada 94, 108, 111–12
    Ireland 94
    United States 225–6
Irish unions
    armed forces associations 144–5
    bargaining right 169
    British-based unions 152, 154, 160
    centralization 157
    closed shops 140
    conciliation 139
    Democratic Left 142
    dispute resolution 139–40
    European Monetary Union 161–2, 173
    European Works Councils 141
    Fianna Fail 142, 143
    Fine Gael 142
    general unions 152, 243
    governance 157–60
    historical development 138
    immunities 139
    incentives for unionization 162–3
    industrial action 139, 144, 145
    international unions 94
    Irish Congress of Trade Unions 5, 154,
        158–9, 161–2, 163
        reviews 163–6
        union recognition 169
    joint consultative committees 141
    Labour Court 139, 140, 169, 170–1
    Labour Party 141, 142
    legislation 138–41
    membership
        composition of 152–4
        decline in 138, 146, 162, 171–2, 173,
            240
        density 137, 146–52, 162, 172, 240
        growth in 138, 147, 240
        private sector 150–1, 171, 172
        public sector 139–40, 150–1, 156,
            171, 241

retired members 145
right to 140
self-employed workers 145
threshold for negotiating licence
 145
time-series indicators 145
trends 145–52
unemployed members 145
women 150, 151
mergers 154–6
militancy 138
minimum wage 139
national pay bargaining 157–8, 159,
 160
negotiating licence 145
neo-corporatism 137–8, 142, 162, 172
Northern Ireland 162
orientation and strategies 160–71
Partnership 2000 144, 161, 165, 166,
 169, 248
pay agreements 157
pay bargaining 157–9, 160
pay drift 172
pay restraint 143–4
police associations 144, 145
Programme for Competitiveness and
 Work 144
Programme for Economic and Social
 Progress 143–4
Programme for National Recovery
 143
Programme for Prosperity and Fairness
 144
Progressive Democrats Party 142–3
recognition 140, 167–71
 union substitution strategies 167
 union suppression tactics 167–8
 voluntarism 169, 170
secret ballots 139
self-employed workers 145
social partnership 161, 163, 165, 171,
 173
strategic partnerships 165
structure 152–6
tripartism 143–4, 147, 148, 160–1, 162,
 171–2
unskilled workers 138
US multinationals 167
white-collar unions 152
worker directors 140–1
worker participation 141
workplace activism 157

workplace partnership 163–6
works councils 141

Labour Parties *see* political parties

membership 239–41
 compulsory, New Zealand 181–2
 decline in 4, 6–8, 240, 249
 Australia 4, 22–3, 28, 32, 34–5, 46–8,
  240
 Canada 113
 Ireland 138, 146, 162, 171–2, 173,
  240
 New Zealand 184, 186–7, 188, 194,
  240
 United Kingdom 63–9, 84, 240
 United States 100, 200, 202, 215,
  227–8, 240
 density 239–41
 Australia 22, 31–4, 48, 239
 Canada 95, 103, 106, 239, 240
 Ireland 137, 146–52, 162, 172, 240
 New Zealand 239
 United Kingdom 63, 239
 United States 208–12, 230, 239
 growth in
 Canada 100–1, 102, 103, 112
 Ireland 138, 147, 240
 United States 201, 202
 minimum size
 Australia 26
 New Zealand 186, 187, 195
 private sector
 Ireland 150–1, 171, 172
 New Zealand 178–9, 188, 195
 United States 202, 206, 212, 228
 public sector 4, 240–1
 Australia 27, 241
 Canada 95, 105, 120, 126, 240, 241
 Ireland 139–40, 150–1, 156, 171, 241
 New Zealand 178–9, 183, 184, 187,
  192, 241
 United Kingdom 60, 63, 65, 68, 85,
  241
 United States 202, 209, 228, 240–1
 racial minorities 11
 United Kingdom 69
 United States 210, 211, 212
 retired members, Ireland 145
 self-employed workers, Ireland 145
 unemployed members

Canada 101
Ireland 145
women 11, 241
Canada 104, 121–2
Ireland 150, 151
New Zealand 184
United Kingdom 68–9, 75
United States 210, 211, 212
young people
Canada 106–7
United Kingdom 75, 76
mergers 242–3, 249
Australia 39–41, 42, 45–7
Canada 112, 121, 242
Ireland 154–6
New Zealand 193
United Kingdom 72, 78, 242
United States 216–17, 218, 228, 242
minimum wage
Ireland 139
New Zealand 177
United Kingdom 62

New Zealand unions
amalgamations 193
anti-union legislation 8
business agent model 194
coalition Government 195–6
collective bargaining 178, 180, 191–2
collective documents 180
compulsory conciliation and arbitration 177, 178, 191
contracts of service 180
economic restructuring 179–80
Employment Contracts Act 180–2, 183,
184, 189, 192, 195, 239
Employment Relations Act 195–6, 247
federations 244
free-loading 195, 196
historical development 177–80
individual agreements 180
Labour Governments 179, 180, 181,
182, 183, 191, 247, 252
Labour Party 182, 195
liberalization programme 179, 180
lobbying 182
membership 183–6, 187, 193
compulsory 181–2
decline in 184, 186–7, 188, 194, 240
density 239
minimum 186, 187, 195

private sector 178–9, 188, 195
public sector 178–9, 183, 184, 187,
192, 241
rules 178
voluntary 180, 181, 182
women 184
mergers 193
minimum wage 177
multi-employer bargaining 192, 193,
195, 196
National Governments 180, 181, 182,
183, 191
New Labour Party 182
New Zealand Council of Trade Unions
181, 188, 189
Search Committee Report 190–1
New Zealand Federation of Labour
188
orientation and strategies 190–4
partnership arrangements 192
patronage 180
loss of 177, 181
political action 182, 191
recruitment and organization 193–4,
243
registration 177–8, 183, 193, 196
service organizations 183, 187–8
single-issue campaigns 191
strike action 182, 192
structure and governance 186–9
Trade Union Federation 188–9, 190–1
workplace reform programs 192–3
North American Free Trade Agreement
100, 221

organization see recruitment and organi-
zation
orientation and strategies 248–51
Australia 43–8, 50–1
Ireland 160–71
New Zealand 190–4
United Kingdom 76–83
United States 218–27

paired studies 13
pay restraint see incomes policies
political parties 4–5, 244–8
Australia 23–5
Communist Party
Australia 23
Canada 118

conservative
  Australia 23, 24
  United Kingdom 57, 60–1, 63, 73,
    80, 247
Ireland 141, 142–3, 250
Social Democratic/Labour Parties 4, 5,
    246, 249, 250
  Australia 22, 23, 24–5, 30, 49, 247,
    249, 250
  Canada 95, 99–100, 118, 126, 131,
    249
  Ireland 141, 142, 250
  New Zealand 182, 195, 249
  United Kingdom 8, 56–7, 60, 61–2,
    80, 83, 84, 85, 250
  United States 221
United Kingdom 56–7, 60
United States 204–5, 221

recruitment and organization 241–4,
    249–50
  Australia 46–7, 48–9
  Canada 119–21, 128, 129, 132
  New Zealand 193–4
  organizing model of unionism
    Australia 47
    United States 224, 230
  United Kingdom 75, 76, 77, 81, 82

United States 214–15, 222–3, 225–6,
    230

secret ballots
  Australia 24
  Ireland 139
service-model unionism 5
  United Kingdom 73
Social Democratic Parties *see* political
  parties
state-union relations 2, 3, 244–8
  Australia 23–30, 245, 246
  Canada 99–100, 246
  Ireland 138–4, 246–7
  New Zealand 180–3, 246, 247
  United Kingdom 58–62, 246
  United States 203–7, 245, 246
strategies *see* orientation and strategies

United Kingdom *see* British unions
United States *see* American unions

wage restraint *see* incomes policies
women *see* membership
works councils
  European 141
  Ireland 141
  United Kingdom 80